The Cultural Politics
of Reproduction

The Cultural Politics of Reproduction

Migration, Health and Family Making

Edited by
Maya Unnithan-Kumar and Sunil K. Khanna

berghahn
NEW YORK · OXFORD
www.berghahnbooks.com

First published in 2015 by
Berghahn Books
www.berghahnbooks.com

Library of Congress Cataloging-in-Publication Data

The cultural politics of reproduction: migration, health and family making /
edited by Maya Unnithan-Kumar and Sunil K. Khanna.
  pages cm
 ISBN 978-1-78238-544-8 (hardback: alk. paper) -- ISBN 978-1-78238-
545-5 (ebook)
 1. Women immigrants. 2. Motherhood. 3. Family planning. 4.
Immigrants--Health and hygiene. I. Unnithan-Kumar, Maya, 1961- II.
Khanna, Sunil K.
 JV6347.C855 2014
 362.198'40086912--dc23
                                                        2014018768

British Library Cataloguing in Publication Data
A catalogue record for this book is available from the British Library

ISBN 978-1-78238-544-8 (hardback)
E-ISBN 978-1-78238-545-5 (ebook)

Contents

Tables

Acknowledgements

This volume has been some time in the making – completing a long but resilient journey from when the issue of movement and social reproduction was first discussed by some of the contributors in 2007. It represents the fruits of transnational collaboration between the co-editors, but also with contributing authors from the US, Europe and Britain. Finally, as with most edited volumes, the book embodies the hard work of a committed set of contributors and labour of supportive colleagues and friends. Our very special thanks to anthropologist, friend and colleague Josephine Reynell, who has generously given her time and meticulously rendered the chapters in publishable form. The volume has benefited, particularly in the final stages, from the encouraging support of colleagues Anastasia Christou and Priya Deshingkar at the Sussex Centre for Migration Research. We would also like to thank Marion Berghahn, Ann DeVita, Molly Mosher and Mark Stanton at Berghahn Books for their patience and support.

Maya Unnithan
Sunil Khanna
August 2013

Migration and the Politics of Reproduction and Health

Tracking Global Flows through Ethnography

Sunil K. Khanna and Maya Unnithan-Kumar

In recent years, scholars have paid significant attention to the broad topic of the politics of health and reproduction. Within this larger domain of knowledge, anthropologists have focused on the political economy of health, often drawing on theoretical trends prevalent in other disciplines to examine health from a cross-cultural perspective. This volume adds yet another dimension to this already complex topic, namely the relationship between the politics of reproduction and health among both internal and external migrant communities. Our key objective in this volume is to develop a fresh perspective, informed by ethnographic research, to examine how migrant communities experience migration, adaptation and assimilation, especially in terms of how the overlapping of these domains changes prevailing ideas and practices associated with reproductive health and healthcare. Since migration is a complex and multi-directional phenomenon, it is important to examine the relationship between migration and reproductive health from both local and global perspectives. We argue that a multi-level examination of migration and reproductive health can help reframe the way anthropologists study this complex issue and move the discourse on reproductive health among migrant groups to the centre of anthropological inquiry.

Increased flows of people, capital, technology and information – the key defining characteristics of globalization – have accelerated the movement of people, commodities, ideas and cultures across the world (Appadurai 1996), thus making spatial and 'cultural' boundaries of limited relevance in describing people (Gupta and Ferguson 1997). In particular, the unprecedented trans-regional and transnational mobility of people can be seen as both a cause and a consequence of changes in livelihood strategies and related conceptions of the self, family, community and nation-state. Tracking the flows of people, goods, capital, ideas, practices and information is one of the most exciting areas of research emerging in a variety of disciplines. While the movement of people has primarily, if not exclusively, been viewed in terms of labour, income and material aspects, anthropologists have adopted a more subjective approach. The latter approach has led to the development of new theoretical perspectives for understanding the experience of migrant groups or communities not only in terms of their adaptation to the 'host' site, but also in terms of their links to the world at 'home' and everything in between. While previously anthropologists focused on processes of assimilation or adaptation with regard to languages, food and identities as an outcome of migration, more recent scholarship has focused on 'reverse' migration, anti-migration movements and policies, transnationalism, global/diasporic citizenship and localization as affective dimensions of migration (Appadurai 1996; Bledsoe 2004; Mahalingam 2006; Bledsoe and Sow 2011).

In the last twenty years, evidence from qualitative studies suggests the need to differentiate a community's migration experience in terms of a host of confounding variables of demography, history and more localized sociopolitical characteristics (Gaetano and Jacka 2004). The majority of scholars agree that ethnographic discourse concerning migration offers an important and nuanced understanding of the migration experience, and thus a useful means for planning effective intervention programs and policies at the community level (Knorr and Meier 2000; Herbert 2008). This assertion results from the success of anthropological writings at analysing hitherto prevalent homogenizing and reductionist discourses on migrants and their experiences. Findings based on community-level studies, adopting a qualitative or ethnographic mode of inquiry and critical reflections on the macro-determinants of healthcare services and policy, suggest that dominant demographic and economic perspectives and linked policies have failed to account for similarities and differences within these broad analytical categories, and for differences at the level of gender, age, class and other sub-cultural categories (Holmes 2006; Llacer et al. 2007; Favell 2008). This critique is most clearly articulated in recent studies on health and reproduction among migrant groups (Lu 2009; Vanderlinden 2009; Varley 2009).

Recent studies of migrant health highlight the heterogeneity of migrant groups and problematize vertical or simplistic models of the assimilation of migrants by healthcare services and systems of host locations (Salant and Lauderdale 2003; Koehn 2006). Studies show that, compared to non-migrants, migrants are less likely to use available health services; more likely to express dissatisfaction with healthcare providers and systems; and have worse health statistics (Derose et al. 2007). A few studies have identified migrant groups as 'vulnerable populations' at risk of poor health outcomes, which are seen primarily as outcomes of structural barriers limiting migrants' access to culturally appropriate and affordable healthcare (Poudel et al. 2004; Grove and Zwi 2006; Derose et al. 2007) in contrast to other studies which find migration to have positive benefits (Deshingkar et al. 2008), or, as chapters in this volume indicate, a simultaneity of positive and negative outcomes.

Within the broader context defined by migration and reproductive health, chapters in this volume focus on the reproductive experiences, desires and practices of migrant communities living in countries including the United States, Canada, United Kingdom, Europe, India, Sri Lanka and Vietnam. Migrant reproductive health has been an area of growing academic interest, and there have been several calls for understanding this issue from an ethnographic and therefore qualitatively informed perspective. Clearly, there is an urgent need to examine the kinds of 'cultural work' associated with migration in the domain of health and reproduction.

Several chapters in the volume address the making and remaking of places through an exploration of a range of issues, challenging the construction of migration as a spatial phenomenon (Qureshi, Unnithan-Kumar, Ally, Olson, all this volume). As Xiang (2010) amongst others argues, the spatial view of migration reinforces the dominance of the modern state based on territorial exclusivity. For Xiang, a focus on temporality rather than space in migration enables us to understand more effectively the ways in which migrants experience and negotiate structural control. We would suggest that it also enables us to examine local reproductive and health strategies linked to migration across the context of internal as well as transnational movement. The chapters in the volume concerned with understanding place-making primarily examine the issue through the lens of social relationality, especially when it is concerned with the birth of children and the resulting production of new relationships (such as parenting, siblingship and so on) that surround such events. Contributors examine the diverse meanings of space and place-making that emerge in migrant reproductive practice, and the effects that these have on the social reproduction of their communities. The link between birth and birthplace is central not only to women's and men's sense of self and identity, but also to relations within families, and between a community and the state.

A critical contribution of a cultural focus on reproduction and health is that it enables the gendered body to be established as an analytic domain within the framework of migration studies. The body is important for migrants in a physical sense, but the ways in which labour migrants, for example, conceptualize their bodies may be as devoid of agency or value, making bodily health a submerged concern within their narratives of migration (Unnithan-Kumar 2004). Through a focus on the 'mindful body' (Scheper-Hughes and Lock 1987), we can examine the interaction between the mind and the body, further complicated by the individual, social and body politic. This analytic shift away from the notion of the mind, the body and the social as separate entities allows us to examine the body as an analytic site, and migrant experience as embodying the exercise of institutional and self control. The cultural construction of bodily difference as manifest through gender in turn reveals how men and women may have different bodily experiences of migration, with different emergent senses of self. Migration then becomes inevitably associated with different forms of gender and reproductive politics, reflected for instance in negotiations around marital responsibilities and appropriate sexual behaviour, the sexual and reproductive division of labour, expectations around conception and contraceptive practices, or in terms of family size and sex composition as preferences linked with the imaginaries of social reproduction (that is, the reproduction of the family, state and nation). The key question here is whether and to what extent migration transforms, supports, reinforces or challenges existing kinship, gender and family-making discourse and practice. To what extent are the norms of mothering constrained, facilitated or reconstituted through the movement of young, married and pregnant women? What are the kinds of emotions that arise as a consequence, and how do they shift and shape practice?

The state looms large in defining migrant experiences, whether in the context of internal or external migration. Several chapters (Locke, Khanna, Griffiths, Challinor, Unnithan-Kumar, Ally, Olson) examine migrant parenthood in the context of a wider set of development, demographic and health discourses. In terms of migrant engagement with state health services, we find these to result in particular forms of 'disciplining', whether these are to do with sexuality in terms of hetero-normativity or fertility in terms of citizenship. Migrant use of public health services also brings to attention the conflict between the authority of 'indigenous' versus 'culturally competent' care providers. Migrant mothers may be pathologized by health workers for their poverty in contexts of internal displacement, but may be simultaneously pathologized and idealized as bearers of culture in contexts of transnational migration (see especially the chapters by Griffiths, Qureshi). Relationships between migrants and the state, as articulated through health services, also bring up the issue of migrant modernity, especially in terms of the ways it is expressed through reproductive healthcare practices. Equally important is the issue of migrant agency. Through careful ethnographic analysis, several chapters in this volume demonstrate new kinds of reproductive agency (strategies, tactics and reticence), and the political deliberation that is imagined and exercised by migrants.

The studies included in this volume are informed by qualitative and ethnographic data, and examine unique as well as shared features of migration experiences and its relationship with healthcare-seeking behaviour across communities. Contributors to the volume have prioritized listening to the stories people tell about their experiences of migration. Such qualitative data is important as health matters and physical well-being are often a more submerged concern within a wider discourse of migrant economic and social mobility (Unnithan-Kumar et al. 2008). A focus on accounts of migration also enables information across different discursive levels (embodied in multi-sited analysis) to be brought together (Unnithan-Kumar and De-Neve 2006). The chapters included in this volume furthermore illustrate how qualitative methods and theoretical approaches can be used to examine migrants' access to healthcare services, and the critical interaction between migrants' knowledge, experience and practices of health and the available biomedical healthcare services.

The combination in the volume of studies on internal and transnational migration illustrates that, however small or large the spatial movement, migrating groups may experience similar gendered and kinship-based control over reproduction. Similarly, state responses may be equally lax in making reproductive health services accessible to both transnational and internal migrants (particularly evident in the case for newly industrializing countries such as Vietnam and India). In our attempt to articulate the experiences and healthcare-seeking behaviour of both internal and external migrant groups, we have found aspects of postcolonial and critical theory useful in examining experiences of migrant communities discussed in the present volume. In particular, postcolonial critiques of the politics of structure (Kapferer 2006) have strongly informed our understanding of how individuals negotiate their everyday lives in a distant alien context.

There are two main themes which cut across the chapters in the volume. These are, first, a focus on the interconnections between migrant motherhood and senses of place and self, and second, an explicit concern with issues of 'culture' in migrant engagement with health services.

Making Parents through Place

Focusing specifically on motherhood, chapters addressing this theme in the volume examine the effects of spatial and social dislocation during childbearing in forging new relations between the body, self and society. The chapter by Qureshi adopts a life-history approach to examine personal identity, motherhood and migration memories of now middle-aged Pakistani women who came to Britain in the 1960s or 1970s as the brides or daughters of industrial workers. Qureshi's study suggests that, although women's identities as mothers are pivotal to their sense of who they were, the migration experience changed the nature and practices of motherhood. Qureshi argues that the so-called 'feminine toil' of migration complicates how belonging is negotiated and exercised through the reproductive body.

Locke, Nguyen and Nguyen's chapter is concerned with internal, rural-to-urban migration of low income families. Set in the context of recent Vietnamese economic and structural reform, Locke et al. analyse the rising trend in the migration of married women to cities as part of the survival strategy of poor rural households. Their chapter focuses on the ways in which young, married, Vietnamese women negotiate conflicting expectations of them by their families and the state in the era of transitional economic reform. Women migrants are caught in the reproductive dilemma of having children and nurturing them appropriately for the social reproduction of the lineage, while being at the same time expected to abandon them to fulfil the expectations of household economic stability met through carrying out their work in the cities. As the authors argue, a creative local response has been that women's migration is increasingly cast as parenting work itself, obscuring any contradictions it has with women's obligations to fulfil everyday care for their children.

Locke et al. trace a set of diverse and dynamic migration strategies, which emerge from within what they see as strongly institutionalized practices of the 'leaving behind' of children. They identify five distinct patterns of migration, the timing and motivation of each being linked to reproductive and family-building strategies. The most dominant pattern is one in which most migrant mothers choose to stay at home for their first birth, and then they 'wean and go', migrating approximately twelve months after the birth. Children's need for their parents is seen as less complex between three years and becoming a teenager. Adolescents are regarded as those in most 'need' of their parents, mothers as well as fathers, for appropriate gender-based instruction and guidance.

The impact of such strategies for reproductive patterns shows that migrant women tend to space their children with a five to seven year gap rather than the two to three years that is more conventionally regarded as appropriate. When pregnant with their second or higher birth-order children, they also tend to delay their antenatal care until they are back in their rural home area. Their access to public healthcare is determined by the way in which healthcare is structured by the state in Vietnam. Social entitlements (including healthcare) are structured in ways that discourage migration, as reflected in, for example, the household registration system, which makes access to maternal care for rural migrants only available in their village of residence.

Unnithan-Kumar's chapter focuses on the gendered experience of migration regarding marriage and childbirth for poor rural women who migrate to cities in North India. Like Locke et al., she is concerned with the effects of internal displacement on experiences of motherhood. She suggests that the chronic movement associated with India's poor has significant implications for the reproductive choices and birth experiences of women who come from and marry into poor families. In particular, she focuses on migrant mothers' accounts of birth and loss. Unnithan-Kumar suggests that the agency of migrants is connected to their perceptions of place (as constituted by intimate social relations that are therapeutic). Following Fassin (2004), she sees the active production of health inequalities associated with poor labour migrants as taking place in the space between the perceptions that migrants have of their claims on health services, and the perceptions of state health workers who see migrants' claims as illegitimate.

With a state that makes little provision for migrants, Rajasthani women migrants move back and forth across rural and urban settings for maternal and child health services in their quest for good birth outcomes based on their evaluation of places as therapeutic. It is 'home', whether in the village or in the slum, which is the favoured place for giving birth. Public hospitals, in contrast with 'home' settings, are places where childbearing is terminated. Not considered appropriate for giving birth, public institutions are, however, sought out for sterilization services. These perceptions also highlight class issues: while middle-class, urban women in India associate institutional births with modernity and high status, for poor migrant women, institutional births reflect the risks of modernity.

Apart from the decision to give birth in places which are primarily socially rather than biomedically constituted, poor migrant mothers in Rajasthan explicitly evaluate place in terms of their ability to nurture and provide sustenance for their children. Good parenting, especially mothering, emerges in the context of place and work which facilitates responsible nurturing and the feeding of children. It is connected with the capacity to 'earn food' rather than access to healthcare per se. Health is a submerged concern within the wider quest for employment.

Challinor focuses on the experiences of unplanned pregnancies among young migrant Cape Verdean women studying or working in Portugal. Migration, like pregnancy, crafts a new relation between the body and the self. Young migrant women who become unexpectedly pregnant face an added sense of disorientation and loss of control over their bodies and social relationships. Challinor uses the metaphor of the labyrinth to explain the interrelation between migrants' inner and outer experiences of unexpected motherhood. The idea of the labyrinth is used as a means to capture the processes through which migrant subjectivity is shaped at the same time as it symbolizes the tension between individual desires and social norms.

Faced with the likelihood of potential parenthood, migrant women are forced to enter into new kinds of negotiations with their communities and families back home. The influence of kinship relations across space remains strong, and Challinor finds that the physical distance between migrants in Portugal and their families in Cape Verde actually serves in large part to uphold traditional views of the morality of childbearing (which may have been reversed if the women were able to meet up with their families). There are also some cases where migrant women have discovered a new sense of independence from their families, but these are relatively few. Their agency emerges especially when they engage with state-sponsored maternal health services. Here, migrant women found that they did not have automatic access to the same maternal healthcare that is provided to non-migrant women, but that they had to be assertive to receive attention in the health system.

Ally's chapter concerns the lives of poor, rural Sri Lankan women and their migration to and from the Persian Gulf. Through an exploration of narratives to do with sexuality, emotion and love towards past, existing or prospective spouses, the chapter examines the ways in which migrant women negotiate, submit to and/or defy negative moral representations, and how spousal relationships are negotiated, reconstructed or eroded across Sri Lanka and the Gulf as women aspire for more honour and respect. Migration for domestic labour is popularly perceived as morally undesirable, due to the stigmatization of women for their sexual vulnerability as domestic workers and supposed sexual promiscuity, and the detrimental effects these perceived changes are thought to have upon families and Sri Lankan cultural values. For Ally, sexuality, and the different ways it is expressed in spousal relationships and through the body, is a crucial dimension of power that shapes and organizes processes of migration and self-(re)making. Judged by traditional, patriarchal norms, the lives of the Muslim migrant women she discusses are particularly influenced by virtues derived from Islam. She examines how these religious moralities intersect with regulatory norms of gender and class to influence the ways in which women are categorized as 'good' or 'bad'.

Olson's chapter examines the complex politics surrounding the location of birth and meanings of birthplace among indigenous First Nation communities in Manitoba, Canada, through the narratives of Aboriginal midwives. In particular, she considers the practice of state-enforced evacuation of pregnant Aboriginal women from their homes in the rural hinterland to give birth in urban health centres. What are the implications of such reproduction-related movement for the experience of giving birth, knowledge and identity of Aboriginal women? Like Challinor, she uses the concept of 'authoritative knowledge' as a way of understanding how Western medical and childbirth knowledge and techniques function as a normalizing practice (Davis-Floyd and Sargent 1997) and, in the First Nations case, serve to rescue pregnant women from the 'risks' posed by indigenous midwifery.

To understand what the relocation of childbirth means to indigenous women themselves, Olson argues it is important to understand the significance of 'place' in the construction of First Nation identity. Place, beyond its material importance, is regarded primarily as embodying relational identities, and it is constituted by histories of social interaction. This social density makes the land occupied by First Nation communities truly nurturing for subsequent generations.

Olson sets her analysis of the movement of birthing practices away from First Nation locations in the context of a history of state-enforced movement of people and practices (to do with health and education) outside their communities. These movements represent attempts by the state to modernize its population through providing them with access to Western (medical and epistemological) practices as a means to improve their overall health and the quality of their lives. But Olson's chapter shows how maternal health for First Nation women cannot be set apart from trauma (physical, mental, social, political) linked to the dislocation of giving birth and the memories of individual and collective illness caused as a result. Her chapter also delineates recent collective, state and individual (local midwife-driven) initiatives to resituate birthing in the community ('bring birthing back'), which is seen as a means to restore (make whole again) social connections and the identities based on them, thus healing the trauma of 'having babies born outside' their home territory.

Cultures of Health Provision in Migrant Experience

The chapters included in this volume examine the relationship between health services and migrants and specifically add to a growing body of qualitative studies that provide an in-depth understanding of migrant identity and the culture of health. These chapters focus on changing views of family size and sex composition and the use of the new reproductive technologies in an internal migrant community in India (Khanna); the complexity of the migrant acculturation processes as examined through experiences of childbirth and later life among migrant women living in the US (Fernandes-Paul); and the cultural particularism and universalism of 'postnatal depression' among Bangladeshi migrants living in the UK (Griffith).

In his study of reproductive choices and the use of new reproductive technologies among Punjabi migrants living in New Delhi, Khanna examines the complex relationship between gender hierarchy, reproductive decision-making processes and power, and family-building strategies. Khanna's ethnography focuses on an internal migrant community from Punjab – part of the region of north-west India viewed in the literature in terms of kinship organization, gender relations, women's decision-making power and levels of women's autonomy. Communities from this region of India practice patrilineal kinship, patrilocal residence after marriage, and village exogamy, and additionally exhibit a strong preference for sons. Scholars have used these cultural characteristics to explain certain demographic outcomes: high fertility rates, large family size, excess female child mortality and masculine sex ratios in the region (Croll 2000; Khanna 2010; Purewal 2010). Khanna offers a critical evaluation of these historical trends of demography and culture by examining how urban residence and increased access to pre-natal diagnostic technologies influences desired family size and sex composition among migrant Punjabi migrant married couples living in New Delhi. In his conclusion, Khanna examines the intricate and intersecting views of parents regarding migration, urban living and the need for regulating family size and sex composition in urban India, and draws parallel with similar research findings in India and elsewhere in Asia. Through his analysis of household demographic data and community-level ethnographic information, Khanna contributes to a growing body of literature on 'situating fertility', or understanding the anthropological and historical underpinnings of demographic outcomes (Greenhalgh 1995), particularly relevant to examining this complex relationship among internal or regional migrant communities in South Asia.

Fernandes-Paul's chapter focuses on an assumption that, on average, immigrants are healthier than those who are native-born. However, as she points out, in the case of post-partum depression, several studies have shown that immigrant women face a significantly higher risk of post-partum depression than native-born women. A wide variety of factors – including age, maternal and foetal health, the cause and duration of migration, fluency in the host country's language, and social support networks – have been found to affect this risk. She discusses the results of a qualitative study involving in-depth interviews with eleven immigrant mothers from nine countries, as well as their healthcare providers, about post-partum depression. She suggests that, in addition to previously identified risk factors, a desire to acculturate acts as an added stressor that is unique to middle- and upper-middle-class women who have earned higher education qualifications in the U.S. Fuelled by a desire to acculturate themselves into the dominant culture of the U.S., during their pregnancies and post-birth period, this group of immigrant women eagerly adopt those lifestyles that are considered traditional for American women. Often these pregnancy and post-birth related lifestyles differ from, and even contradict, the beliefs and practices that are followed in the home cultures of these women. Hence, a continued connection for migrant women to their home cultures and families involves 'straddling', which could increase the risk of post-partum depression.

Griffith's chapter investigates the narratives of Bangladeshi mothers to examine the role of culture as presented in both self-conscious and implicit terms, and examines the claims that are based on these conceptions. Griffith chooses health and motherhood as the loci where personal experience, social institutions and notions of 'culture' all intersect. To stress only that the experience of motherhood is undeniably a feature of shared humanity would be to ignore the fact that reproduction is also culturally mediated and reconstructed. Through discussions such as those concerning the nature of 'postnatal depression', depicted as having both universal and culturally specific elements, debates around ethnicity and class are also brought into sharper focus. Bangladeshi mothers as 'bearers of culture' are both pathologized and idealized in equal measure.

To conclude, the research included in this volume provides ethnographically nuanced case studies that problematize 'homogenizing' images and narratives of migrant communities and their health experiences. Breaking new ground by offering ethnographic insights into reproductive health experiences among migrant groups, the volume reveals the complex relationship between different and often competing health beliefs and health systems and policies in 'host' locations. The conclusions drawn are thus grounded not only in the experiences of those who undergo migration, acculturation and adaptation to a new healthcare environment, but also in understanding these experiences in a myriad of local, regional and global domains. The insights provided by the chapters in the volume contribute not only to more nuanced understandings of the relationship between reproduction and migration, but also potentially to better reproductive healthcare policy for migrant groups.

References

Appadurai, A. 1996. *Modernity at Large: Cultural Dimensions of Globalization*. Minneapolis: University of Minnesota Press.

Bledsoe, C. 2004. 'Reproduction at the Margins: Migration and Legitimacy in the New Europe', *Demographic Research* 3: 87–116.

Bledsoe, C., and P. Sow. 2011. 'Family Reunification Ideals and the Practice of Transnational Reproductive Life among Africans in Europe', in C.H. Browner and C.F. Sargent (eds), *Reproduction, Globalisation and the State: New Theoretical and Ethnographic Perspectives*. Durham, NC: Duke University Press, pp.175–92.

Croll, E. 2000. *Endangered Daughters: Discrimination and Development in Asia*. London: Routledge.

Davis-Floyd, R.E., and C.F. Sargent (eds). 1997. *Childbirth and Authoritative Knowledge: Cross-cultural Perspectives*. Berkeley: University of California Press.

Derose, K.P., J.J. Escarce and N. Lurie. 2007. 'Immigrants and Healthcare: Sources of Vulnerability', *Health Affairs* 26(5): 1258–68.

Deshingkar, P., P. Sharma, S. Kumar, S. Akter and J. Farrington. 2008. 'Circular Migration in Madhya Pradesh: Changing Patterns and Social Protection Needs', *European Journal of Development Research* 20(4): 612–18.

Fassin, D. 2004. 'Social Illegitimacy as a Foundation of Health Inequality: How the Political Treatment of Immigrants Illuminates a French Paradox', in A. Castro and M. Singer (eds), *Unhealthy Health Policy: A Critical Anthropological Examination*. Lanham, MD: Altamira Press, pp.203–15.

Favell, A. 2008. 'The New Face of East–West Migration in Europe', *Journal of Ethnic and Migration Studies* 35(5): 701–16.

Gaetano, A.M., and T. Jacka (eds). 2004. On the Move: Women in Rural-to-urban Migration in *Contemporary China*. New York: Columbia University Press.

Greenhalgh, S. (ed.). 1995. *Situating Fertility: Anthropology and Demographic Inquiry*. New York: Cambridge University Press.

Grove, N.J., and A.B. Zwi. 2006. 'Our Health and Theirs: Force Migration, Othering, and Public Health', *Social Science and Medicine* 62(8): 1931–42.

Gupta, A. and J. Ferguson (eds). 1997. *Culture, Power, and Place: Explorations in Critical Anthropology*. Durham: Duke University Press.

Herbert, J. 2008. *Negotiating Boundaries in the City: Migration, Ethnicity, and Gender in Britain*. Aldershot: Ashgate.

Holmes, S.M. 2006. 'An Ethnographic Study of the Social Context of Migrant Health in the United States', *PLoS Medicine* 3(10): 1776–93.

Kapferer, B. 2006. 'New Formations of Power, The Oligarchic-Corporate State, and Anthropological Ideological Discourse', *Anthropological Theory* 5(3): 285–99.

Khanna, S.K. 2010. *Foetal/Fatal Knowledge: New Reproductive Technologies and Family-building Strategies in India*. Belmont, CA: Cengage/Wadsworth.

Knorr, J., and B. Meier (eds). 2000. *Women and Migration: Anthropological Perspectives*. New York: St Martin's Press.

Koehn, P.H. 2006. 'Globalization, Migrant Health, and Educational Preparation for Transnational Medical Encounters', *Globalization and Health* 2(2): 1–16.

Llacer, A., M.V. Zunzunegui, J. Amo, L. Mazarrasa and F. Bolumar. 2007. 'The Contribution of a Gender Perspective to the Understanding of Migrants' Health', *Journal of Epidemiology and Community Health* 61: 4–10.

Lu, Y. 2009. 'Rural–urban Migration and Health: Evidence from Longitudinal Data in Indonesia', *Social Science and Medicine* 69: 1–8.

Mahalingam, R. (ed.). 2006. *Cultural Psychology of Immigrants*. New York: Routledge.

Poudel, K.C., M. Jimba, J. Okumura, A.B. Joshi and S. Wakai. 2004. 'Migrants' Risky Behaviors in India and at Home in Far Western Nepal', *Tropical Medicine and International Health* 6(8): 897–903.

Purewal, N.K. 2010. *Son Preference: Sex Selection, Gender and Culture in South Asia*. Oxford: Berg.

Salant, T., and D.S. Lauderdale. 2003. 'Measuring Culture: A Critical Review of Acculturation and Health in Asian Immigrant Populations', *Social Science and Medicine* 57: 71–90.

Scheper Hughes, N., and M. Lock. 1987. 'The Mindful Body: A Prolegomenon to Future Work in Medical Anthropology', *Medical Anthropology Quarterly* 1(1): 6–41.

Unnithan-Kumar, M. 2004. 'Spirits of the Womb: Migration, Reproductive Choice and Healing in Rajasthan' in F. Osella and K. Gardner (eds), *Migration, Modernity and Social Transformation in South Asia*. Delhi: Sage, pp.163–89.

Unnithan-Kumar, M., and G. De-Neve. 2006. 'Producing Fields, Selves and Anthropology', in G. De-Neve and M. Unnithan-Kumar (eds), *Critical Journeys: The Making of Anthropologists*. Aldershot: Ashgate, pp.1–17.

Unnithan-Kumar, M., K. McNay and A. Castaldo. 2008. 'Women's Migration, Urban Poverty and Child Health in Rajasthan', Working paper T-26. Brighton: Sussex Centre for Migration Research, University of Sussex.

Vanderlinden, L.K. 2009. 'German Genes and Turkish Traits: Ethnicity, Infertility, and Reproductive Politics in Germany', *Social Science and Medicine* 69: 266–73.

Varley, E. 2009. 'Targeted Doctors, Missing Patients: Obstetric Health Services and Sectarian Conflict in Northern Pakistan', *Social Science and Medicine* 69: 1–10.

Xiang, B. 2010. 'Rushing, Waiting and the Suspended Life: Temporal Anxieties in Labour Outmigration from Post-socialist China', unpublished seminar presentation, University of Sussex 15 October.

CHAPTER I

Migration, Belonging
and the Body that Births
Pakistani Women in Britain

Kaveri Qureshi

This chapter explores the life histories of middle-aged Pakistani women who migrated to Britain in the 1960s and 1970s as the brides or daughters of industrial workers, did piecework at home or labour jobs, and brought up their children to adulthood. As this generation of women entered their fifties and sixties, they were preoccupied with their ageing bodies and deteriorating health, which brought back for them memories of migration, building their lives in a new place and passing through the life course. Their identity as mothers was central to their sense of who they were, yet migration changed the nature and practices of motherhood and made, over time, for different kinds of relationships with their children. The labour they foreground in their life histories raises important questions about the complexities of inhabitance, and the ways in which belonging is negotiated and exercised through the reproductive body.

One of the women, Mariam, was told by her GP, 'if you're over the age of forty, you just have to accept being ill'. This depressing advice is supported by the findings of health surveys that report that from the age of thirty, and cumulatively with each successive decade of their lives, Pakistanis, and particularly Pakistani women, bear an excess and premature burden of chronic illness compared to other ethnic groups in England. A large part of this excess burden of ill health can be accounted for by their economic and political marginalization, which engenders inequalities in health and access to health-care (Evandrou 2000; Nazroo 2006). The middle-aged women I worked with had been diagnosed with a litany of conditions, including diabetes, high blood pressure, heart disease, arthritis, back pain, kidney disease, stomach ulcers, gall stones, thyroid and gynaecological conditions, and a number of them suffered from other chronic complaints that their doctors could not diagnose. The women talked about their chronic conditions in such a way that they seemed to materialize their emotional and mental distress, waxing and waning in relation to other stresses in their life courses. Their talk about their health echoes accounts of 'embodied metaphors' (Low 1994) in which the body emerges as a mutable mediator between self and society. Their bodies were shaped by life history and relational experience as well as collective identities.

In life history interviews and conversations, the women talked about the onset of chronic illness by emphasizing their feminine toil and reproductive labour, invoking a narrative structure which I elaborate below. Looking back over their lives and talking about their illness and sense of ageing before their time, many of the women invoked migration histories, repeated pregnancies and obstetric trauma, the hard and intricate work of bringing up children in a new place alongside engaging in paid work to provide for their families financially. They used a rich, bodily vocabulary to talk about motherhood and the toll that reproductive labour took on their health. My data suggests that these stories were not merely told for my benefit, but were co-produced, or to use Carrithers's (1995) term, 'confabulated' with other interlocutors in their everyday worlds of family and community. I found echoes of these stories, often mythologized, in the discourse of their adult children, who talked about their mother's ill health as an expression of their collective lot as 'Asian women', oppressed by their families and the capitalist-imperialist system alike.

These women's accounts of their health in terms of their biographies resonate with a vein of migration studies that attends to the complicated relationships between place, body and identity. Steven Feld and Keith Basso's edited volume *Senses of Place* goes beyond earlier work which identified place with immobility and staying put, and theorizes place in conditions of diaspora and displacement. Their lens turns towards the process of 'emplacement', the 'cultural processes and practices through which places are rendered meaningful – through which ... places are actively sensed', alongside the 'complex ways in which places anchor lives in social formations ranging widely in geographic location, in economic and political scale, and in accompanying realms of gender, race, class and ethnicity' (Feld and Basso 1996: 7). In the same volume, Edward Casey (1996) stresses the relationship between emplacement and embodiment, the body as the vehicle between self and place, bodies engaging with places through practice, and places sedimented through daily activity. Through the language of Bourdieu's conceptualization of habitus, Casey sees bodies, differentiated by gender, race and class identity, as carriers of 'traces of places' in the memories and dispositions people bring to their ways of being in the world.

This work paves the way for empirical studies exploring how migrants' ways of talking about health and illness are embedded in their experience of place. Isabel Dyck (1995, 2006), writing about immigrant women in Canada, sees their accounts of health and illness management as moral tales about 'being in place' constructed about the body at different scales. Describing their practices of health-seeking, self care and cooking, these are narratives about bodily experience that differed between Canada and their places of origin – but equally, the women equate social well-being with a sense of bodily rootedness in Canada. Others have emphasized more the inscription of relations of political economy on migrant bodies, commenting on how labour processes are felt and become marked on the body. Abdelmalek Sayad (2004) describes how Algerian immigrants in France relate to their bodies through contradiction, caught between the economic rationalism of the factories they work in, which value their bodies in terms of output in production cycles, and their own experience of their bodies as a way of being and existing in the world. Katy Gardner's (2002) work with Bengali elders in London picks up how men and women narrate their bodily deterioration in differing ways, men recalling the hard labour of their jobs, and women stressing their caring roles and transnational worries about their families in Bangladesh. Usefully, she stresses the material effects that places have on migrants' lives, feelings and bodily experiences, but also how 'changing bodies play an important role in how places are perceived and acted upon' (ibid.: 213). However, I suggest that what needs to be made more explicit is the centrality of reproductive work and the reproductive body to these processes.

Irene Gedalof (2009) offers theoretical orientations for approaching the specific identity and subjectivity of the migrant 'body that births'. She argues that maternal practices have been misrepresented in writing about migration, which – with the emphasis on the dynamic reconstructions of transnational families – privileges displacement as the motor that injects transformation, and reinforces a problematic view of reproduction as otherwise repetitive and uncreative. Gedalof outlines the significance of interventions by Irigaray (1985), Young (1990), Cavarero (1995) and Battersby (1998) in thinking through alternative approaches to subjectivity from the perspective of a body that births, complicating our understandings of the repetitive reproductive work undertaken within the domestic sphere, and of non-singular, relational senses of self and identity that might emerge from a repeated play of embodied care practices. However, Gedalof argues that these writers privilege sexual difference over other forms of difference, and overlook the intersections of sexual difference with race, ethnicity and other forms of collective identity.

This is a particularly important omission for understanding migrant women, whose reproductive practices are often mobilized and constrained within discourses of national, ethnic and racialized identities (see Yuval-Davis and Anthias 1992). Black feminists have been more insistent on linking physical reproductive work to processes of reproducing collective identities. For bell hooks (1991), for example, women's role in building a stable 'home-place', where a sense of self and belonging can be affirmed, is necessary. The work of producing domesticity may be a conventional role assigned by patriarchy, but what is important is that black women took this conventional role and expanded it, using the home as a site from which to educate their families as part of building communities of radical resistance.

Gedalof's work suggests ways for thinking about the importance of reproduction for emplacement, the complexities of inhabitance, the innovation and negotiation that are worked in to reproductive labour in the context of migration, and the new senses of self shaped by motherhood that come out of this process, as I will explore in this chapter.

Research Setting

My research set out to explore the social course of illness in Pakistani families, looking beyond individual biographical reconstructions to how illness experience is embedded in the realms of kinship and neighbourhood, structure and culture (Kleinman 1999). The research was mainly situated in the docklands borough of Newham, a predominantly working-class borough in London's East End, between inner-city Tower Hamlets and the more prosperous commuter suburbs of Essex. Among remarkably complex waves of migration which fed its changing industries, Newham is home to about 19,000 Pakistani Muslims (LBN 2006), mostly of Mirpuri/Kashmiri and northern Punjabi heritage. The old London borough of West Ham was known as the industrial heart of the south-east, but its industries have been in decline since 1900 (LBN 1972, 2002). From the 1950s to the 1970s, Commonwealth migrant workers sustained these dockland industries at a time when they would have otherwise been economically unviable, allowing workshops and factories to remain profitable through low pay and poor health and safety standards (IRR 1991).

As elsewhere in Britain, Pakistani women began to migrate to Newham in appreciable numbers in the 1970s, in the context of tightened immigration and citizenship laws, as a result of which female spouses and dependent children were some of the few remaining classes of people eligible for entry. The first generation of women migrants were engaged in the garment industry or 'rag trade' in the East End, which was at that time coming under pressure from globalization, and the only way it survived in any form was by cutting costs and relying on ethnic minority women to work for very low pay (Hirst and Zeitlin 1989). Pakistan in the 1970s was a country with one of the highest fertility rates in the world, where a woman could expect to have at least six children (Sathar and Casterline 1998). Most migrant women from this generation kept up this high level of fertility, and had an average of four children per woman (Berthoud 2000). This has been understood in relation to the traditional high value placed on childbearing and maintaining the joint family system (Saxena et al. 2002), although here I explore how women spoke of large families in relation to diasporic ethnic assertion.

Emplacement

In men's accounts, wives were depicted as passive – often missed and longed for in the early days, but better placed in Pakistan until they were required to follow at their husbands' bidding. Women were in accordance at times with this official narrative. For example, one woman described her group of friends as *England ki brides* ('brides of England'), amid appreciative laughter from the rest. However, around this official narrative were more differentiated stories of migration, stressing their resistive agency and involvement in the decision to join their husbands in England.

The story of Mumtaz's mother Sugra illustrates the capacity for resistive agency in these pioneering women. In the early 1970s, Mumtaz's father was living with a Russian woman whom he had met in Bradford. Sugra, who has now passed away, came to know about the affair through multiple channels of communication that existed between the migrants and their kin and village friends. Mumtaz remembered that her mother felt ashamed and vulnerable; she wrote to her husband, requesting him to send her a visa and money for her ticket, but he ignored her letters. So, she travelled through other channels. A family who were neighbours in her parents' village were coming to England by road, and Sugra requested that they take her with them for a small sum of money that she raised by herself. Entirely unsupported by her husband, she brought her children overland on a two-month journey to England. The women therefore had some space to negotiate migration, their agency supported by strong relationships with husbands who could be convinced to call them over, or failing that turning to their natal kin (see Unnithan-Kumar 2001).

Most of the women's first impressions of England were of disappointment with the environment, the dirt, and the poverty they saw in the docklands. They remembered London as very 'quiet' in those days, by which they meant that there were relatively few Asian people to be seen out and about, and that it lacked the hustle and bustle of Pakistan. As Zubia remembered, 'there were hardly any shops at that time. You used to find no shops for food, you know, the things we eat. And there was so much snow ... You used to go far to get paraffin in the big bottles'. They had to adjust to the new climate and way of living, as well as to the White people living around them. They also had to 'adjust' to their husbands, who for some were relative strangers, and for others had changed after coming to England.

Nusrat, who was from Karachi and educated to degree level, told stories about the difficulty of accomplishing everyday tasks when she first came to England. Though she and her husband were unusual in that they both spoke good English, he was not confident in speaking to English people, and she remembered how he used to send her out to do the shopping. She found the informal Cockney language hard to grasp. 'They swallow half the word', she said, '"because" becomes "cos" and library becomes "libry"'. She added, signalling the labour of 'adjustment', that 'it wasn't just going to a new place, but I had to get to know him, I had to *acquire* him'.

Domestic life, family-building, sisterhood and friendship were important in creating a sense of 'emplacement', a process in which people 'encounter places, and invest them with meaning' (Feld and Basso 1996: 8). Haseena felt quite alone when she first came from Pakistan but, she said, 'slowly slowly I found friends who I could share with, talk to like I'm talking to you'. Her best friend was a woman who lived on the same street, but it took them many years to find each other. She remembered:

I used to drop my kids and she used to pass by me and drop her kids. And then I found out she's only living here on this road. She'd just say, '*Salaam aleikum, walaikum salaam*'. I never knew her name. And then the kids were talking one day, and she goes, 'Oh, do you live here?' And I said, 'Yes, it's not far, it's just here'. And then she introduced herself and I introduced myself, and since then we've become good friends.

Haseena's memory conveys a sense of belonging that was sedimented through the daily activity and sociability of dropping their children at the school gates.

Now middle-aged, their initial feelings of upheaval and loss had given over to a sense of embedding in London, as their children had grown up and established their lives in England. It was their adult children's growing up and settling down in this place that was the permanent turning point. They told me, often, that nowadays it was London that they missed when they visited Pakistan, as all their family was there. Fauzia told me she had already bought the *chador* (cloth) ready for her funeral shroud. She wanted to be buried in London because, 'I eat in London, I live in London, so I'll die in London'.

Maternity

Many women talked about their deteriorating health as the result of physical fatigue. They felt tired and weak: 'When you get to a certain age, and with everything that I've been going through, you know your body's not the same any more'; 'I get tired, now I feel that I have become very *kamzoor* (weak) in my body'; 'my hands shake like an old person'. They said they were worn out from years of hard work endured in the early years of migration and settlement in England. For many, their ageing bodies were rooted in childbearing. Illness narratives often began with complications of pregnancy and childbirth. For some, gestational diabetes was the precursor for type 2 diabetes, whilst others said that they had been subjected to malpractice during maternity care. Zubia had three of her children with epidurals, and 'they done something wrong in my back as well, they stuck a pin and it went wrong. It just tore the tissue in my spine'. She felt that all her troubles with back pain started after that. For two years, she said, she was in and out of her GP's surgery trying to make him see that she was not suffering mere muscular pain but that real damage had been done, but he took no notice. Obstetric trauma was inseparable from their experiences of hospitalized maternity as a site of control and complete loss of agency, and as Gardner (2002) argues, these circulating stories of clinical malpractice have to be seen as a complicated politics of complaint about their feelings of not being treated well, or equitably, by Britain's National Health Service.

Successive pregnancies were weighed out in the women's life histories in conjunction with other stresses in their life. As Caroline Bledsoe (2002) has argued, ageing is not a cumulative process but measured out in accordance with a conjunctural life course. Khadija remembered her fourth pregnancy as the point at which her health began to decline, a critical event binding together concerns about her marriage, her family's financial state, worries about her parents back in Pakistan and obstetric trauma. Her husband, trained in the Pakistan army, had migrated to England in the early 1970s and retrained as an electrician. In 1975 he was overlooked for promotion, and had a younger, less experienced white colleague appointed as his supervisor. He was resentful, lost his job and became abusive, and it was at this point Khadija recalled that she had began to suffer from *kamzoori* (weakness) 'because of the worries … I was carrying a baby, I used to think, the child that is to be born … who will feed this child, there are so many expenses when a child is born'. She remembered that when she went to her GP, several months before the due date, she had been told that she had 'no blood in her body', and was sent straight to hospital for a traumatic pre-term delivery.

Motherhood

The theme of sacrifice was woven into the women's life histories in other ways, too. The experience of motherhood was laced with ambivalences associated with bringing up children in a place that they sometimes felt was inimical in terms of values. In Britain, the outside environment was potentially threatening as children could be led astray by a morally deficient multicultural society. As Shaheen, mother of three, explained:

> it's a big thing to bring up the children correctly, according to our culture and our religion. Keeping them on the straight road is a very difficult thing. There are too many outside influences – *English log, kale log* [English people, black people], the children do get influenced. It's hard to bring them up in your own religion. Even the big *namazis* [those who are pious] can be let down by their children.

As mothers, they felt they had to compensate for the outside environment and actively inculcate in their children many things that they would have picked up automatically had they been in Pakistan. They had a kind of folk notion of habitus (Osella and Osella 2008: 170), linking their children's dispositions to the places they bore traces of within them, and observed the way that their children's spontaneous gestures of behaviour departed from those that they would have desired. Continuing her life history, Shaheen told me: 'in our parents' time there was that thing about *izzat*, respect – we've lost all of that in this country. My parents didn't even dare to raise their eyes to each other. Here we've lost our culture, our roots. We have to make sure that we can teach our children in this country'. This required conscious effort, such as taking children to the mosque because 'they don't get that at school'. The women often regretted that their children had not learnt to speak 'their own language' as fluently as they would have liked, but they agreed that religion was something that could not be compromised upon. Generalizing her situation to that of her generation, Shaheen emphasized again their collective sacrifice and toil: 'because of our family responsibilities, bringing up children is very important. We don't think of anything as housework. It's nothing. To better our next generation is very important. It they make a mistake, you need to be there to pick it up and correct it'.

As Kanaaneh (2002: 203) argues in her ethnography of Palestinian women in Israel, reproduction is a key terrain on which the relationships between identity and nationalism, the body and the self, are worked out. These processes involve a tight connection between physical reproduction and cultural reproduction, centring not only on women's position as mothers, but as mothers of nations. However, the women's reflections on bringing up their children as Muslims in a non-Muslim society imply that this cannot be seen as a reproduction of fixed traditions, but an active negotiation of difference. Mrs Begum, now in her early sixties, had more than twenty grandchildren, and interacting with them was the only time I would ever see her using English; she would sing them lullabies and rhymes such as 'Twinkle, Twinkle, Little Star', 'Rub-a-Dub-Dub' and 'Solomon Grundy', illustrating how the local ways of motherhood in East London had been incorporated into her repertoire of maternal practices over a long period of interacting with her own children, as they themselves were shaped by their schooling. This bricolage of practices entailed coming to terms with her daughters' school uniform in the 1970s: knee-length skirts and bare legs. As they entered their teenage years in the 1980s though, she remembered her daughters as becoming 'too free'. Looking through family photo albums from the 1980s and seeing her daughters smiling boldly in jeans and blouses, in *salwar kameez* (traditional Punjabi suit) with the *dupatta* (scarf) slung across their chests, or without a dupatta at all, I got some sense of the kinds of embodied practices that were entangled with questions concerning her competences as a mother and her children's place within the community. Rather than risking them completing secondary school, she removed her daughters from school at the age of fifteen and sent them to Pakistan for marriage, to keep them out of 'bad company' and protect them from romantic affairs. As mothers and daughters, women embodied notions of cultural tradition and collective identities, yet what can be discerned in their reproductive labour is a process of negotiation rather than unchanging tradition.

Children's upbringing was talked about by women as a kind of test of their abilities as mothers to transmit culture and religion in the face of an uncaring outside society. However, motherhood was not only about meeting community expectations; it was about meeting their hearts' desires, joy and solace in an unfamiliar place. Khadija, whose husband became abusive, told me that in the hardest days of her marriage she would force herself to be strong for the sake of her children: 'my children were the support of my life … I used to keep looking at them and feel happy, and think that once they grow up they will reduce my troubles, that my life would be easy when they grew up'. This sense of hopes invested in children was repeated through the interviews and conversations. Education was a primary means through which the women talked about redeeming the hardships of migration vicariously through their children, in contrast to the struggle they had faced in England themselves. Nasreen was fiercely ambitious for her children and tried to instil this in them: 'my life's goal is for them to be able to do what I couldn't do'. She said she had always tried to protect her children: 'until I survive and have soul in my body, the children should not have any problem … They should study, because we have suffered ourselves'.

Now that their children had grown up, studying at university or getting married, seeing how their adult children turned out gave cause for self-reflection about their competences as mothers. Sayeeda felt that her children's strong-willed stubbornness over their marriages was an indictment of the excessive control under which they had brought them up: 'it's a culture problem. We impose our culture from Pakistan onto our children and they rebel, and then because of that the children have stress with their mothers and fathers'. Other women felt that there was something positive about the ways in which their daughters had grown up to question things. Nasreen said approvingly: 'The children from here – the girls are more aggressive than boys. They watch their mothers suffering and they say "Why? I don't want any part of it". They've become a bit more selfish, they fight for their rights'. She liked the way that her daughters went beyond merely 'following' their religion prescriptively but instead interrogated it and got to the bottom of its principles. This gave them a platform to live their lives freely and defend themselves from mindless tattle, she felt. Comparing her two daughters, she said: 'My older daughter has a degree in languages, she says she needs to wear the *dupatta*, but my other daughter wears clothes that are like this [she smooths down the material on her waist], all short and tight. She says she doesn't care, she says she knows what's in the Qur'an and what's necessary. It's a habit'.

In middle age, then, the women reflected on ways in which motherhood in England was stressful, invoking the substantial community pressures relating to, and judgements made about, their competence as mothers, all of which had also contributed to their poor state of health. However, woven into these accounts of motherhood was also a dynamism, as their reproductive labour engaged place and was simultaneously acted upon by place.

'The Fruit of My Own Sweat and Blood'

Unlike Shaheen, who had never done paid work and emphasized the extent to which she and her generation had immersed themselves in the intricate labour of raising their children, for other Pakistani migrant women, motherhood in Britain entailed working shoulder-to-shoulder with their husbands to bring in money to support their families as well as dependants 'back home'. Mrs Sharif's story is a good example of the physical toll that paid work was felt to have taken on their bodies. When I asked her about how her ill health had come on, she took me all the way back to the first years after coming to England and told me about her hard life. When she came to London in 1965, her husband was working in a factory in Southall, and they were poor. They shared a house with two other families from Lahore. They were trying to make ends meet for their six small children on her husband's meagre wages, and all of the children needed food and clothing. The Sikh women she had made friends with in her neighbourhood told her about work making garments, so she bought a sewing machine and started doing piecework at home, stitching shorts for a clothing manufacturer. A couple of Jewish men would bring the material for a hundred pairs of shorts at the beginning of the week, and she would earn a penny for each completed pair. She used her income for the housekeeping and for the children, so that her husband could save money for the deposit on their first house. She stressed, 'if my husband was making £12 a week, I was making £6', emphasizing her financial contribution to their becoming established in England. They bought a shop in Southall, and set up a clothes business selling clothes sewn by Mrs Sharif. 'We made such a lot of profit on that shop', she reminisced. She bought machines for sewing, cutting and embroidering, and continued to do sewing, although on better terms. At one time, she recalled, she was sewing for West End boutiques and making good money. 'So much hard work in those days', she recalled, 'so much hard work. But that was how we managed to make money – it was my own *khoon pisine di kamai* (the fruit of my own sweat and blood)'. Her repeated phrase, *khoon pisine di kamai*, which was echoed by other women, used strongly bodily language to stress her economic contribution to family life, and located her ill health in having sacrificed herself beyond the feminine domestic realm.

Paid work was laced with moral questions about being a 'good woman' and a 'good mother'. Many of the women who had worked took pains to stress that they were not working out of greed but to bring in some extra money to help with the children's clothes or the housekeeping: 'It's not that I'm spending it on gold'. The necessity of not compromising on the children's upbringing made many women look for paid work that could be carried out within the home, machining for the garment trade, painting toys or preparing food for others. Paid work alongside bringing up children required resourcefulness and hard work. Rabia ran up against deadlines because she would be so busy with the children that she would only find time to run the sewing machine after they had gone to bed: she would be regularly up sewing until 4 AM, and the workman who came to collect the garments would be on her back. She'd fall behind and have to tell him she wasn't ready, but it was like talking to a brick wall. Sewing itself hurt the body. As another woman emphasized: 'I did sewing work for ten years. Now I've got this tight muscle in my neck here when I move. I can't even sit'. The fact that this culturally novel engagement in industrial paid work was always referred to and legitimated with reference to the material needs of their children is a powerful illustration of the inherent dynamism of the reproductive sphere – the women emphasized that the changes they introduced were in order to effect continuity in reproducing their families.

This narrative of tired bodies was also reiterated by their children's generation, who would talk about their mothers' ill health as the result of their hard lives living in cramped, shared housing, having to look after large families and other young children who had come over, and years spent bent and squinting over sewing machines. Twenty-three-year-old Ayesha told me about the reasons her mother's health problems had come on:

> I really do think that with Asian women, because they have so many children, but it does seem that the older they get … although they all say it's because of their children, they've not turned out quite right, but a lot of them do have problems … They're not very old, like my mum's younger than your mum, she's forty-seven, that's all, she's not old at all … But because she's always had kids and then more kids, she never had the opportunity to go out, she was always working to earn money for her kids.

The way she links her mother's individual life history to that of other Asian women illustrates the collective 'confabulation' (Carrithers 1995) of the suffering of migration, which has been passed down through inter-generational storytelling, mythologized and turned into a theory of premature ageing.

Pnina Werbner (1980), analysing the surprising emphasis on shared experiences of poverty in the oral histories of otherwise competitive Manchester Pakistani entrepreneurs, writes of this as a 'community of suffering' narrative. This is a term she borrows from Victor Turner: 'the affliction of each is the concern of all; likeness of unhappy lot is the ultimate bond of ritual solidarity' (Turner 1957: 302). Werbner suggests that this common consciousness can only be understood in relation to racism. To confront experiences of racism culturally and symbolically, she argues, Manchester Pakistanis used their life histories to redefine themselves. The 'community of suffering' narrative culturally transformed the physical and emotional hardships of migration into a myth of endurance and sharing. Here, I suggest that in later life, this narrative is being put to work again in transforming feminine toil into tired and prematurely aged bodies as the legitimate result of sacrifices undergone on behalf of their families. The women's use of collective language such as 'Asian women' to talk about their own circumstances as reflecting those of other migrant women of their generation signals their awareness of how the patriarchal relations of the post-war migrants were constituted in articulation with capitalism and racism as interlocking systems. They managed to pass this collective narrative down to their children in their stories of migration – using the 'homeplace' (hooks 1991) as a site from which to educate their families.

Grandmothers, Mothers, Daughters

Early work on middle-aged women suggested that women experience the end of childbearing years as somehow masculinizing, as their role transforms from a ritually polluting menstruating, childbearing woman to a non-polluting, androgynous older woman (see Brown 1982). The women I knew did not see it that way: there was no sense in which they talked about a loss of feminine roles or becoming 'manlike'. They continued to be active mothers even after their children had grown up; they became mothers-in-law, and continued to be highly involved as care-givers after the arrival of grandchildren. Although the metaphoric extension of motherhood is more developed in Rasmussen's ethnographic example of Tuareg women's healing rituals, due to their identification with the matrilineal ancestor spirits, there are still strong resonances with her observation that in the social roles of mother-in-law and grandmother, 'women are transformed from child-bearers to culture-bearers' (Rasmussen 2000: 94).

From the women's life histories I collected, it emerged not only that children continued to be important throughout women's life courses, but also that migration had introduced substantial changes into the kinds of relationship that the women had with their adult children. Looking across the fifty-odd families I worked with, my data shows there has been an increased emphasis on matrilateral kinship in England. In middle age, as their health was ailing, the women reflected at length on their preference for spending time with, and being looked after by, their daughters as compared to their *bahus* (daughter-in-laws). They felt that the *khidmat* (care) done by a daughter for her parents was more free and loving. Moreover, they had close and spontaneous friendships with their adult daughters. Safina's daughter had got married and moved away, but as Safina and her husband were not keeping well, the daughter had managed to persuade her husband to live nearby so that she could visit them on a daily basis. Safina reflected on how lucky she felt that the in-laws had agreed to the arrangement, as 'when I think that if my daughter wouldn't have been here, and if her husband wouldn't have compromised to stay nearby, then god knows what would have happened. Usually the in-laws do not think'. Her daughter was everything to her: 'she is my first friend ... she is my daughter, my sister, everything ... I share everything with her'. The closeness of relationships between mothers and adult daughters, and the husband as the one who 'adjusts', is similar to kinship practices among working-class White East Enders in the 1950s (Young and Willmott 1957).

Writing on Manchester Pakistanis in the 1980s, Werbner (1988) describes an emerging matrilateral bias among second-generation women, with closer relationships being maintained by female kinswomen, particularly mothers, daughters and sisters. Shaw (2004) relates this practice to the preference for transnational marriage, such that young women marrying spouses from Pakistan will live with the wife's parents' household for a period of some months or years, or until children have been born, before moving out to a council flat or their own house in the same area. However, according to Sylvia Vatuk's study of urban kinship in North India in the 1970s, rural to urban migration is often associated with bilateral kinship tendencies. Many urban women married within their own neighbourhood, which made for much more active and dense social interaction with their natal families, and for a blurring of statuses as daughter and bride: 'the strong emotional ties between parents and daughter, which would have been compartmentalized by traditional residence rules and clear role definitions, are allowed active expression' (Vatuk 1972: 142). It is not only international migration, then, that introduces transformation in the family.

Through local matrilateral kinship, the women remained mothers at the apex of a female-centred family, hyperbolizing their maternal roles. Mrs Anwar's two daughters had persuaded their husbands to buy houses on the same street as the 'main house' they had grown up in, where Mrs Anwar lived with her eldest son Nazir. Next door to the 'main house' was Mrs Anwar's eldest daughter, Naseem. The two houses were connected at the back, as they had a joint patio and the family left the back doors unlocked so that they could walk freely from one house to the other without going onto the street, and they sent round food or borrow furniture if extra were needed. Although all her children were now grown up, Mrs Anwar still continued to provide for them as a mother. She cooked for her daughters and sent round enormous volumes of food, even though they told her not to because standing up hurt her arthritis and made her head spin. On Saturdays, when her daughters would do their shopping, she would order from them six bottles of fizzy drinks. Her daughters would bring them to Mrs Anwar, and she would then gift them back to the three households on her street, providing sweet things as a treat. Since she did not see eye to eye with her daughter-in-law, Mrs Anwar would spend most of her time at Naseem's house, watching Indian dramas on TV and interacting with her grandchildren. Mrs Anwar would drop off to sleep on the sofa, but rouse herself in the small hours of the night to cross the patio back to the 'main house', as she felt it improper to stay the night in her married daughter's home.

Not all the women upheld the prohibition on staying at their married daughters' houses. Shaheen's mother Mrs Malik, whose husband had recently died, had a council flat but rarely slept in it. She would move between her children's houses following a fixed rota over the weekends, and during the week Shaheen's younger daughter or one of her maternal cousins would stay with her at the council flat. *Nani maan* (maternal grandmother) was a huge figure in the children's lives, and they shared close relationships. Shaheen explained this system in a practical manner, making no big deal of the ways in which the relationships among women in her family were in stark contrast to official kinship practice:

> We have all set days, like my mum comes to me on a Saturday, she goes to my brother on a Sunday, she goes to Bilqeez on a Friday, on a Thursday she's at my other sister's, then during the week I take my mum out shopping or whatever. I don't want her to be on her own, so she doesn't feel she's on her own. And during the winter months I bring her over to me more often cos the days are short and that's when she feels more lonely. Cos my brother works, my sister-in-law works, and I believe – although my brother does everything for my Mum – well, my sister-in-law can't do what we can do for our own mum. She can't feel the same thing as we can feel for our mum, because it's her mother-in-law, it's not her mother.

Conclusions

Recent work on migration has demonstrated that 'the body is both experienced through place and engages place' (Dyck 2006: 5). The accounts I have discussed in this chapter illustrate furthermore the centrality of the reproductive body in the process through which migrant women encounter places and time and invest them with meaning.

In middle age, the women reflected on their deteriorating health as a consequence of their difficult migration histories. They explained how their bodies bore the mark of obstetric trauma and what they recalled as their unjust and medicalized treatment from the National Health Service. Their situation as migrants heightened their awareness that they were not only mothers but mothers of nations, raising concerns about their competence at providing their children with an upbringing and inculcating dispositions that would have been second nature to them had they been in Pakistan. Motherhood was an intricate labour, and they insisted that it took its toll on their health, but it also gave space for pleasure. The women explained how their bodies had been marked by paid labour which they carried out shoulder-to-shoulder with their husbands, culturally unusual but performed to effect continuity in reproducing their families. I have suggested that the physical toll of feminine labour on which they dwelled must be comprehended as the product of a collective consciousness of upheaval. In the migration stories they told their children, they educated them about their poor lot as 'Asian women', and gave them an awareness of racism and patriarchy.

As their children grew up, they transformed 'from child-bearers to culture-bearers' (Rasmussen 2000: 94), their identities as mothers not flattened but hyperbolized through their relationships with adult children and grandchildren. Importantly, though, they were not bearers of official cultural traditions, but effected complex negotiations and innovations, which gave them new and unconventional ways of being a mother.

Gedalof says that we need to know more about how women construct migrant and transnational identities in the face of processes of displacement, non-belonging and isolation. But she asks: 'are we only hearing Odysseus' narrative of agency – still making the hero(ine) of migration narratives the uprooted, dislocated and solo actor remaking her identity in a new world? What about a migrant Penelope's story of emplacement, belonging and connectedness? Can we unpick the complexities of her small stories to reveal another site in which identities are made?' (Gedalof 2009: 97). This chapter should go some way towards thinking about alternative approaches to migrant subjectivity from the perspective of a body that births, the everyday sedimented activities of reproductive labour giving way, over time, to a complicated and relational sense of belonging and inhabitance.

Acknowledgements

This chapter comes from doctoral research funded by the ESRC, and was written up during a postdoctoral research fellowship funded by the John Fell Fund and Wolfson College, Oxford. This research set out to explore the social course of illness among Pakistani Muslims in the context of health inequalities, which mean that ethnic Pakistanis in Britain are disproportionately afflicted by chronic illness. I rented a room with a Pakistani family in Newham for two years (2005 to 2007) and met other Pakistani women through my fieldwork families, through four Asian women's groups which I attended in community centres, and through the women-centred networks that extended from these. Data were generated through ethnographic methods and recorded in fieldnotes. I also collected life histories and illness narratives in English and Urdu with fifty people living with chronic illness, of whom nineteen were women over the age of thirty-five. I am very grateful to Sarah Salway for doctoral supervision, to Punita Chowbey who assisted me with nine of the Urdu life histories, and to Alison Shaw, Filippo Osella and Maya Unnithan-Kumar for their mentoring and insights.

References

Battersby, C. 1998. *The Phenomenal Woman: Feminist Metaphysics and the Patterns of Identity*. Cambridge: Polity.

Berthoud, R. 2000. *Family Formation in Multi-cultural Britain: Three Patterns of Diversity*. Colchester: Institute of Social and Economic Research, University of Essex.

Bledsoe, C. 2002. *Contingent Lives*. Chicago: University of Chicago Press.

Brown, J. 1982. 'Cross-cultural Perspectives on Middle-aged Women', *Current Anthropology* 23(2): 143–56.

Carrithers, M. 1995. 'Stories in the Social and Mental Life of People', in E. Goody (ed.), *Social Intelligence and Interaction*. Cambridge: Cambridge University Press, pp.261–77.

Casey, E. 1996. 'How to Get from Space to Place in a Fairly Short Stretch of Time: Phenomenological Prolegomena', in S. Feld and K. Basso (eds), *Senses of Place*. Santa Fe, NM: School of American Research Press, pp.13–52.

Cavarero, A. 1995. *In Spite of Plato: A Feminist Rewriting of Ancient Philosophy*. Cambridge: Polity.

Dyck, I. 1995. 'Putting Chronic Illness in Place: Women Immigrants' Accounts of Their Healthcare', *Geoforum* 26(3): 247–60.

——— 2006. 'Travelling Tales and Migratory Meanings: South Asian Migrant Women Talk of Place, Health and Healing', *Social and Cultural Geography* 7(1): 1–18.

Evandrou, M. 2000. 'Ethnic Inequalities in Health in Later Life', *Health Statistics Quarterly* 8(Winter): 20–28.

Feld, S., and K. Basso (eds). 1996. *Senses of Place*. Santa Fe, NM: School of American Research Press.

Gardner, K. 2002. *Age, Narrative and Migration: The Life Course and Life Histories of Bengali Elders in London*. London: Berg.

Gedalof, I. 2009. 'Birth, Belonging and Migrant Mothers: Narratives of Reproduction in Feminist Migration Studies', *Feminist Review* 93: 81–100.

Hirst, P., and J. Zeitlin. 1989. *Reversing Industrial Decline? Industrial Structure and Policy in Britain and Her Competitors*. Oxford: Berg.

Hooks, B. 1991. *Yearning*. London: Turnaround.

Irigaray, L. 1985. *Speculum of the Other Woman*. Ithaca, NY: Cornell University Press.

IRR. 1991. 'Newham: The Forging of a Black Community'. London: Institute of Race Relations.

Kanaaneh, R. 2002. *Birthing the Nation: Strategies of Palestinian Women in Israel*. Berkeley: University of California Press.

Kleinman, A. 1999. 'Moral Experience and Ethical Reflection: Can Ethnography Reconcile Them? A Quandary for the New Bioethics', *Daedalus* 128(4): 69–97.

LBN. 1972. 'Background to the Borough'. Report available at the Archives and Local Studies room at Stratford Library, London.

———— 2002. 'The Newham Story: A Short History of Newham'. London: London Borough of Newham.

———— 2006. 'Focus on Newham: Local People and Local Conditions'. London: London Borough of Newham.

Low, S. 1994. 'Embodied Metaphors: Nerves as Lived Experience', in T. Csordas (ed.), *Embodiment and Experience: The Existential Ground of Culture and Self.* Cambridge: Cambridge University Press, pp.139–62.

Nazroo, J. 2006. 'Ethnicity and Old Age', in J. Vincent, C. Phillipson and M. Downs (eds), *The Future of Old Age*. London: Sage, pp.62–72.

Osella, C., and F. Osella. 2008. 'Nuancing the "Migrant Experience": Perspectives from Kerala, South India', in S. Koshy and R. Radhakrishnan (eds), *Transnational South Asians: The Making of a Neo-diaspora*. New Delhi: Oxford University Press, pp.146–80.

Rasmussen, S. 2000. 'From Childbearers to Culture-bearers: Transition to Postchildbearing among Tuareg Women', *Medical Anthropology* 19(1): 91–116.

Sathar, Z., and J. Casterline. 1998. 'The Onset of Fertility Transition in Pakistan', *Population and Development Review* 24(4): 773–96.

Saxena, S., P. Oakeshott and S. Hilton. 2002. 'Contraceptive Use among South Asian Women Attending General Practices in London', *British Journal of General Practice* 52(478): 392–94.

Sayad, A. 2004. *The Suffering of the Immigrant*. Cambridge: Polity.

Shaw, A. 2000. *Kinship and Continuity: Pakistani Families in Britain*. Amsterdam: Harwood Academic Publishers.

———— 2004. 'British Pakistani Elderly without Children: An Invisible Minority', in P. Kreager and E. Schroeder-Butterfill (eds), *Ageing without Children: European and Asian Perspectives*. Oxford: Berghahn, pp.198–221.

Turner, V. 1957. *Schism and Continuity in an African Society*. Manchester: Manchester University Press.

Unnithan-Kumar, M. 2001. 'Emotion, Agency and Access to Healthcare: Women's Experiences of Reproduction in Jaipur', in S. Tremayne (ed.), *Managing Reproductive Life*. Oxford: Berghahn, pp.27–51.

Vatuk, S. 1972. *Kinship and Urbanization: White Collar Migrants in North India*. Berkeley: University of California Press.

Werbner, P. 1980. 'Rich Man, Poor Man, or a Community of Suffering: Heroic Motifs in Manchester Pakistanis' Life Histories', *Oral History Journal* 8(Spring): 43–48.

———— 1998. 'Taking and Giving: Working Women and Female Bonds in a Pakistani Immigrant Neighbourhood', in P. Westwood and P. Bhachu (eds), *Enterprising Women: Ethnicity, Economy and Gender Relations*. London: Routledge, pp.177–203.

Young, I.M. 1990. *Throwing Like a Girl and Other Essays*. Bloomington: Indiana University Press.

Young, M., and P. Willmott. 1957. *Family and Kinship in East London*. London: Routledge.

Yuval-Davis, N., and F. Anthias. 1992. *Racialised Boundaries: Race, Nation, Gender, Colour and Class and the Anti-racist Struggle*. London: Routledge.

CHAPTER 2

To Be or Not to Be?
Cape Verdean Student
Mothers in Portugal

Elizabeth P. Challinor

This chapter focuses on how the experience of motherhood, within the context of migration, shapes migrant subjectivities, posing a challenge for Cape Verdean women to renegotiate their relations with themselves and with the wider world. The experience of migration, when familiar social relations are disrupted and new relations are forged, coupled with the experience of pregnancy and maternity, when a new relation between body and self develops that disrupts the immediacy of non-reflective self-knowledge (Gadow 1982), constitutes a rich source for ethnographic investigation into how displacement shapes notions of identity.

The experience of birth and pregnancy, like migration, may alienate women from their own bodies, which are transformed into objects over which they lose control. Jordan's concept of 'authoritative knowledge' has had an enormous influence upon studies of how biomedical knowledge subjugates other forms of knowing in the birth process (Davis-Floyd and Sargent 1997). Resistance to the hegemony of biomedical knowledge has resulted in the emergence of movements in favour of 'natural' births, such as the National Childbirth Trust of the United Kingdom with its emphasis on the right to choose. Nevertheless, gaining access to medical assistance, particularly in the South and amidst immigrant communities in the North, may be a more compelling issue than 'natural' birth. In her study of poor women in India, van Hollen (2003) found that, rather than criticize the excessive use of technology, these mothers complained that they had been denied access to it and were thus unable to reap its benefits.

Unnithan-Kumar, following Strathern, also points out that 'bodies do not belong to persons but are composed of the relations of which a person is composed' (Unnithan-Kumar 2003: 189). The women she has studied in Rajasthan 'experience their bodies through the collective membership of their social group' (ibid.: 189). The issue of individual control over their bodies is thus inseparable from the social relations of which their bodies are a part. Nevertheless, this is not to deny women the possibility of self-reflection. Unexpected pregnancy – 'a journey into vulnerability' – prompts 'an inner dialogue with uncertainty' (Marck et al. 1994: 269).

Researching how migrant experiences of unexpected pregnancy affect the self requires engaging at an intimate level with informants, whilst at the same time paying attention to the broader, structural context that impacts upon their sense of self. The methodological challenge lies in finding the right set of tools to be able to look both ways: inwards towards the self-understanding of informants, and outwards towards the phenomena of social and collective worlds. Drawing on the analytical concept of identity, together with its qualified variants such as 'fluid' or 'multiple' identities, may help to capture some of the processes at work as women are seen to 'negotiate' their 'multiple identities' as mothers, students, workers, immigrants and so forth; however, its underlying connotation of a flippant 'pick and mix' approach towards the self not only ignores structural constraints, but also the intensity of the emotions involved.

I propose the concept of 'subjectivity' as an alternative conceptual tool for examining these processes. As young women grapple with the challenges unplanned pregnancy presents them with, they are also engaged in a process of constructing their subjectivity, described by Biehl et al. as the 'continuous process of subjective experimentation – inner, familial, medico-scientific and political' (Biehl et al. 2007: 345). They embark upon an inner journey which compels them to reflect upon their own identity in their engagements and interactions with the wider world around them.

Relevant here is Bradley's (1996: 25) suggestion that we distinguish between three levels of social identity: passive, active and politicized. 'Passive identities', of which individuals are not particularly conscious, are derived from the relationships in which individuals are engaged during their everyday life. 'Passive' identities are thus not acted upon, and individuals do not usually define themselves by them unless a particular event occurs that draws their attention to their everyday relationships in a new way. This describes the position of many of the young women before they left Cape Verde. It was only after they had arrived in Portugal and were confronted with a new context in which their ethnic identities, for example, came to the fore. 'Active' and 'politicized' identities are those of which individuals have become conscious and which present a base for action which may, in some cases, be in response to the restrictive influence of wider structures. The ethnographic material discussed below examines the processes through which 'passive' social identities become 'active' (or 'politicized').

New Life in New Lives

Located 500 kilometres off the west coast of Senegal, the archipelago of Cape Verde is profoundly influenced by migration. Settled by Europeans in the 1460s, the islands developed a plantation economy with slaves taken from the African mainland, and became a transit point in the Atlantic slave trade. A mixed European and African population eventually emerged. Famine, drought and a poor resource base were among the major causes of mass emigration over the centuries. Portugal, the former colonial power in Cape Verde, continues to be a relatively popular destination for Cape Verdeans in search of a higher education which symbolizes the key to a wider world of potential prosperity.

The ethnography in this chapter derives from fieldwork conducted between May 2008 and December 2009 in Porto, Portugal, which included in-depth interviews with mothers and fathers, participant observation of appointments with doctors and nurses, and visits to nannies. Over thirty women were contacted, fourteen of whom were formally interviewed, and eleven were accompanied to appointments. I also conducted formal interviews with six fathers.

Unexpected pregnancy that interrupts higher education or work plans is experienced, by the majority of women contacted and interviewed, as oscillating between a sense of helplessness – struggling with pregnancy coupled with a range of difficulties, before, during and after birth – and of delight in a new found agency. Mothers claimed that overcoming difficulties contributed towards expanding their sense of self as individuals capable of taking on new and unexpected challenges.

At the onset of pregnancy, the implications of early unexpected motherhood within a context of immigration are experienced as overwhelming, with a sense of disorientation and loss of control. Personal relations are immediately affected, sometimes resulting in the inability or refusal of the fathers – and often the grandparents back in Cape Verde – to provide support.

After birth, reconciling motherhood with studies or work (or indeed both) and affordable childcare represents another hurdle to be overcome. Separation from family in Cape Verde deprives mothers of their customary support networks. The waiting lists for state funded childcare leave some women isolated at home, interrupting studies or work until a vacancy appears. Some of the mothers who share accommodation with fellow Cape Verdean students have occasional, informal babysitting arrangements so that they can go out to work, for example, at weekends, when nurseries are closed. Like the Cape Verdean migrant workers in Lisbon (Wall 2008), others opt to send their babies to Cape Verde, to be looked after by their family whilst they continue their studies in Portugal. The following provides more detailed ethnographic material of how women and men experienced unexpected parenthood. All of the names have been changed in order to guarantee anonymity.

No One Is an Island

Nearly all of the Cape Verdean mothers interviewed spoke of the difficulties they had faced when revealing their pregnancies to their family. The transition towards assuming motherhood far from home rendered their pregnant bodies sites of negotiation and contestation over which they had differing degrees of control. The way in which family relations become implicated in the decision-making processes of whether to go ahead or terminate an unexpected pregnancy corroborates Unnithan-Kumar's (2003) thesis of the importance of the collective, and brings to light the inseparability of personal and social identities.

Elsa had a close relationship with her mother: 'I tell her everything', she said. When she and her boyfriend had decided on an abortion, she communicated this to her mother over the phone, but her mother advised her to keep the baby. Abortion (legalized in 2007 in Portugal and in 1986 in Cape Verde) was illegal in Portugal at the time. Aware of the life-threatening risks of illegal abortion, Elsa's mother offered to look after the baby for her in Cape Verde instead: 'Better to have one more child than to end up without any'. Elsa finally decided to keep the baby with her in Portugal: 'I was more enthusiastic now that my mother had encouraged me'.

The case of Célia, demonstrates very clearly how the individual control that women have over their pregnant bodies cannot be separated from their social relations. Célia had arrived in Porto at the age of twenty-two to study, but she was unknowingly pregnant. Ignoring early signs of pregnancy, it was her uncle, with whom she was living, who insisted she take a pregnancy test. Her uncle communicated the positive result, by phone, to her father, resident in Lisbon, whose initial reaction was one of anger. He urged his daughter to give up her studies and come to live with him in Lisbon. Célia's uncle managed to persuade him otherwise after contacting relatives in Cape Verde, who also rang Célia's father in order to convince him that she should continue her studies. Abortion was not yet legal in Portugal and Célia claims that it never crossed her mind:

It never crossed my mind to do anything to stop her from being born. But my father's neighbours, they asked, 'How many months pregnant is she?' And my father said, 'Less than four months'. And they said, 'Well, she still has time'. But my father replied, 'She is not the first one to have a baby. There are many out there who are younger than her who had a baby. So she can have hers too'. My father didn't listen to them; but if he had done, I think I would have had to follow his decision, because he was paying for everything … Fortunately he reacted the way he did; he was an excellent father.

The role Célia's relatives had played in persuading her father to allow her to continue her studies suggests that she may have also been able to turn to them in order to keep the baby. What is clear, in either case, is that the power to do as she wished depended upon the outcome of negotiations between relatives that were not totally within her control.[1]

The cases discussed here suggest that issues of individual control and personal choice cannot be analytically separated from the influence of kinship relations upon individual decision-making processes, and that geographical distance does not appear to have weakened their influence, especially since, in most cases, the women were financially dependent upon relatives.

The Autonomous Subject?

Two women interviewed whose studies were not financed by relatives displayed more signs of independence from their families in their decision-making processes; however, this is not to say that they were immune from the influence of local interactions. The case of Maria reveals how new social relations made in Portugal altered her initial decision to abort.

Maria had tried everything within her powers to abort at a time when abortion was illegal in Portugal. She was given the contact of a woman who carried out clandestine abortions but, despite various attempts, never managed to meet her. The pills Maria took for a self-induced abortion were also ineffective. After these failed attempts, an older work colleague, whom she knew from her part-time job at a bank, noticed that Maria was looking unhappy and invited her for a coffee. Maria succumbed to her insistent questions and confided in her. Maria's work colleague immediately told her not to have an abortion because she and her husband had always wanted to have a 'coloured' child, and that they would take care of everything. The couple provided financial, material and emotional support. Maria claims that if it had not been for her Portuguese colleague, whom she described as 'like an angel from heaven', she would have continued in her efforts to abort. Maria only informed her family in Cape Verde that she was pregnant after she had decided to keep the baby. She felt, nonetheless, apprehensive about her mother's reaction, and asked a sister to break the news to her elderly, religious mother, who did so by posing the rhetorical question of whether she preferred her daughter to have an abortion or a baby.

Meanwhile, Luisa had received the news of her unexpected pregnancy with elation, but had suffered financial difficulties, to the point of going hungry, while she was pregnant. Coming from a large family, her parents could not afford to pay for her studies, which had originally been financed by a Portuguese boyfriend: a businessman resident in Cape Verde. Luisa was proud of having taken the decision to break off the relationship with him, and to find work in Portugal to finance her own studies. At first it had been very difficult to find work. Friends who had stayed close whilst money was no object abandoned her. Luisa was very disappointed by one of her sisters, resident elsewhere in Portugal, who had refused to lend her money, saying, 'You have made your choice'.

Luisa had left her Portuguese boyfriend for a Cape Verdean student in Portugal, who turned out to be unable to support her. It was, nonetheless, a choice that she did not regret having made, and she felt imbued with a sense of her own power:

> I thought that with the first difficulty I would … go straight back to Cape Verde. But I look at myself and say, 'Look, I am much stronger than I thought' … For my son, I can, I can do anything. Believe me. I think if it wasn't for [my son] I wouldn't have the strength to fight. Everyday, when I was pregnant and had difficult situations, I would say like this: 'For you baby, for you, mummy does everything'.

Here we see the transition from a 'passive identity' to a new 'active' social identity (Bradley 1996: 25) as a mother. Luisa's touching words to her baby in the womb illustrate the powerful influence of this new, emergent identity upon her sense of self. Her account also highlights the dialectical processes involved: restriction, disorientation, loss of control and isolation, as well as the potential to choose new directions, to make new social relations, to exercise power.

Upholding the Family Name Overseas: Stretching a Tradition?

During an interview, Maria justified to me her late father's reaction, years ago in Cape Verde, when he had thrown her older sisters out of the house on two separate occasions upon hearing that they were pregnant: 'In Cape Verde as soon as you become pregnant you're on the street. You may even come back home after three days, but it is a tradition so as not to dirty the family name. This is the way it is at the beginning ... They just cut off all contact'. Maria recalled that one of her sisters, who was eighteen years old at the time, was not allowed back home until the baby was born: 'When my parents saw the baby, their hearts softened and she came back home'. The Cape Verdean women in Porto had already left home, so they could not be physically thrown out. This section examines how this tradition was nonetheless upheld, and considers whether it was affected by geographical distance.

For women who are living at home and financially dependent upon their parents, pregnancy is usually unwelcome. According to Maria, it is a matter of family honour to expel the daughter. According to another informant, this may also be a way of trying to make the father of the baby take responsibility for the child. In some cases, the parents of the father take the pregnant woman in. Pregnancy outside marriage is not, in itself, stigmatized. In the interviews I conducted, it became apparent that the gender ideology supporting this tradition was much harder on women than on men.

Katia, twenty-five years old, had received warnings from her parents in Cape Verde not to follow her sister's example by becoming pregnant before completing her studies in Porto. When Katia broke the news to her father, he responded with anger, and demonstrated his disapproval by diminishing the monthly allowance he had been paying for her to study. Katia appeared to be more upset by her mother's reaction, from whom she had expected more support; however, her mother refused to talk to her on the phone and Katia spent the first two weeks crying in bed.

Much of the strength Katia had found to take on the responsibility of becoming a mother came from her partner, Miguel, who in turn found his strength from his parents. A 21-year-old student in his final year, Miguel immediately rang his parents in Cape Verde, as soon as Katia's pregnancy test was confirmed positive, to gauge their reaction. He told me, with satisfaction, how they had responded positively, having been themselves young parents, and that this had given him the necessary confidence to take on the responsibility.

Edgar, a 24-year-old father interviewed, told me how his mother had broken out into uncontrollable laughter when he gave her the news over the phone that Pamela, his nineteen-year-old girlfriend had discovered she was pregnant. Like Miguel, Edgar claimed that his mother's joyful reaction took a weight off his shoulders. Pamela, on the other hand, anticipating a negative reaction, waited for four months before telling her father, who also punished her by freezing and then permanently reducing her monthly allowance.

Although they had both sent photographs, neither Pamela nor Katia had had the opportunity to return to Cape Verde with their babies – they could not afford to pay for the flight – nor had their parents come to visit them. Pamela's Cape Verdean housemates claimed that once her father saw the baby in the flesh he would change his attitude; however, Pamela's son was six months old and Katia's daughter was fifteen months, and neither of their father's hearts had softened yet. Pamela knew from more sympathetic relatives that her father had publicly stated that he did not have a grandson. There may be a case for arguing that the physical distance between the women and their parents served to prolong the traditional period of estrangement required for upholding the family name.

The following section looks at how new social relations which emerge as a result of migration may produce a more reflexive attitude towards traditional practices as a 'passive' cultural identity becomes 'active' in the face of a new cultural context. Although active identities serve as a conscious base for action, they are not drawn upon in a continuous or consistent manner, since it is the context that will determine to what degree an 'active identity' will be promoted (Bradley 1996: 25).

'Respecting Both Sides': Negotiating Tradition

The Cape Verdean traditional ritual to 'look after' or 'keep' the baby's head (*guarda cabeça*), more commonly known as the 'seventh day', was intended to protect newborn babies from the supernatural powers seen as the cause of frequent deaths that occurred within the first week of life. Although it is still widely practised in Cape Verde, it is currently more of a social event, which brings together family and friends for a long night of eating, drinking, talking, playing cards, playing loud music and dancing. All of the noise and activity was traditionally supposed to frighten away witches, and after the seventh day had passed the witches no longer had any power over the baby's life (Lopes Filho 1995: 34).

Some parents had celebrated the seventh day in Porto; others claimed that circumstances had prevented them from doing so. Some mothers were still in hospital recovering from Caesareans, and others, recovering at home, found it required too much work at a vulnerable time without extended family support.

Diana, a 32-year-old pregnant Cape Verdean woman who had been living with a Portuguese family for five years, having helped to look after a terminally ill member of the family, had become so involved in these new social relations that it affected her decision of whether or how she should celebrate the seventh day. Due to move out and live with her partner after the baby was born, she knew that on the seventh day she would still be living with the Portuguese family, who had invited her to organize the celebration at their home. Nevertheless, Diana had reservations regarding what, in Cape Verde, would have been a self-evident celebration:

> The way in which the Portuguese do parties is different. They sit down, everybody talks, and everybody likes to listen to what the other person is saying … The Portuguese prefer silence and talking. Not Cape Verdeans! There is music, there is dance, people talk as well, but it is totally different … For example, the woman in this house likes to talk, but she doesn't like loud music; Cape Verdeans like loud music … The Portuguese invite less people; the godparents are Cape Verdean, they could invite lots of people.

Diana told me she wanted to 'respect both sides', since her partner was keen to have the party. Her partner's niece, Célia, had also offered her flat, but Diana felt that it would be rude to take the baby off elsewhere for the celebration. Both agreed that it was a complicated situation, and that one way out was to postpone the celebration until they had moved into their new flat, which meant that it would not take place on the seventh day.

Diana's sensitivity towards the differences between Portuguese and Cape Verdean parties indicates how developing a more active cultural identity had the paradoxical effect of distancing herself from Cape Verdean cultural existence and, in the words of van Binsbergen, of 'objectifying [culture] and making it a topic of conversation' (van Binsbergen 2003: 462). Diana did not identify herself totally with either side; rather, she could be seen as what van Binsbergen describes as one of the 'bearers of explicitly different cultural orientations capable of establishing at least a measure of communication between their respective cultural orientations' (ibid.: 519). In other words, since coming to live in Portugal, her identity, formerly shaped by Cape Verdean social relations, was now also shaped by social relations with her hosts that prompted a questioning of self, bringing to light the contingency and performativity of culture. Yet the idea of 'bearing' cultural orientations also needs to be handled with care, since it may paint an over static picture and attribute too much substance to the concept of culture.

Getting to Grips with the System: Seeking Healthcare

The struggles and silences that characterized encounters between Cape Verdean parents and health professionals elucidate the interplay between inner passages of self-reflection and outer passages of active engagement as parents sought to find their way around the labyrinth of the Portuguese health system. Most of the Cape Verdeans in the study considered the quality of maternal healthcare services to be better than in Cape Verde. Many of the women interviewed had had Caesareans, and only a few expressed their disappointment at not having had a natural birth. Like the Indian women studied by van Hollen (2003), access to services, information and knowledge was a more pressing concern.

A study of Cape Verdean immigrant utilization of medical services in the Netherlands argues that the necessary tools required to exercise 'medical citizenship' are care users' participation in health services and 'health literacy': 'the ability to make sound health care decisions in the context of every day life' for which reflexivity is identified as an essential feature (Beijers and de Freitas 2008: 237, 246). Beijers and de Freitas (ibid.: 251) attribute the low levels of health literacy amidst Cape Verdeans in the Netherlands to their disadvantaged socio-economic position, limited access to information and limited contact with other ethnic groups. The different degrees to which Cape Verdean parents exercised their medical citizenship in Porto are exemplified below.

Issues of Access: Fighting for Rights

The local health centre is the basic unit of the national health service in Portugal, which provides primary healthcare to the population. Upon registering at the health centre in their area of residence, patients are issued with a temporary document which is later substituted by a user card (*cartão de utente*). There are not enough general practitioners – family doctors – for the whole population, so patients on waiting lists for a family doctor may not always be seen by the same doctor.

The information booklet issued by Portugal's High Commission for Immigration and Intercultural Dialogue (ACIDI 2007), which informs immigrants of their rights and obligations whilst living in the country, states that foreigners with work visas, temporary residence and residence permits are entitled to user cards, and that foreigners who lack these documents may still register at their local health centres with residence certificates issued by their local authorities. The booklet notes that all individuals should be registered and issued with a user card. Family doctors are only mentioned in brackets in the booklet, stating that individuals should be registered 'if possible, with a family doctor' (ibid.: 74). My ethnography reveals that access to the kind of healthcare desired by Cape Verdean pregnant students was not always automatic, and involved taking an assertive stance vis-à-vis the state. Although 'active identities' are 'positive elements in an individual's self identification', they can also be 'promoted by the experience of discrimination' (Bradley 1996: 25–26).

The unsolicited accounts of Luisa, Katia and Miguel of their struggles with health centres, given within the context of an open interview on their experiences as young parents, display a high degree of reflexivity, and demonstrate how standing up for their rights, exercising 'medical citizenship', had become an integral part of their experience of consolidating their expanded sense of self.

Katia and Miguel told me that the biggest battle they had to fight in the first months of pregnancy was managing to register at a health centre that would guarantee them a family doctor, since they both felt that it was important that Katia be seen by the same doctor throughout her pregnancy. When she went to register at her local health centre, Katia was issued with a temporary document and told that she did not have the right to a card because she was a foreign student – 'sporadic' in the words of Katia. 'Do you think it is correct that I should be seen by a different doctor each time I come?' she had asked, making a moral claim in the form of a rhetorical question. The couple insisted that they wanted a family doctor, so they were advised to try at a new health centre that had opened. This constituted another 'battle' because they did not want to register her there. Once again Katia made a moral claim by simply exclaiming, 'I am pregnant'. Eventually, an exception – which the health centre insisted was 'irregular' – was grudgingly made to accommodate her.

Miguel criticized the inconsistencies of the health system. He said he had Cape Verdean student friends, some of whom had managed to register and obtain cards at their local health centres, whilst others had not. Why this dual approach? Miguel, a law student, was equipped with the necessary tools to enforce the rights he was entitled to. He told me that the right to health was independent of a person's legal situation.

Luisa had already managed to obtain a card from a health centre – the one that had refused to issue Katia with one – when she arrived from Cape Verde to study and before she became pregnant. Luisa claims that at first she received a temporary document and was told that the card would arrive later, but that when she went to ask for the card the woman who attended her issued another document. 'What has happened? Why can't you give me the card like you said you would?' she asked. The woman replied that people from PALOP (African lusophone countries) did not have the right to a card. Luisa claims to have retorted, 'Why don't I have the right? I am a citizen as well, aren't I?' The woman finally agreed to have a card issued to her. Luisa told me proudly that most of her Cape Verdean colleagues did not have cards, and that she had only received one because she had complained. Exercising medical citizenship meant having to speak out.

Ernestina, a shy young student mother, had attempted to make clear the inconvenience that a nurse's proposed home visit would cause on the date suggested through her body language. The nurse insisted upon the proposed date and Ernestina acquiesced. Having come to Portugal to study accountancy, Ernestina was certainly less aware of how to defend her own interests than the law student Miguel. Her shyness had manifested itself in Ernestina's refusal to allow me to record the interview I conducted, and in the reserved nature of her responses to my questions. We always communicated in Creole, and there may be a case for arguing that having to respond to the nurse in Portuguese undermined her self-confidence to speak out.

Keeping quiet does not necessarily signify low levels of health literacy. Although Diana was keen to go to preparation classes for her birth at the maternity hospital, she never brought up the subject herself during her routine appointments at the health centre. When she was around thirty-three weeks pregnant, the nurse casually asked her if she was already attending classes. Diana went to the maternity hospital the same day, where she was told that it was too late for her to start.

When I asked her why she had not brought up the issue of classes with the doctor, Diana explained to me that she had presumed that it was part of routine medical care to be informed at the appropriate time. Her passive attitude may thus be interpreted as displaying faith in the workings of the Portuguese health system, and indicating a desire to behave as an exemplary migrant patient, integrated into the host society. Nevertheless, her outward passivity in the appointments should not be interpreted as a sign of powerlessness. I had witnessed how Diana could stand up for her rights in exchanges with a Portuguese official who refused to acknowledge that Cape Verdean driving licences were valid in Portugal. Her passivity suggests, instead, a high degree of sensibility towards the 'other'. The ethnography below explores the way in which the authority of medical knowledge was constituted through social relations.

Protecting Relationships and Identities

Mothers with low incomes were entitled to apply for state-funded childcare, and although there was always a waiting list for nannies, students were usually given priority. Mothers whose babies were cared for by state-funded nannies were requested by social security to give the nannies lists of permitted baby foods. Nurses routinely gave mothers pamphlets with this information, but the social educator responsible for supervising the nannies' work specifically asked mothers for doctor's lists. I witnessed, on various occasions, the confusion that this caused, with the reluctance or refusal of doctors to write them. The social educator's desire to protect her nannies by giving them clear guidelines thus encouraged deference to doctors, and contributed towards the hegemony of expert medical knowledge which resulted in the incongruous situation of resistance by the doctors. Infant nutrition consequently became a hot potato which, as the case below demonstrates, was sometimes left in the parents' hands.

Miguel and Katia received a card through the post with an appointment for their one-year-old daughter with a paediatrician. The last time she was seen by a paediatrician their daughter was only two weeks old, and both parents were eager to get more specialist advice. When the parents picked their child up from the nanny, she asked them to check whether their daughter could consume regular cow's milk instead of formula. Although regular cow's milk has traditionally been considered appropriate for infants at the age of one, this has been questioned because cow's milk is harder to digest than formula as it contains high concentrations of protein and minerals. Some chemists in Portugal claim that paediatricians are now recommending infant formula until the age of three. A paediatrician that I consulted upon the matter dismissed this recommendation, invoking market interests.

During the appointment, the 'hierarchy of relations between specialists and patients' (Davis-Floyd and Sargent 1997: 21) was evident in the failure of both the paediatrician and the nurses to introduce themselves to the parents, or to explain the nature of the tests they had conducted. After they had finished, the paediatrician announced that the parents could leave. Miguel then said that they had a few doubts that they would like to clarify. Katia remarked that their daughter wasn't eating very well, and that they wanted some advice about food. The doctor replied:

> That isn't a question for this appointment. This appointment is just for these developmental tests. If you want to ask those kinds of questions then you have to ask your family doctor. If you want to ask your doctor to refer the baby to me for an appointment, then that is possible, but you have to go through him because I don't want to interfere with your doctor. If it were just a one off question, I could answer, but I don't want to interfere. It is a matter of professional ethics.

On the way back home, both parents expressed indignation at the paediatrician's response. Katia commented that her family doctor was not much help either, claiming that when she had requested him to provide a list of appropriate foods, his reply had left her speechless: 'I don't have children. I have no idea what they eat'.

Miguel said that he could understand if it were a family doctor not wishing to interfere with the paediatrician, but he found it difficult to understand that it should be the other way round. The paediatrician was the expert; he was the one with the special knowledge that they could not expect a family doctor to have. He noted that it was not actually the doctor's fault: it was the fault of the system. Nevertheless, Miguel still did not agree that priority should be given to the relationship between the two doctors: he felt that the paediatrician was more concerned to protect his relationship with the family doctor than to help them.

Notwithstanding the parents' genuine desire to consult an expert, behind their request for advice on nutrition also lay the social educator's attempt to safeguard the social responsibility of state nannies that triggered a reaction in doctors to protect their own professional identities. Although this kind of experience was not limited to immigrants, the social educator's request could, nonetheless, impact upon the way in which doctors perceived migrant patients to be less health literate than they actually were, since it made them request information that they had already received from nurses. This in turn brings to light the importance of distinguishing between external categorization and self-understanding (Brubaker 2004: 54), an approach that opens more fruitful theorizations of the concept of identity.

Theorizing Identity

The idea of multiple, fluid identities has become so commonplace that the concept has lost its cutting edge in social analysis (Brubaker 2004), taking away depth and understanding from conceptions of self (Biehl et al. 2007). Bradley's three levels of social identity help us to see how identifications are contextually activated through different social relations. 'Politicized identities' have not been discussed here because these refer to political action that leads to collective organization (Bradley 1996: 26). The ethnography has nonetheless revealed the ways in which 'passive identities' become 'active' and serve as a basis for carrying out new actions, as individuals take on the roles of mother and father, of bearers of new 'cultural orientations' and of members of an ethnic minority demanding access to health services. The ethnography suggests that identity is a never-ending process of subjective experimentation and self-making, influenced by tensions between individual aspirations and the demands and expectations from collectivities and kin.

The purpose of my analysis has been to explore how the ethnography of inner and outer experiences of 'displacement' among migrants who experience unexpected pregnancy may provide a new angle for theorizing identity. I have argued elsewhere, following Eriksen (1993: 59–60), for the need to study both reflexive constructions of self identity and processes of identification as an expression of social relations (Challinor 2008: 89). According to Eriksen, it is not the social anthropologist's business to probe into the psychology of people's minds; yet, the degree of the anthropologist's engagement should be dictated in my view by the nature of the subject matter. Entering into the private realm of Cape Verdean women's experiences of motherhood requires engaging at a deeper level. Moreover, the ethnography presented in this chapter shows that reflexive constructions of self-identity also express social relations. I have found the distinction between processes of internal and external categorization (Jenkins 1994) a useful tool for elucidating tensions between the individual and the collective (Challinor 2008); however, for the study of experiences of migrant motherhood, it does not take us deeply enough into the self. Brubaker's distinction between external categorization and self-understanding (Brubaker 2004: 54) is more helpful here, for it is when we are faced with uncertainty in relation to our situation that we may talk with ourselves, to try to reach understanding. In the case of the Cape Verdean women discussed above, addressing the uncertainty of family reactions to their pregnancies and negotiating the bureaucracies that provide services and support in Portugal constitutes an ongoing process of decision making, the nature of which cannot be captured through neither deterministic nor rational-choice models. Jonhson-Hanks's (2005) analysis of the uncertainty that women face in Cameroon suggests that it is 'the pathways' which partially determine women's goals: particular events prompt individuals to call into question their actions, ideas and goals, providing the opportunity for embarking upon alternative routes of thought and action. In order to further understand how women plan, formulate strategies and take action in the face of uncertainty, Johnson-Hanks calls for a 'rich ethnography of reasoning' (ibid.: 383). I have attempted to demonstrate how this involves paying attention to the workings of the mind and the influence of emotions, and to examining how these are both affected by the choices and opportunities that are (and are perceived to be) structurally available.

Acknowledgements

My research was funded by the Foundation for Science and Technology (FCT), Lisbon, Portugal in the Centre for Research in Anthropology (CRIA) at the University of Minho (UM). It began as a post-doctoral grant (SFRH/BPD/36914/2007), and is now funded within the ambit of the Programa Ciência 2008 and the project 'Care as Sustainability in Crisis Situations' (PTDC/CS-ANT/117259/2010). I wish to thank Maya Unnithan for inviting me to contribute towards the volume and for her insightful comments.

Notes

1. For a more in-depth discussion of this case, see Challinor (2011: 201–3).

References

ACIDI. 2007. 'Imigração em Portugal: Informação Útil 2007/2008'. Lisbon: Alto Comissariado para a imigração e o diálogo intercultural.

Beijers, H., and C. de Freitas. 2008. 'Cape Verdeans' Pathways to Health: Local Problems, Transnational Solutions', in L. Batalha and J. Carling (eds), *Transnational Archipelago: Perspectives on Cape Verdean Migration and Diaspora*. Amsterdam: Amsterdam University Press, pp.237–54.

Biehl, J., B. Good and A. Kleinman (eds). 2007. *Subjectivity: Ethnographic Investigations*. Berkeley: University of California Press.

Bradley, H. 1996. *Fractured Identities: Changing Patterns of Inequality*. Cambridge: Polity Press.

Brubaker, R. 2004. *Ethnicity without Groups*. Cambridge, MA: Harvard University Press.

Challinor, E.P. 2008. *Bargaining in the Development Market-place: Insights from Cape Verde*. Berlin: Lit Verlag.

——— 2011. 'Cape Verdean Migrants and Extended Mothering', in M. Walks and N. McPherson (eds), *Mothering: Anthropological Perspectives*. Bradford, ONT: Demeter Press, pp.196–208.

Davis-Floyd, R.E., and C.F. Sargent (eds). 1997. *Childbirth and Authoritative Knowledge: Cross-cultural Perspectives*. Berkeley: University of California Press.

Eriksen, T.H. 1993. *Ethnicity and Nationalism: Anthropological Perspectives*. London: Pluto Press.

Gadow, S. 1982. 'Body and Self: A Dialectic', in V. Kestenbaum (ed.), *The Humanity of the Ill: Phenomenological Perspectives*. Knoxville: University of Tennessee Press, pp.86–100.

Jenkins, R. 1994. 'Rethinking Ethnicity: Identity, Categorization and Power', *Ethnic and Racial Studies* 17(2): 197–223.

Johnson-Hanks, J. 2005. 'When the Future Decides: Uncertainty and Intentional Action in Contemporary Cameroon', *Current Anthropology* 46(3): 363–85.

Lopes Filho, J. 1995. *Cabo Verde: Retalhos do Quotidiano*. Lisboa: Caminho.

Marck, P.B. 1994. 'Unexpected Pregnancy: The Uncharted Land of Women's Experience', in P.A. Field and P.B. Marck (eds), *Uncertain Motherhood: Negotiating the Risks of the Childbearing Years*. London: Sage, pp.82–138.

Marck, P.B., P.A. Field and V. Bergum. 1994. 'A Search for Understanding', in P.A. Field and P.B. Marck (eds), *Uncertain Motherhood: Negotiating the Risks of the Childbearing Years*. London: Sage, pp.268–98.

Unnithan-Kumar, M. 2003. 'Reproduction, Health, Rights: Connections and Disconnections', in M. Jon and W. Richard (eds), *Human Rights in Global*

Perspective: Anthropological Studies of Rights, Claims and Entitlements. London: Routledge, pp.183–209.

Van Binsbergen, W. 2003. *Intercultural Encounters: African and Anthropological Lessons towards a Philosophy of Interculturality*. Munster: Lit Verlag.

Van Hollen, C. 2003. *Birth on the Threshold: Childbirth and Modernity in South India*. Berkeley: University of California Press.

Wall, K. 2008. 'Managing Work and Care for Young Children in Cape Verdean Families in Portugal', in L. Batalha and J. Carling (eds), *Transnational Archipelago: Perspectives on Cape Verdean Migration and Diaspora*. Amsterdam: Amsterdam University Press, pp.221–36.

CHAPTER 3

'Good Women Stay at Home, Bad Women Go Everywhere'

Agency, Sexuality and Self in Sri Lankan Migrant Narratives

Sajida Z. Ally

Women are used to coming and going. They have no family life, no values. That's not the life. We are Buddhist, we are very strong. The families who migrate don't have strength … Migrant remittances have not been so helpful. It is a useless journey. If they could manage their money properly, they could manage from here. But going abroad has become a style.

—Sinhala Buddhist female high-ranking government official,
North-Western Province, Sri Lanka

This chapter focuses on issues of agency, sexuality and self within the lives of low-income, rural Sri Lankan women migrating to and from the Persian Gulf. While women emphasize the economic concerns underlying their migration, I argue that despite their poverty, their motivations also need to be understood in terms of their emotional involvement and desires towards spouses, as well as their aspirations for honour and change in their lives. Defining agency as a capacity for action and self-transformation that historically-specific relations of South Asian domestic workers' subordination create, I suggest that women act as moral agents engaged in processes of making a more embodied self as they re-imagine their lives. Migration for domestic labour is popularly perceived as morally undesirable due to women's sexual vulnerability and supposed promiscuity, and the perceived detrimental effects arising from these concerns. Within these, sexuality, and the different ways it is expressed in spousal relationships and women's bodies, is a crucial dimension of power that shapes and organizes processes of migration and 'self re-making'. I contend that sexuality structures judgements of women's moral integrity, the cumulative effects of which can be embodied physically and emotionally. This essay examines the ways in which migrant women negotiate, submit to and/or defy negative moral representations of them through the renegotiation of spousal relationships spanning Sri Lanka and the Gulf. My findings are based on ethnographic fieldwork conducted between 2009 and 2011 in the rural locality of Kalpitiya in north-western Sri Lanka and in Kuwait.

Kalpitiya in the district of Puttalam is viewed in national terms as an under-privileged and remote area of Sri Lanka. In 2009, the district sent the sixth highest number of domestic workers (6,793) out of Sri Lanka, the largest proportion of whom (1,789) were from Kalpitiya sub-division (SLBFE 2009). Kalpitiya is ranked as the fifth-poorest sub-division within the country,[1] with poor socio-economic indicators, such as a low average income, high incidence of unemployment and an unequal system of land ownership that makes men and women reliant on exploitative and low-paid *coolie tollil* or day labour in the form of agriculture, salt production or fishing. There are particular economic constraints on women seeking work outside day labour, and socio-cultural constraints against their migration to urban centres to work in the garment or service sectors. These constraints translate into pressure upon them to migrate to the Persian Gulf for domestic work, which occurs against the backdrop of South Asian migration to West Asia.[2] The latter has brought significant social transformations, particularly through migrants' accumulation of economic and symbolic resources that they use to move through social hierarchies (Gardner and Osella 2004). Over three-quarters of Sri Lankan overseas workers move to West Asia, with Saudi Arabia hosting the largest group of over 500,000, and Kuwait hosting the second-largest of more than 200,000. Sri Lanka is the leading South Asian country deploying foreign domestic labour (SLBFE 2009).[3]

While the economic necessity of women's transnational migration is widely upheld, the social and moral consequences of this migration are issues of contention within Sri Lankan society. Notions of morality towards women's mobility are thought to be influenced by nationalist and communal state ideologies that have historically emphasized women's primary role as mothers, and paid labour as their secondary, less respected role (Jayawardena and De Alwis 1995). The Sri Lankan Bureau of Foreign Employment (SLBFE) – the key, state agency regulating migration – has been seeking to reduce female migration for domestic work, yet it provides women with the institutional means to migrate and is unable to suggest viable alternatives.[4] Partly as a result of the SLBFE's efforts to reduce female migration, the proportion of domestic workers among all Sri Lankan transnational economic migrants had declined from over 80 per cent in the 1990s to around 50 per cent in 2007.

State practices regarding female migration mirror the sentiments of many religious leaders, which transcend ethnic and religious boundaries, as most leaders of the central faiths in Sri Lanka (Buddhism, Islam, Hinduism and Christianity) voice broader social unease towards women migrating for domestic work. My observations suggest, however, that state migration practices and the moral discourse of local religious leaders do not adequately address the economic reality of labour markets in the Gulf that demand low-paid female, rather than male, labour, as well as women's socio-cultural and personal motivations for migration. I have chosen to focus on the stories of Muslim women in the case studies below not because sexuality and agency are more prominent concerns for them than they are for other women, but because I lived most closely among Muslim women, and this proximity enabled them to share their intimate lives with me.

Kalpitiya is characterized by a high concentration of Tamil-speaking persons, these being 'Muslims' and 'Tamils',[5] and the presence of a significant population (70,000) who were forcibly displaced from Northern Province in the early 1990s and who have since been living a semi-settled existence. My primary research informants were derived from an inter-connected Muslim minority population of *ur aalkal* (host community) and *muhaam aalkal* (displaced or 'camp' people),[6] and I consider the stories of three women that illustrate the various sorts of change that occur in women's agency, sexuality and self over the course of the period of their migration.

Sexuality and Honour in Migrant Marriages

The emphasis of this chapter is on migrant women's agency and sense of self within migratory experiences, wherein I use sexuality as a central axis of analysis as it is deeply implicated within women's relationships with past, prospective or existing spouses, which in turn influence their sense of honour. I contend that migrant women's aspirations for their lives and migration need to be understood in connection with prevailing sentiments towards migrant female sexuality and honour as these shape women's sense of self more markedly than other factors.

I address these issues through a synthetic understanding of sexuality and gender as being both distinct and complexly interrelated (Butler 2004),[7] an approach widely used within recent anthropology on sexual health. Correa et al. define sexuality as, 'the domain of bodily and social experience produced through ever-changing discourses, norms and regulatory practices that operate where desire, behaviour, identity and institutional power meet' (Correa et al.

2008: 7). Borrowing from Cantu (2009) to address migrants' sexuality more specifically, I view sexuality not merely as a uni-dimensional variable, but as a dimension of power in a system of stratified relations that needs to be incorporated into analyses of migrants' experiences.[8]

My approach contrasts with emerging studies of migrants' sexual cultures, which tend to focus on the experiences of migrants as 'sexual minorities' or 'sexual migrants' who migrate as a direct consequence of sexuality (Herdt 1997; Ahmad 2009; Cantu 2009a: 22).[9] While recognizing the variety of sexual attachments that can motivate migration (Mai and King 2009), particularly among those who migrate from a constraining space to one imagined as offering greater sexual freedoms, it must be said that Muslim women from Kalpitiya are migrating from the constraints of their village to another constraining space, that of their employers' homes in Gulf societies. While the latter provide women with new spaces to meet potential spouses and/or develop intimate feelings, I suggest that their migration is primarily motivated by aspirations for honour, rather than the seeking of new sexual experiences, though such experiences may be unintended or secondary outcomes. Here, it is important to stress the primacy of hetero-normative spousal relations within women's aspirations, wherein prospective or existing relations largely frame desire.[10]

The imagined or real intimate actions of migrant women challenge normative Sri Lankan views of sexual morality, which are part of meta-narratives that highlight the various 'social ills' of female migration – abuse, rape, prostitution, sexual promiscuity, dissolving marriages, neglected children – and how these contribute to the erosion of 'Sri Lankan cultural values'. Unlike male migrants, whose sexuality is not subjected to the same level of moral scrutiny,[11] women are seen as tainted for having engaged in extra-marital or pre-marital affairs, transgressing norms of virginity and fidelity, regardless of whether they have engaged in intimate relations while abroad or not.

While research has found that Sri Lankan women do engage in intimate relationships while abroad (Moukarbel 2009a, 2009b; Smith 2010), more needs to be understood regarding the prevalence and motivations underlying these relationships. Smith (2010) has documented the ways in which Sri Lankan women have ambivalent desires for independence and new intimate relationships on the one hand, and for motherhood/wifehood on the other, while they change notions of what is morally permissible to match new desires and practical needs. My observations of women in Kalpitiya and Kuwait, particularly from the perspective of their sense of self, indicate something different: these women do continue to conform to notions of morality dominant in Sri Lanka even while they are abroad, and though some adapt aspects of their sexual and bodily culture – for example, in their dress and ways of searching for potential spouses – they remain largely within the same moral order of their *ur* ('homeland' or 'community').

The social construction of migrant women's sexual culture is integrally linked to the historical development of notions of sexuality within South Asia, where particular rules of respectability for women have been constructed. Women's behaviour has become the target of control, and their bodies symbolize the space of the nation and have been subject to manipulation by nationalist-revivalist ideologies (Jayawardena and De Alwis 1995). Mobile women are often seen as loose women who have transgressed assumptions of their immobility and disrupted traditional gender roles (Lynch 1999), challenging attempts to control their sexuality through confinement in the home and being kept in subordinate and familial positions.[12]

While notions of sexuality and women's mobility cut across ethnicity and religion,[13] the desires and understandings of rural Muslim women in north-west Sri Lanka are shaped within a particular social and historical context and way of belonging to interconnected communities of *ur aalkal* and *muhaam aalkal*. My observations are consistent with an anthropology that warns against the reification of particular groups of people as a 'culture' (Abu-Lughod 2002; Fassin 2001a), as many of the obstacles faced by my Muslim women informants were political and material rather than 'cultural' in nature. Their lives are influenced by 'Muslim identity', which has been described by some as a reactive ideology developed in relation and response to Sinhala and Tamil ethno-nationalistic ideologies, while also being rooted in global socio-political conditions (Nuhman 2007). In Kalpitiya, the existence of a permanently displaced community may have exacerbated Muslims' move towards reasserting their own identity (Haniffa 2002). It is unsurprising that homogenizing tendencies within the Muslim communities of Kalpitiya are magnified within discussions on female migration – a prime issue highlighted by the national media and a platform for ideological propagation – especially as sexuality is a central site where social identities are contested and inter-communal relations are expressed (Sargent 2006; Tober et al. 2006).

As such, I contend that the pronouncements of *imams* and *maulavis* are as inextricably linked to socio-political factors as they are to Islamic 'traditions' and juridical practices, while women's material needs remain undeniable. Many leaders whom I interviewed encouraged the institution of strong restrictions upon women's physical mobility in order to preserve their safety and purity, and, perhaps most importantly, the moral uniqueness of 'Muslim communities'.[14] In the words of a local preacher, expressed in a flyer as part of a commentary on 'women and morality', 'good women stay at home, bad women go everywhere'.[15] While such reductionist views are rarely propagated in print, they are echoed within daily conversations in the *ur*. They are also thought to be rooted in unequal and defensive reactions towards women that have been historically instituted in the form of legal protections – justified to safeguard against heterosexual involvement outside marriage among people living under Muslim laws (Mernissi 2003).[16] As such, one needs to recognize how Islamic leaders are shaped by socio-political conditions, and the constraints they face in making statements that are inconsistent with institutional ideologies. During informal conversations in their homes, I found certain *maulavis* empathetic towards women's poverty, admitting that they should not be judged for simply needing to provide for their families.[17]

In response to the various pressures in their lives, my women informants appear to have differently structured desires, and they are, in the words of Abu-Lughod, 'called to personhood, so to speak, in a different language' (Abu-Lughod 2002: 788). Most of these women value appropriate Muslim feminine behaviour, characterized by veiling and restricted mobility (*parda*), and the inculcation of the notions of shame (*vekkum*) and honour/respect (*mariada*). They appreciated staying at home, being provided for or not having to travel far for work, and living closely with their families. Rather than objectifying the readings of these characteristics as a sign of 'unfreedom', it is important to consider the motivational force of women's desire for freedom and mobility in the light of other desires that are culturally and historically located (Mahmood 2001). Not one of my informants failed to highlight the backwardness and impoverished state of their *ur*, the urgent need for improved roads, schools and healthcare facilities, an end to domestic violence and making a decent living so that their children could grow and live safely in ways that would necessitate confrontation with the power relations that underpin socio-economic conditions.

These ideas also need to be analysed against academic writing on the gendered effects of migration, particularly upon families and marriages. More than half of all Asian migrant women leave behind small children, and consequently migration inevitably and significantly affects family roles and marriages (Samarasingha 1989; Parrenas 2001; Kottegoda 2006). It is popularly thought that marriages do not collapse when men migrate, while female migrants' chance of separation increases upon return. Zlotnik (1995) suggests, however, that female migration itself does not increase marital instability, as women who face difficulties within their marriages are more likely to migrate than those in stable unions. Other scholars have also documented social perceptions of marriages being weakened by male migration and the leaving behind of female-headed households (Pathirage and Collyer 2011).

Agency and Self in Migrant Women's Sexuality

Having laid out the ways in which Sri Lankan women's migratory experiences are influenced by sexuality and gender norms, I now discuss the connections between these issues and women's agency and their sense of self. I argue that women migrate largely due to their emotional involvement and desires towards spouses, as well as their aspirations for honour and for change in their lives. Defining migrant women's agency as a capacity for action and self-transformation that the historically specific relations of South Asian women's and domestic workers' subordination enables and creates, I assert that women act as moral agents engaged in processes of making a more embodied self as they re-imagine their lives. Within these processes, sexuality, and the different ways it is expressed in spousal relationships and women's bodies, is a key dimension of power that shapes processes of migration and women's 'self re-making'. I contend that sexuality structures judgements of women's moral integrity, the cumulative effects of which can be embodied physically and emotionally.

My usage of the definition of women's agency – as a capacity for action and self-transformation within historically specific relations of subordination – is derived from the work of Saba Mahmood, who calls for agency to be seen 'not as a synonym for resistance to relations of domination, but as a capacity for action ... that [is] related to women's desires, aspirations and capacities that inhere in a culturally and historically located subject' (Mahmood 2001: 203). Referring to Egyptian women involved in patriarchal religious traditions such as Islam, Mahmood suggests that agency needs to be understood differently in the context of lives that have been shaped by non-liberal traditions, and where moral virtues are accorded an important place. While drawing upon Judith Butler's idea of 'subjectivation' – that the very processes and conditions that secure a subject's subordination are also the means by which they become a self-conscious identity and agent (Butler 1997; see also Foucault 1980, 1983) – Mahmood differs from Butler in her consideration of agency as other than the capacity to subvert norms. Instead, she defines it as the capacities and skills required to undertake particular kinds of acts (Mahmood 2001: 210), urging us to think of 'agentival capacity as not only those acts that result in progressive change, but also those that aim toward continuity, stasis, and stability' (ibid.: 212).[18] Drawing upon Das (1999), Mahmood explains that women's ability to survive the presence of pain can be viewed in terms of the 'doing of little things' that do not have the sense of 'passive submission but of an active engagement' (Das 1999: 11–12).

To address agency within sexuality and spousal relations, I combine Mahmood's contrasting concept of agentival action with some of Unnithan-Kumar's (2001) work on reproductive agency. Unnithan-Kumar suggests that the contestation of authority may be a related but perhaps a largely unintended, secondary outcome of women's motivation and desire to seek out reproductive healthcare. Discussing poor women in rural Rajasthan, India, she describes women's experiences of forgoing contraception as part of their doxa, the taken for granted, normalized part of their lives (ibid.: 33). In this and another study (Unnithan-Kumar 2003), she suggests that women's sexual and reproductive well-being are influenced more by loyalties and desires towards spouses and poverty, rather than by notions of 'rights'.[19] The idea of agency not necessarily involving resistance or the contestation of power relate well to the context of Muslim women in Kalpitiya, who are strongly motivated by notions of morality and virtue, rather than those of an autonomous free will. I suggest that by viewing these women as moral agents in their self-transformation, the language of their aspirations and pain can be better understood.

The agentival action of migrant women relate closely to the changes that occur within their sense of self and emotion. As persons who need to have the capacity to describe who they are, and to grasp and communicate this to other people, migrant women negotiate their selves through new interactions with their changing social worlds and relations.[20] Women's personhood is constructed largely through aspirations for and/or within marriage, wherein they are propelled by virtues of honour to seek enhancements in their moral status through changes in spousal relations. As women migrate, they are confronted by new realities within host-country workplaces, and they make sense of these by propelling their sense of self to undergo changes, some of which are dislocating, while some provide opportunities for the re-imagination of their lives. Consistent with analyses of emotions being socially constructed and embodied (e.g. Scheper-Hughes 1988; Lutz and Abu-Lughod 1990), my women informants rarely discussed their emotions in relation to themselves as individuals, but in terms of their obligations towards children and spouses, or in relation to physical health.[21] Notions of 'I' (the individual) need to be seen in relation to those of the self/'me' (the social person), and women's 'real' expressions of grief as an individual are less important than the collective importance of their suffering (Lutz and Abu-Lughod 1990).

Finally, an inextricable link needs to be made between issues of agency and sexuality on the one hand and embodiment processes and biopolitical mechanisms on the other, all of which involve moral discourse and state policies on migration. I develop my analysis along the lines of recent medical anthropology that has highlighted how national government policies tend to inscribe themselves on the body of (im)migrants by means of a dynamic relationship between the exercise of sovereign power and the agency of the (im)migrant (Fassin 2001b, 2005). In the context of Asian migrant women, these processes have been described most closely by Parrenas as 'multiple dislocations', these being 'the positions into which external forces in society constitute the subject of migrant domestic workers' (Parrenas 2001: 3). Dislocations are manifested as migrants' subordinate conditions as low-wage, temporary workers and racialized women, and they impact profoundly on the self. Such dislocations, in the words of Anderson, create the conditions for the appropriation of domestic workers' 'personhood', particularly in their relationships with employers – a dehumanizing process that leaves them 'socially dead' (Anderson 2000: 121).[22] These dislocations conflate with more visible ones. They are constituted by migration regimes that I contend structure the ways in which sexuality and agency are negotiated, namely the separation of families and the strains placed upon migrant marriages. While domestic workers' conditions of formal employment under the *kafala* or sponsorship system seriously limit their opportunities for social communication, Gulf Cooperation Council labour migration policies prevent low-status migrants from bringing in dependent, non-working spouses.[23] Consequently, spouses separated by migration often lead separate lives. I now turn to ethnographic case studies of migrant women that illustrate how experiences of dislocation are inscribed on their bodies and experiences, yet, despite constraints, how they nonetheless engage in agentive actions that lead to transformations of their lives and selves.

Three Case Studies

I now turn to the experience of agency, sexuality and self of three Muslim migrant women, Amina, Shafna and Jansila, with whom I became close over the course of one to two years.[24] They worked as domestic workers in Kuwait or Saudi Arabia, and they came from neighbouring *urs* or resettlement villages in Kalpitiya. Their stories illustrate how disruptions to their sense of self and emotions played a decisive role in leading them to migrate, including their experience of widowhood or of being unmarried, the state of their spousal relations and their aspirations for honour. Women did not articulate goals of self-transformation as part of their motivation for migration, but their migration did catalyse changes involving various dimensions of their selves – in their virtues, their ideas of themselves and their views of their lives – as well as those relating to social relationships and metaphysical entities such as Allah. They did not speak of moral discourse or state policies, yet the effects of these could be easily understood.

Amina

Amina, a mother of three sons and in her early thirties, migrated to Kuwait after the death of her first husband, who died in the crossfire of the ethno-

political conflict in Jaffna. The pain of her husband's death and her conse-
quent feelings of losing respect as a widow transformed in Saudi Arabia as she
began to court an Indian Tamil Muslim man who was working as a driver. She
eventually married, and her new marriage helped her to renegotiate her social
status after her return from Saudi Arabia. She and her husband re-imagined
their lives together, and they created plans for migrating once again, but this
time together and with the aim of saving money towards the future creation
of a sustainable livelihood. Amina was born in Jaffna in the Northern
Province, and her family left Jaffna in 1992 and went to Mannar.

> My husband was killed in the fighting. Your book is not enough to capture
> my pain Sajida … I loved Azfar so much. He did everything for us. I did
> not have to worry about money. He always asked me what special foods
> I wanted to eat, and no matter how hard it was, he'd find a way to buy
> them for me. [She starts crying.] I felt loved and respected by him. Men
> don't respect women, but Azfar respected me. He always used to say, 'If I
> can't give food and clothing to my family, what kind of man am I?' My job
> was to look after and raise our sons. His work (*tollil*) was difficult, but he
> didn't want me to work. When he died, I felt the pain of losing his love,
> and losing a friend … My husband was no longer there to protect me, so
> I also lost respect in society … Our people always like to talk and blame.
> Without a husband, they started saying all kinds of things … that I can't
> look after my sons properly, I must be looking at other men, those kinds
> of things … I felt like a dead person. There was fighting happening all
> around us, but I couldn't really think about it. How was I going to feed
> my sons? … I couldn't stand the pain of being in the world without him.
> So I decided to go to Kuwait.

Following her husband's death, Amina worked in Kuwait for a year, but
then returned to Sri Lanka after the death of her mother. She migrated a
second time as she found no other means to support herself and her sons, and
she continued to feel alone and marginalized in Kalpitiya. In the following
excerpt, she describes how she met her second husband in Jeddah, Saudi
Arabia:

> AMINA: Saadiq was the driver in the house where I was working … I
> couldn't talk to him, I couldn't even look at him. We would both get in
> trouble. But I kept looking at him from the side of my eyes. And he was
> looking at me too. I would feel myself blush sometimes, and I was worried
> madam would notice … I liked the way he went about his work. He was
> quiet and dutiful, but always had a sense of dignity about him. I felt shy

when I caught Saadiq looking at me from the corner of his eye because I knew he liked me.

S.A.: How did you know?

AMINA: I just knew. [She smiles, giggles, and bows her head.] ... Saadiq saw me and treated me as a human being. Before I met him, I'm not sure what I felt about myself [while she was in Saudi Arabia]. I was a machine, I had to work. I had to forget about Azfar so that I could send money home ... I started talking to Saadiq almost every evening [on a mobile phone hidden from her employer], but I was scared ... I felt it was inappropriate to talk to him too much. But when we would talk, I remembered I was human, that Allah did actually exist. And I kept thinking about my sons – they needed a father again. I told him that I was only interested in marriage. Saadiq was a good man. He wasn't looking at my body ... He called my brother in Sri Lanka and told him he wanted to marry me ... We finished our contracts and went back to our countries ... At the beginning [of her second marriage], I don't know if I was happy. I was glad to be married.

S.A. Do you love him?

AMINA: Now I do, but it took time. He's very different from Azfar, who would do any kind of work so that we could live well. Saadiq can't do hard labour. He can drive and do electrician work. It's hard for him to find that kind of work in Kalpitiya, it's not his *ur*. If I didn't work, we would not be able to eat.

Amina did not talk readily about her love for Saadiq but of her respect for him. She felt disappointed about the difficulty he was facing in finding work. But during one visit, I observed their interactions as Saadiq was departing to work in a quarry for a couple of weeks. She was quiet in between her bursts of advice to him. Her body was still and tense, and her eyes lined with tears. He was not his normal talkative self. As he walked out the door, he told me to visit her more while he is gone. They did not touch each other, but his gaze rested on her and he smiled. After his departure, Amina and I sat together quietly.

He can't tolerate that kind of work ... It will be too hard for him. I was close to him when he worked before, but now he will be far away. *Inshallah* Sajida, it's going to be hard without him. I will miss him ... It's good Saadiq has been here with me. Life is still very difficult, but I don't worry as much about what people think. I have no peace/sense of calm (*nimadi*). My fate (*naseeb*) is to work. But he is here. After we both work abroad for a few more years, we will have money to set up our own work (*tollil*), we can finish building our house. My sons will finish their studies properly. I hope my heart/being (*mana*) will be at peace. Allah knows how our lives will be.

Shafna

Shafna, a woman in her late twenties from Kalpitiya, said that it was her husband's infidelity, violence and alcoholism that drove her to migrate to Saudi Arabia. She had hoped that her transnational migration would improve her economic position, help her to renegotiate her relationship with her husband and provide her with a new sense of respect among his kin. But things did not turn out well for her while she was abroad, and her migration did not drastically change the state of her marriage. She explained how the traumatic experiences she had while abroad changed her and made her more determined to create a better life for herself and her children.

My parents had both gone to Saudi Arabia so that we would grow up well … They gave me away [in marriage] with lots of gold. Within a year, it was almost all gone. Azeem had sold it … The first time he beat me was when I told him I was pregnant. It was a month after our wedding. He didn't believe that I was carrying his child. He called me a prostitute, and said I was sleeping with other men. I had his child in my stomach, but he kept beating me. I realized then that Azeem did not love me. I feel much love/care (*paasam*) for him. Maybe I'm crazy. But I know he's a good person. They [his immediate kin] all treat him badly. He was beaten a lot as a child … Azeem thinks that someone did witchcraft (*seyvinna*) on him, and that he will never be happy married. He had wanted to marry another girl he loved, but his parents had wanted him to marry me for my money …

The first time I found out that he had slept with another woman, I shouted at him and could only cry. I asked him how he could betray me. He would come home drunk, then beat me. If you look at Hashim [her second child], he is like a stick. I was beaten while he was in my womb, and I ate little … He told me to leave him, he didn't want me. I didn't have money anymore … They [his kin] say that I am a bad wife who doesn't know how to hold my tongue. And I can't control my husband. My parents are too far away to help. Anyway, I can't say much to them because I went against their advice to not marry Azeem …

I went to Saudi because I could not bear seeing my children with no food. But the hardest thing was the pain I felt knowing that he would not come to me [to have sex] … I wanted to save money to build a house for myself and my children. Then maybe Azeem would change when he sees that I have a way to survive. I was unlucky. Allah gave me the chance to migrate, but I came back with nothing.

In Saudi Arabia, Shafna was sold by her *kefil* (sponsor) to a racket of men engaged in trafficking, and for two years she was made to work without pay and to change houses and employers every two to four weeks.

I was not able to call home. Nobody knew what had happened to me. My parents went to the [recruitment] agent in Maradana [Colombo, the capital], and they were told that I had jumped, escaped [left her sponsor's house]. One day, I managed to call Azeem. I thought he would be happy to hear from me, but he said, 'You jumped so that you could work outside and sleep with Arab men. Don't come back, I don't want you anymore!' He cut the line. Can you believe him? [She starts crying.] With all my suffering, he couldn't even say one comforting word to me.

She also talked about the physical pain in her body that had developed while she was abroad, and how it had worsened upon her return.

I started having pain in the middle of my wrists. First I noticed it after lifting heavy carpets up to the top floor of the house. Once I fainted. I was carrying a gas cylinder up to the top floor. I felt a sharp pain ripping through my chest. I could not stand it. Sometimes you can't even place a finger on my body … It started to come in the night when I could not sleep, and I would start thinking about Azeem, about him sleeping with other women. How could I still love him when he was so bad? … The pain is always there now. But it gets worse when he beats me, and when I think about my life too much. I am pained thinking that he doesn't love me, that he thinks I slept with other men. I ask Allah why I am being treated this way. I cry a lot. I ask Allah for forgiveness, and to make him [Azeem] see differently … It's the pain in my heart that's hard. [She starts to cry.] … I'm still here because I don't think about these things for too long. I would not be able to care for my children. It's for them that I live. Look at her [pointing to her daughter], how can you not smile? [She relaxes and smiles.] They are a gift from Allah …

The bad things about going abroad is all this pain, and that I came back with nothing. The good thing [she pauses for a while] is that Allah gave me a way to come back. I prayed, I always found my strength. When I was in the shelter in Saudi, I had just finished praying my fortieth *raqat* [a series of non-compulsory prayers] one day, and the social worker came to tell me that I could leave the next day! My prayer (*du'a*) was answered just as the words left my heart. I have been given a second chance in life

… Even if things with Azeem have not changed, I came back with courage … I now have a plan to set up my own shop somehow, so I have some money and my children will study well. I don't want people to talk about me, I know that I am on the straight path [the way of faith].

At the time this chapter was written, Shafna was in the process of getting the local religious leadership to intervene to help stop the violence at home. She was also in the process of applying for a loan to set up a small shop.

Jansila

Jansila is an unmarried woman in her late twenties who has been migrating for the past decade between Kalpitiya, Kuwait and Saudi Arabia, and at the time this chapter was written, she was still working in Kuwait. She said that she first migrated to save money for her dowry, and to ease financial strains in her household. As she continued to migrate, her family grew dependent on her remittances; however, though migrating for the fifth time, she still did not have savings. She said that she 'doesn't feel right' anymore when she returns to Kalpitiya. She was sad that she could not marry a boy with whom she had fallen in love, and she disliked the ways in which 'people talk' about her being unmarried. She had been enduring hard working conditions in Kuwait, but felt that she could finally begin saving money for her dowry. She talked constantly about 'a different kind of life' with a prospective spouse.

Jansila's traumatic experience of rape as an eighteen-year-old by a goat herder in Saudi Arabia had pervasive effects on her self-esteem and her aspirations for intimacy with a man. She had a negative conception of the physicality of her body: she both desired and feared 'being with a man', and she was ambivalent about getting married. Though she said that she does not feel that she has been 'spoiled' by her experience of rape as it was not her fault, she used to have periodic attacks of breathlessness and anxiety when men looked at her in a particular way, even in public places. She also began suffering from epilepsy after her rape. Moreover, she expressed her concern that perhaps no potential spouse would find her attractive, as she thought she was 'dark and fat'.

Soon after her arrival in Kuwait, she became attracted to a man – Farook – who worked as a driver in her neighbourhood. She tried to court him. Farook helped her to buy a mobile phone and to send things home, and he has been the only person in Kuwait to whom she can talk. While she giggled and evaded my questions when I asked her directly about physical attraction and sex, I observed from her flirtatious interaction with Farook that she was seeking attention from him.

Farook worked for me as my driver and research assistant in Kuwait, and he became a trusted informant. After some time, he confided in me about his relationship with Jansila, describing the sexual innuendos that were a part of his conversations with her. He claimed that he had declined both her invitation for sex and her proposal for marriage. He felt that she was not a virgin, as she 'expresses things only an experienced woman would know', suspecting that 'she has been spoiled'. He says that most women domestic workers desire sex when they have been in Kuwait for a while because 'the loneliness and stress drives them crazy. After all, they are human too, how can one blame them for not wanting it?' So while he appeared empathetic to a migrant woman's sexual needs, he himself did not want to marry one, preferring instead to find a wife back in his village who is 'poor and innocent'.

Hence, I received two different stories about Jansila's intentions. Rather than deciding on which version was 'correct', I saw both stories as indicative of her psycho-social reality as she grappled with various moral judgements as a young, single migrant woman, desiring both intimacy and an eventual marriage.

Discussion

Agency within Spousal Relations: Desire, Love and Honour

The ethnographic cases presented above highlight the different ways in which migrant women's sense of self and their aspirations for their lives transform in the course of their migration, and in connection to spousal relations. Through their transnational migration, women defy gendered norms of mobility that are prevalent in rural Sri Lanka, but at the same time they remain largely within its cultural order, continuing to place importance upon traditional virtues of perseverance, humility and the need to be respected by spouses, kin and community. Their feelings of being judged in their *ur* combine with those of dehumanization as they live as domestic workers in the Gulf. Yet while they may not articulate awareness of their agency, and despite their continued experience of moral judgement and relative poverty, I suggest that the ways in which migrant women redefine aspirations for their lives and for honour constitute agential action.

Unsurprisingly, variations exist in migrant women's experiences. Amina's story demonstrates a sense of the enhanced respect that followed her last migration, as she met her future spouse in Saudi Arabia, and her social status consequently transformed from that of a widow to a married woman. However, Shafna's sense of (dis)honour remains problematic following her return due to the continued infidelity and violence of her husband, and the ongoing judgements she receives from his kin. In contrast, Jansila's self-image appears to worsen with her continued unmarried status. But even if Shafna's and Jansila's migrations have provided them with greater communal respect, they are still engaged in transforming their aspirations and desires.

I found that women's verbal expression of being loved and loving their spouses is integrally tied to being provided for financially, as a man who provides for the family conveys respect for women's primary role of mothering. Women always said that it was a man's duty to be the breadwinner, even though in reality this was not always the case. For example, the way in which Amina expressed her 'love' towards her husband is closely connected to her need to be respected and provided for financially. Her strong sense of entitlement as a wife and mother contributed to her disappointment in her second husband's limited ability to provide for her.

Turning to the perspectives of men, I found that men often expressed being emasculated by the conditions of poverty, which prevented them from fulfilling their financial obligations towards the family and compels women to migrate. Consequently, spousal separation had the potential to create either enhanced distance or intimacy within spousal relations. Men's sense of being incapable could worsen with the migration of their wives, as they were left to tend to the feminine work of childcare and running the household. Those who had not migrated themselves found it difficult to understand what their wives were experiencing. I noted prevalent perceptions of male emasculation, and how it was thought to influence the occurrence of extra-marital affairs. While the men whom I interviewed did not speak of their direct involvement in affairs, they did discuss the incidence of affairs among men and women known to them. At least a quarter of the women I interviewed across Sri Lanka talked about incidents involving their husbands (or the husbands of their close women relatives or friends) in extra-marital affairs, and a smaller number reported husbands filing for separation or divorce during or following their migration abroad. That said, I also interviewed numerous husbands and brothers of migrant women who discussed feelings of depression and uselessness with me.[25] Many manoeuvred their new roles with love, demonstrating genuine feelings of loss towards their wives' absence while often adopting their new responsibilities in childcare with humour and care.

I suggest that women responded to these experiences while abroad by seeking, in a sense, to re-humanize themselves through emotional support from spouses and children back home – through phone conversations or the exchange of letters, or from prospective spouses and love interests whom they would meet near or within the confines of their employers' homes. The need for women to be respected by their spouses was part of their sense of integrity and self-worth. When spouses failed to provide emotional support while they were abroad, women felt they were being denied the chance to receive love and care – the very things, in the words of one interviewee, that 'makes me human and not a dog'. In Shafna's case, her husband's allegations about her supposed infidelity deepened her pain, even though she was still able to highlight the positive outcome of her experience. On the other hand, women who received spousal empathy and understanding felt greater intimacy and desire towards them, and this strengthened their marriage bond.

Women shared certain embodied experiences with spouses or courtship interests who had also migrated before. As they had both inhabited similar physical and emotional worlds abroad, this helped to create understanding between them. For example, one informant who was a returnee migrant, Farida, had been able to forge a close relationship with a returnee migrant man to whom she is now married – a relationship she feels developed largely because of their respective migration experiences. After the birth of their child, her new husband re-migrated to Saudi Arabia, and they were able to maintain a loving and healthy marriage despite the distance. They are now presently working together in the same household in the UAE. Farida is considered fortunate within the *ur*, as she has a house – built with her own earnings – a child, and a financially responsible husband who loves her and with whom she envisions establishing a small business. Similar experiences were also shared among several other close informants and their husbands.

In other cases, migration provided the chance and physical space for women and men to meet and court potential spouses. Amina may not have had the opportunity to remarry had she remained in Sri Lanka, but after meeting Saadiq in Saudi Arabia and sharing the experience of working for the same employer, she decides she wants to marry again. Saadiq explained how he had fallen in love with Amina as he admired how hard she worked and he could understand her pain. With the case of Jansila, it remains to be seen whether she too will find her spouse while in Kuwait and/or resolve her feelings of ambivalence towards marriage.

Honour and Relations with Kin

Kin relations simultaneously served to encourage and discourage migration with various causes and consequences, and they played a fundamental role in the moral judgements delivered upon migrating women and their spouses. As the ways in which women cared for their husbands and children changed in the course of their migration, so did opinions among kin about whether they were 'good' or 'bad' wives and mothers. Meanwhile, their husbands were often viewed as weak and irresponsible. On the whole, I found that women who had more social support from families tended to have a more positive sense of self-respect and honour.

For example, in the case of Farida, her close relationship with her elder brother, and his financial support for her first migration, motivated her to migrate and made her feel respected despite prevalent stigmatizing views in the village. Her brother's support, she says, also gave her the confidence to seek a well-established spouse. However, Shafna's difficult circumstances before she migrated did not improve after her return, in part because her husband's kin privileged his moral integrity over hers – this despite his alcoholism and infidelity. Though the only money she earned in her first three months abroad was used to buy the land upon which her house is now built, Shafna was blamed for coming back 'empty handed'. She attributes part of her pain to the constant criticism of her mounted by her husband's kinswomen, who assert that Shafna had undertaken the moral risks of migration yet failed to increase the family's standing.

Sexuality and Embodiment

Female migration is often discussed at various levels of society in relation to the effects that migration is thought to have on spousal relations, families and 'cultural values', but I suggest that what lies at the core of these discussions is the moral integrity of the woman migrant, which is integrally structured by sexuality. The ethnographic cases detailed above demonstrate how sexuality, as a fundamental domain of power, shapes kin and communal ideas of women's honour, and how it arises as a fundamental concern at different stages of migration. The sexual stigmatizing of migrating women for their perceived sexual promiscuity and vulnerability in the private confines of employers' houses, and women's culpability for strained, broken or non-existing spousal relations, structure the moral images that are created of them. Most of the returning migrant women I met were identified and judged by their neighbours in terms of changes in their body, dress, behaviour and relations with spouses, children and/or other kin. For example, Farida – considered fortunate by her neighbours for having a husband and stable economic position – also defies norms of femininity and respectability as she is viewed as being over-assertive and dresses in ways that are thought to be disrespectful of local styles.

Migrant women's physical appearance and body language were a constant focus of attention of kin and community. In my own observations I sought to go beyond such communal meta-narratives to penetrate the physical and emotional dimensions of women's experiences. In my attempts to talk about sexuality directly, I was most often confronted by embarrassment or denial of its importance. However, women indirectly provided descriptions of their desires and emotions relating to sex as part of broader narratives of health, spousal relations and daily life. For example, the stories of Shafna and Jansila highlight the physiological effects of violence and their unmet desires towards their spouses or love interests. Shafna's embodiment of trauma is reflected in her anxiety attacks and the physical pain she feels in her chest. The meaning she assigns to this pain appears to be a complex conflation of betrayal, unfulfilled love and sexual desire, and repeated physical, emotional and moral violence inflicted on her by her husband and her in-laws. In the case of Jansila, her ambivalent feelings towards her physical appearance, marriage, sex and men often arose as part of her discussions of her physical health, her anxiety and her experience of epilepsy and breathlessness. I suggest that her traumatic experience of sexual violence as an eighteen-year-old migrant has had lasting effects upon her self-image, her internal sense of honour and her sexuality.

Agency and Projects of Self Re-making

Despite the different effects of migration upon women's sense of self-respect and spousal and communal notions of honour, women were nonetheless able to act as moral agents engaged in processes of making a more embodied self as they hoped for change in their lives. As migrants move transnationally, they begin to reframe their understandings of themselves and their emotions, and these understandings are renegotiated and reconnected along with changes in their sense of place within communities, societies and nations. The ethnographic cases above demonstrate how transformations of self can be understood in relation to emotional, existential and/or spiritual changes in women's views of their lives and futures. For many, the pain they experience in being denied empathy and care by their spouses in Sri Lanka while they worked in the Gulf relates not only to a loss of love, but to a form of existential questioning as to whether or not they are human and whether their lives were worth living or not. As a way of finding meaning for this pain, some talk of spiritual transformation, while others focus their imaginations on their future. In doing so, women's own political interests in desiring more independence often conflict with their internalized sense of cultural order. They struggle to make sense of their roles in the face of new economic, cultural and social realities associated with migration and recreate their realities, at times appearing to defy structures of power and inequality without necessarily challenging them. They aspire to be seen as respectful and honourable women among kin and community, and they seek to maintain virtuous, moral and socially respected marriages, while also hoping for some degree of economic autonomy. For some women, such as Shafna, the virtues of piety, gratitude, humility and perseverance are important in helping her to alleviate pain, make sense of her experiences and reconstruct notions she holds of her self through a perceived connection to a transcendental entity, Allah. For others, they appear to outwardly adopt the language of piety and virtue to counter negative representations and preserve self-respectability.

One can say that women's actions, imaginations and capacities to transform their selves can be viewed as part of projects of 'self re-making', which need to be understood within the historical context of rural Muslim Kalpitiya and its transnational connection with the Persian Gulf. For Amina, in some senses the emotions arising from her relationship with her new spouse not only served to re-humanize her after the sudden and tragic death of her first husband, but they restored her sense of self-respect and led to a new sense of acceptance of her need to continue working. As for Shafna, despite the hardships she has had to endure, the emotional resilience she developed through migration has given her the determination to create a better life for herself and her children, and to decide that she is no longer willing to submit to the violence inflicted on her by her husband. And even if Shafna and Jansila's sense of honour within the *ur* were not drastically changed, what is crucial is that they feel their lives have the potential to transform.

Conclusions

While economic causes tend to dominate popular perceptions and policy discourse on transnational migration, I argue that women's decisions to migrate stem from their emotional involvement and desires towards spouses, as well as their aspirations for honour and for change in their lives. These spousal-influenced decisions can be seen as part of 'projects for self re-making', within which women act as moral agents in seeking to enhance respect. They look to affect change in relations by desiring the creation of more stability and love within relations, or to escape feelings of neglect, betrayal or bereavement, as migration leads to relationships being renegotiated regarding the ways in which they are strengthened, negotiated, eroded or sustained. While women's experiences may, on the one hand, appear to reinforce popular perceptions of migration decreasing communal respectability, my findings elucidate the ways in which women's re-imagination of themselves, their lives and their spousal relations transform their self-respect. I argue that these subjective dimensions of migrants' experiences require urgent attention, as they are often inadequately examined despite being a crucial motivating factor for women's migration.

This knowledge enables the migrant domestic worker to be seen as a complex, feeling being and a moral agent, rather than a 'victim' of poverty and prejudices, or a threat to culture and religion. I suggest that a closer examination of migrant women's experiences in terms of agency, self-transformation and sexuality through extensive ethnography can help to debunk stereotypes and meta-narratives of the perceived immorality of migrating women. The ethnographic cases I have discussed of migrant women's feelings regarding their selves, lives and migration are experiences that are often overlooked and misunderstood by kin, fellow community members and policy makers alike. They also illustrate the ways in which women manoeuvre the structural and moral confines of their lives, stressing the challenges faced by migrants and their spouses in enjoying fulfilling married and sexual lives, and suggesting the need for instituted improvements within the present migration regime to ensure a form of migration that supports their life aspirations and well-being.

Notes

1. This ranking, accorded by the Department of Census and Statistics in 2006/7, excludes the war-affected sub-divisions of the northern and eastern provinces, which were under the political administration of the Tamil separatist regime at the time. According to the same survey, 40.3 per cent of the population of Kalpitiya had a monthly expenditure per capita below the official poverty line in Sri Lanka.

2. West Asia covers the two sub-regions of the Gulf Cooperation Council (Kuwait, Saudi Arabia, Qatar, UAE and Oman) and the Levant (Jordan, Lebanon, Israel and the Palestinian Occupied Territories).

3. Overall migrant remittance earnings were the largest source of foreign direct investment, standing at almost \$3.4 billion or 390,000 million Sri Lankan rupees (SLBFE 2009).

4. The SLBFE has been seeking to reduce domestic work migration by encouraging women to retrain and migrate as 'care givers' or nurses, and by actively promoting men to migrate for 'semi-skilled' work. Simultaneously, it seeks to improve the regulation of domestic work migration through provisions for mandatory pre-departure training, social insurance schemes and attempts to forge bilateral agreements with host countries. See Dias and Jayasundere (2001) and HRW (2007).

5. Tamil-speakers in Kalpitiya comprise 64,908 persons or over 60 per cent of the sub-division's population. Their proportion in Kalpitiya is three times greater than the national average. Forty-two per cent of people in Kalpitiya are Sinhalese, 39 per cent Muslim, and 19 per cent Tamil, compared to the national average of 82 per cent Sinhalese, 8 per cent Muslim, and 9.4 per cent Tamil (DCS 2001). While the Sinhalese and Tamils are identified by the language they speak rather than religion, Muslims have chosen to be identified by religion. Tamils and Muslims are distinct groups with their own political and cultural histories, but they have a shared linguistic bond (Nuhman 2002) and shared experiences of marginalization and discrimination (Haniffa 2008; ICG 2007, 2010).

6. Regarding this distinction, the Tamil word *ur* has a varied meaning that can be broadly translated as village, homeland and 'community'. *Ur aalkal* literally means 'people of the homeland', and it refers to the 'host community' or people from families that have been native to the locality for several generations.

7. The study of sexuality and its link with gender has not been without argument. Butler explains that, 'sexual and gender relations, although in no sense causally linked, are structurally linked in important ways' (Butler 2004: 259). Foucault (1978) describes sexuality as a domain of power, but one where gender norms are always at stake.

8. Cantu's (2009) definition of sexuality being an axis of power relations stems from Hondagnue-Sotelo's (1994) definition of gender being more than a variable of migration, but a dimension of power that shapes and organizes migration.

9. Much of this work focuses either on groups whose sexuality is 'visible' as it is perceived as problematic (e.g., homosexuals and commercial sex workers). The heterosexual cultures of 'more ordinary' migrant groups in advanced industrialized countries have also been studied by Gonzalez-Lopez (2005) and Ahmadi (2003), but Hirsch (2003) suggests the need to focus more on migrants' sexuality in Third World societies.

10. Whether this is a genuine reflection of women's sexuality, or whether women only expressed to me what they perceived was socially permissible, is important to consider. However, I do not analyse this here as it was not a focus of my conversations with women.

11. Social awareness and acceptance of the sexual freedom enjoyed by male migrants is widespread in Sri Lanka, as studies by Gamburd (2000), Smith (2010) and Pathirage and Collyer (2009) show. Studies of Mexicans migrating to the US by Hondagnue-Sotelo (1994) and others also indicate existing double standards in male–female sexual practices, though Gonzalez-Lopez (2005) and Hirsch (2003) have found that these are rapidly changing. The fact that sexual expression is less restricted among men has also been extensively documented across cultures. Dinnerstein (2002: 5) discusses the bases for asymmetric human sexual privilege in white, middle-class USA, which drives men to insist on unilateral sexual prerogatives and inclines women to consent to their insistence.

12. As Caitrin Lynch's (1999) work on 'good girl' Sri Lankan factory workers has shown, once migrant women become mobile subjects, they challenge patriarchal society, an order which partly rests on ideas of women's sexuality and the policing of women's bodies.

13. The sexual and moral codes imposed on women, codified and disseminated through patriarchal institutions such as the state, the law, religious tenets and their interpreters, and the family, share many similarities despite being categorized as Muslim, Christian, Hindu, Buddhist and so on.

14. Thangarajah (2004) argues how returning migrant women most often respond to religious reformism by adopting orthodox practices in their styles of dress, appearing to be active agents in processes of Islamization as they gain status through their new, pious behaviour.

15. This comment was extracted from a flyer that was issued by a local religious group affiliated with the Tabligh Jamaat. I was handed a copy of it as it was being distributed on the streets of Kalpitiya in November 2010.

16. Fatima Mernissi (2003, 2002) suggests that it is the disruptive power of female sexuality, rather than sexuality itself, that poses as a symbol of disorder (*fitna*). Her feminist interpretation of Imam Ghazali's *The Revivification of Religious*

Sciences – the key Islamic text that codified sexual practices in the eleventh century – stresses the fear within Muslim societies of women's active female sexuality, and the difficulty of satisfying female sexual desire (Mernissi 2002: 303), which justifies women being constrained. Without constraints, men would be faced with irresistible sexual attraction that inevitably leads to *fitna* or chaos.

17. I documented the views of the religious leaders described in this paragraph during interviews from July 2010 to January 2011 with eight different *maulavis*, *imams* and *seyvinna* (folk healing, witchcraft) healers in Kalpitiya.

18. Mahmood (2001) draws attention to the fact that notions of self-realization also existed in pre-modern history, and were not an invention of the liberal tradition. For example, Plato discussed self-mastery over one's passions, and notions exist in Buddhism and mystical traditions of Islam and Christianity of realizing oneself through self-transformation (ibid.: 207).

19. For other work from which this discussion stems, see Taylor (1985) for writing on positive and negative freedom, and Carter (1995) for passive and active notions of agency as they relate to demography.

20. Anthropological conceptions of 'self' are linked to those of 'personhood', which is a social construct, a composite of social relations and a process involving social, cultural, political and other factors/conditions. You are not a 'person' when you are born, but you become a person through your interaction with others over time (Scheper-Hughes and Lock 1987; Jackson 1990).

21. Anthropologists studying emotion, human suffering and/or well-being suggest that emotion can best be understood through the body, as it is physiologically and crucially linked to one's state of feeling and sense of well-being (see also Lutz and Abu-Lughod 1990; Lawrence 2000; Gronseth 2001; Unnithan-Kumar 2001). Good (1994) describes the body as an agent in the construction of meaning, and Scheper-Hughes and Lock (1987) discuss the body as a symbol of what is happening in societies and politics, and the control held over it by underlying institutional agendas.

22. Anderson writes, 'By "dehumanising" the maid and choosing to view her as a human being who is not yet a real human being – with likes and hates, relations of her own, a history and ambitions of her own – but a human being who is socially dead, employers exercise an extreme form of power that is uncommon in other employer–employee relationships' (Anderson 2000: 121).

23. The *kafala* or sponsorship programme in the Arab states stipulates that an employer is required to sponsor a migrant worker's visa and assume full economic and legal responsibility for them during the contracted period. In the case of a domestic worker, the programme makes it mandatory for them to remain in their employer's/sponsor's homes, and prevents them from changing sponsorship. The system is thought to breed exploitation of migrant workers (HRW 2007).

24. These ethnographic case studies are based on data that I collected during four to six interviews and ethnographic encounters, and over a period of one to two years in Kalpitiya.

25. See also Gamburd (2000) on this point.

References

Abu-Lughod, L. 2002. 'Do Muslim Women Really Need Saving? Anthropological Reflections on Cultural Relativism and Its Others', *American Anthropologist* 104(3): 783–90.

Anderson, B. 2000. *Doing the Dirty Work? The Global Politics of Domestic Labour.* London: Zed Books.

Ahmad, A.N. 2009. 'Bodies That (Don't) Matter: Desire, Eroticism and Melancholia in Pakistani Labour Migration', *Mobilities* 4(3): 309–27.

Ahmadi, N. 2003. 'Migration Challenges Views on Sexuality', *Journal of Ethnic and Racial Studies* 26(4): 684–706.

Butler, J. 1997. *The Psychic Life of Power: Theories in Subjection.* Stanford: Stanford University Press.

———— 2004. *Undoing Gender.* New York: Routledge.

Cantu, L. 2009a. 'Sexuality, Migration and Identity', in N.A. Naples and S. Vidal-Ortiz (eds), *The Sexuality of Migration: Border Crossings and Mexican Immigrant Men.* New York: New York University Press, pp.21–38.

———— 2009b. 'Towards a Queer Political Economy of Sexuality: Places, Spaces and Shifting Identities', in N.A. Naples and S. Vidal-Ortiz (eds), *The Sexuality of Migration: Border Crossings and Mexican Immigrant Men.* New York: New York University Press, pp.163–70.

Carter, A. 1995. 'Agency and Fertility: For an Ethnography of Practice', in S. Greenhalgh (ed.), *Situating Fertility: Anthropology and Demographic Inquiry.* Cambridge: Cambridge University Press, pp.55–85.

Corrêa, S., R.P. Petchesky and R. Parker. 2008. 'Introduction', in S. Corrêa, R.P. Petchesky and R. Parker (ed.), *Sexuality, Health and Human Rights.* London: Routledge, pp.1–11.

Csordas, T.J. 1994. 'Introduction: The Body as Representation and Being-in-the-world', in T.J. Csordas (ed.), *Embodiment and Experience: The Existential Ground of Culture and Self.* Cambridge: Cambridge University Press, pp.1–24.

Das, V. 1999. 'The Act of Witnessing: Violence, Poisonous Knowledge, and Subjectivity', unpublished paper presented at the conference 'Practices of Violence and Post-colonial Modernities', Berkeley, University of California, 9 April.

DCS. 2001. 'National Census 2001'. Department of Census and Statistics, Ministry of Finance and Planning, Sri Lanka. Retrieved 20 December 2011 from: www.statistics.gov.lk/.

———— 2008. 'Kalpitiya Divisional Poverty, 2006/7'. Report provided by the Puttalam district office of the Ministry of Finance and Planning.

Dias, M., and R. Jayasundere. 2001. 'Sri Lanka: Good Practices to Prevent Women Migrant Workers from Going into Exploitative Forms of Labour', Series on Women and Migration. Geneva/Colombo: International Labour Organization.

Dinnersten, D. 2002. 'Higamous-Hogamous', in C.L. Williams and A. Stein (eds), *Sexuality and Gender.* Oxford: Blackwell Publishers, pp.5–19.

Fassin, D. 2001a. 'Culturalism as Ideology', in C.M. Obermeyer (ed.), *Cultural Perspectives on Reproductive Health.* Oxford: Oxford University Press, pp.300–16.

———— 2001b. 'The Biopolitics of Otherness. Undocumented Foreigners and Racial Discrimination in French Public Debate', *Anthropology Today* 17(1): 3–7.

———— 2005. 'Compassion and Repression: The Moral Economy of Immigration Policies in France', *Cultural Anthropology* 20(3): 362–87.

Foucault, M. 1978. *The History of Sexuality*, Vol. 1. New York: Pantheon Books.

———— 1980. 'Truth and Power', in C. Gordon (ed.), *Power/Knowledge: Selected Interviews and Other Writings 1972–1977*. New York: Pantheon Books, pp.109–33.

————. 1983. 'Subject and Power', in M. Foucault, H. Dreyfus and P. Rabinow (eds), *Beyond Structuralism and Hermeneutics*. Chicago: Chicago University Press, pp. 208–26.

Gamburd, M.R. 2000. *The Kitchen Spoon's Handle: Transnationalism and Sri Lanka's Migrant Households*. Ithaca, NY: Cornell University Press.

Gardner, K., and F. Osella. 2004. 'Migration, Modernity and Social Transformation in South Asia: An Introduction', in K. Gardner and F. Osella (eds), *Migration, Modernity and Social Transformation in South Asia*. New Delhi: Sage, pp.1–24.

Gonzalez-Lopez, G. 2005. *Erotic Journeys: Mexican Immigrants and Their Sex Lives*. Berkeley: University of California Press.

Good, B.J. 1994. 'The Body, Illness Experience and the Life World', in *Medicine, Rationality, and Experience*. Cambridge: Cambridge University Press, pp.25–64.

Gronseth, A.S. 2001. 'In Search of Community: A Quest for Well-being among Tamil Refugees in Northern Norway', *Medical Anthropology Quarterly* 15(4): 493–514.

Haniffa, F. 2002. 'Power Dressing', *Options Magazine*. Colombo: Women and Media Collective.

———— 2008. 'Piety as Politics amongst Muslim Women in Sri Lanka' *Modern Asian Studies* 42(2/3): 347–75.

Herdt, G. 1997. 'Sexual Cultures and Population Movement: Implication for AIDS/STDs', in his G. Herdt (ed.), *Sexual Cultures and Migration in the Era of AIDS: Anthropological and Demographic Perspectives*. Oxford: Clarendon Press, pp.3–22.

Hirsch, J.S. 2003. *A Courtship after Marriage: Sexuality and Love in Mexican Transnational Families*. Berkeley: University of California Press.

Hondagnue-Sotelo, P. 1994. *Gendered Transitions: Mexican Experiences of Immigration*. Berkeley: University of California Press.

HRW. 2007. 'Exported and Exposed: Abuses Against Sri Lankan Domestic Workers in Saudi Arabia, Kuwait, Lebanon, and the United Arab Emirates', Report 19: 16 (C). New York: Human Rights Watch.

ICG. 2007. 'Sri Lanka's Muslims: Caught in the Crossfire', Asia Report No. 134. Colombo/Brussels: International Crisis Group.

———— 2010. 'Sri Lanka: A Bitter Peace', Asia Update Briefing No. 99. Colombo/Brussels: International Crisis Group.

Jackson, M. 1990. 'The Man Who Could Turn into an Elephant: Shape Shifting Among the Kuranko of Sierra Leone', in I. Karp and M. Jackson (eds), *Personhood and Agency: The Experience of Self and Other in African Cultures*. Uppsala/Washington: Uppsala Studies in Cultural Anthropology, pp.59–78.

Jayawardena, K., and M. De Alwis. 1995. 'Introduction', in K. Jayawardena and M. De Alwis (eds), *Embodied Violence: Communalising Women's Sexuality in South Asia*. London: Zed Books, pp.ix–xxiv.

Jayaweera, S., M. Dias and L. Wanasundera. 2002. *Returnee Migrant Women in Two Locations in Sri Lanka*. Colombo: Centre for Women's Research.

Kottegoda, S. 2006. 'Bringing Home the Money: Migration and Poverty in Gender Politics in Sri Lanka', in A. Agrawal (ed.), *Migrant Women and Work: Women and Migration in Asia*, Vol. 4. New Delhi: Sage, pp.47–91.

Lawrence, P. 2000. 'Violence, Suffering, Amman: The Work of Oracles in Sri Lanka's Eastern War Zone', in V. Das (ed.), *Violence and Subjectivity*. Berkeley: University of California Press, pp.171–204.

Lutz, C., and L. Abu-Lughod (eds). 1990. *Language and the Politics of Emotion*. Cambridge: Cambridge University Press.

Lynch, C. 1999. 'The "Good Girls" of Sri Lankan Modernity: Moral Orders of Nationalism and Capitalism', *Identities* 6: 55–89.

Mahmood, S. 2001. 'Feminist Theory, Embodiment and the Docile Agent: Some Reflections on the Egyptian Revival', *Cultural Anthropology* 16(2): 202–36.

Mai, N., and R. King. 2009. 'Love, Sexuality and Migration: Mapping the Issue(s)', *Mobilities* 4(3): 295–307.

Mernissi, F. 2002. 'The Muslim Concept of Active Female Sexuality', in C.L. Williams and A. Stein (eds), *Sexuality and Gender*. Oxford: Blackwell, pp.296–307.

———— 2003. *Beyond the Veil: Male–Female Dynamics in Muslim Society*. London: Saqi Books.

Moukarbel, N. 2009a. *Sri Lankan Housemaids in Lebanon: A Case of 'Symbolic Violence' and 'Everyday Forms of Resistance'*. Amsterdam: Amsterdam University Press.

———— 2009b. 'Not Allowed to Love? Sri Lankan Maids in Lebanon', *Mobilities* 4(3): 329–47.

Nuhman, M.A. 2002. 'Understanding Sri Lankan Muslim Identity', ICES Course Series 4. Colombo: International Centre for Ethnic Studies.

———— 2007. 'Sri Lankan Muslims. Ethnic Identity within Cultural Diversity', ICES Sri Lanka Program. Colombo: International Centre for Ethnic Studies.

Parrenas, R.S. 2001. *Servants of Globalization: Women, Migration and Domestic Work*. Stanford: Stanford University Press.

Pathirage, J., and M. Collyer. 2009. 'Capitalizing Social Networks: Sri Lankan Migration to Italy', *Ethnography* 12(3): 315–33.

Rozario, S. 2002. '"Poor and Dark": What Is My Future? Identity Construction and Adolescent Women in Bangladesh', in L. Manderson and P. Liamputtong (eds), *Coming of Age in South and Southeast Asia: Youth, Courtship and Sexuality*. Guildford: Biddles, pp.42–57.

Samarasingha, G. 1999. 'The Psycho-social Implications of Middle East Migration on the Family Left Behind', report for UNICEF Sri Lanka. Colombo: Centre for Women's Research.

Sargent, C.F. 2006. 'Reproductive Strategies and Islamic Discourse: Malian Migrants Negotiate Everyday Life in Paris, France', *Medical Anthropology Quarterly* 20(1): 31–49.

Scheper-Hughes, N. 1988. 'The Madness of Hunger: Sickness, Delirium, and Human Needs', Culture, *Medicine, and Psychiatry* 12(4): 429–58.

Scheper-Hughes, N., and M. Lock. 1987. 'The Mindful Body: A Prolegomenon to Future Work in Medical Anthropology', *Medical Anthropology Quarterly* 1(1): 6–41.

SLBFE. 2009. 'Annual Statistical Report on Foreign Employment'. Battaramalla: Research Division, Sri Lankan Bureau of Foreign Employment.

Smith, M.A. 2010. 'The State of Sexuality and Intimacy: Sri Lankan Women Migrants in the Middle East', PhD diss. Singapore: Department of Geography, National University of Singapore.

Taylor, C. 1985. 'What's Wrong with Negative Liberty?' in *Philosophy and the Human Sciences: Philosophical Papers*, Vol. 2. Cambridge: Cambridge University Press, pp.211–29.

Thangarajah, C.Y. 2004. 'Veiled Constructions: Conflict, Migration and Modernity in Eastern Sri Lanka', in K. Gardner and F. Osella (eds), *Migration, Modernity and Social Transformation in South Asia*. New Delhi: Sage, pp.141–62.

Tober, D.M., M.H. Taghdisi and M. Jalali. 2006. '"Fewer Children, Better Life" or "As Many as God Wants"?: Family Planning among Low-income Iranian and Afghan Refugee Families in Isfahan, Iran', *Medical Anthropology Quarterly* 20(1): 50–71.

Unnithan-Kumar, M. 2001. 'Emotion, Agency and Access to Healthcare: Women's Experiences of Reproduction in Jaipur', in S. Tremayne (ed.), *Managing Reproductive Life: Cross-cultural Themes in Sexuality and Fertility*. New York: Berghahn, pp.27–51.

——— 2003. 'Reproduction, Health, Rights: Connections and Disconnections', in R. Wilson and J. Mitchell (eds), *Human Rights in Global Perspective*. London: Routledge, pp.183–208.

Zlotnik, H. 1995. 'Migration and the Family: The Female Perspective', *Asian and Pacific Migration Journal* 4(2-3): 253–71.

CHAPTER 4

'That's Not a Religious Thing, That's a Cultural Thing'

Culture in the Provision of Health Services for Bangladeshi Mothers in East London

Laura Griffith

This chapter looks at the experiences of motherhood among Bangladeshi women in Tower Hamlets, in the East End of London. The analysis focuses on the concept of authoritative knowledge: knowledge 'that counts' and on the basis of which choices are enacted. I move beyond simply describing what we might presume to be the dominance of biomedical knowledge, or the standardization of Islamic practice, and look at the multiple sites in which different types of authoritative knowledge are produced and reproduced. The majority of research on the Bangladeshi diaspora in the East End has concentrated upon male public and political identities (e.g., Eade 1989, 1990). However, more recent work has investigated Bangladeshi women's roles in public and private spheres (Gavron 1997; Gardner 2002; Ahmed 2005). Whilst the borough of Tower Hamlets is not deprived by global standards, it has that reputation nationally. Within London, it is a borough always considered to be beset by problems; conversely, its diversity is celebrated and hailed by others. It is often referred to by workers in the health services, public sector workers and the local press as a 'unique' environment. Whilst it is true that poverty is rife, this never tells the whole story, and certainly does little to detail the way people experience statistics of deprivation emotionally.

Newborns and Breastfeeding: Diagnosing the Problems

The Bangladeshi diaspora in East London exists in a rapidly changing social geography, and during fieldwork conducted over a period of eighteen months in 2003 and 2004 I collected accounts of Bangladeshi motherhood in a variety of formal and informal settings such as playgroups, mother and baby clinics, households, parents' centres and at local meetings. In addition, I conducted forty-five interviews with a series of different health professionals and mothers. This chapter is based on interviews with just two women whom I knew well, and to whom I refer using pseudonyms. These participants were deliberately selected as Bangladeshi mothers with whom I had a good relationship, and who were in contact with the health services. Written consent was gained and the interviews were recorded and transcribed verbatim; these were then subsequently analysed from a narrative point of view. This chapter represents an in-depth narrative analysis, and therefore is focused on only two narratives, chosen from a set of fifteen longer transcribed narratives of mothers that I interviewed, and countless other stories that I heard, to highlight the complexity of the formation of individualized opinions about becoming a mother. However, these narratives are contextualized with reference to the entire data set.

Shurma

The first narrative discussed in this chapter is from a woman whom I shall call Shurma, who was in her early twenties and lived in Spitalfields and Weavers. Her natal family had lived in England for about thirty years. She was fluent in English and Sylheti, and had married a British Bangladeshi from a family that had come to Britain in the last five years. He was also bilingual. She had just had her second child at the time I interviewed her. When she had her first baby (three years prior to the interview) she was in her in-laws' house on a housing estate in Spitalfields and Weavers, and she was 'living in a two-bedroom flat and we were all so squashed. Overcrowded and no space, no privacy, nothing'. At the time of the interview, she had moved to live in a flat with her husband and two small children, close to both her parents and her in-laws.

During the course of the interview, Shurma told me that after the delivery of her first baby her health visitor put in her notes that she was experiencing postnatal depression. What follows is her account of what happened after she returned from hospital.

> I came home and he [the baby] was just screaming, and I just wanted someone to take him off me. He was crying because he didn't have no

bottle milk. I was breastfeeding and there was no breast milk, that's why he was crying. My husband's family were like, 'He's hungry, he's hungry, give him breast milk'. I was thinking, 'Oh, okay, he's having it, he's sucking', but he wasn't getting any. He kept on screaming, so they went out and got milk from the next-door lady, she just had a baby two weeks ago and they got milk from her.[1]

During the interview, Shurma said that she was advised to breastfeed by the midwives and her in-laws, but that this wasn't 'successful'. According to her, it was her own family and the next-door neighbours who intervened to help her (by fetching formula milk), providing her with the thing that she needed to stop her baby screaming. It was the advice of the midwives that was found wanting. When I spoke to the health visitors who worked for a local family-based health initiative, they often talked about mothers not being able to breastfeed as they felt that they somehow weren't producing enough milk for their babies – the implication being that they couldn't measure it as they could with formula. In this instance, Shurma told me that the midwives just told her to breastfeed, but then did not help her or realize the difficult circumstances she was struggling with. However, Shurma knew that she had been given the wrong advice as her son needed formula milk and was suffering from the lack of it.

Amina, a breastfeeding support worker, commented on a 'lack of understanding' amongst second-generation migrants:

[With the] second generation you get things like, 'Is it true you are supposed to throw away the colostrum?' They think that the colostrum is in there for nine months and that you need to throw this away. So I get a lot of questions relating to colostrum, and whether it is dirty, also whether breast milk is enough because they can't see how much the baby is drinking, purely because with a bottle you can see just how much the baby is drinking in ounces.

Here Amina refers to the suspicion of colostrum (*shaldood*), and to the fact that mothers saw her as someone who was knowledgeable about the medical aspects of breastfeeding. In Tower Hamlets, breastfeeding was a contentious issue, and health visitors regularly explained the benefits and advised against feeding babies hot water (*gorom fani*), sugar water (*misri fani*) or honey (*modhu*) on the tip of one's finger. However, Shurma's decision represents neither the ignorance of a biomedical model nor the result of direct pressure from her in-laws to bottle feed, but rather what she saw as an entirely pragmatic decision to halt the suffering of her child and herself. After the birth of her second child, she bottle fed, her baby did not scream so much and she felt much better as a result.

In the rest of Shurma's interview she explained how it was when she was a first-time mother, saying that she and her husband were very inexperienced parents and unfamiliar with various medical procedures. Shurma was sixteen when she fell pregnant, and seventeen when she gave birth. She gave a positive account of her labour and she was very comfortable talking with me about her time in hospital. In her interview she particularly remembered a student who was kind to her and stayed with her throughout the delivery. Shurma liked having a student there because, she related, it was nice having another young woman who showed her personal kindnesses and support: 'The one girl was really nice, a student she was. It was better like that, if you get a student, they aren't so bored by it and are nicer to you. I don't think she was that ... that experienced, or didn't know that much about nothing, but she was nice'.

Shurma did not find her doctors or the midwives particularly useful in supplying the information she needed during her first pregnancy: 'No, actually the midwives didn't say anything it was ... I heard it from my friends that had already had a baby. They said like, don't use epidural because you are going to get back pain. Don't do this, don't do that. So it was my friends that I found out from not the doctors or the midwives'. There was a certain set of information about the hospital that to Shurma was a way of resisting hospital practice. These 'little things' sometimes turned out to be very significant, and not only to Shurma herself. As Shurma did not have the same midwife throughout her pregnancy, other serious problems were overlooked:

> After my second baby was born, the midwife throughout the whole nine months – I saw different midwives – and it's like none of them cared. It's nice when a midwife says, 'Oh how are you, you don't look good', or whatever, 'You all right?' When you say things like that it makes you happy, but last year it was like different midwives every appointment. My last appointment ... the midwife, she found out like I was really like anaemic.

In this example, Shurma talks about how the attention to personal detail – 'You don't look good', presumably in comparison to her normal appearance – would help the midwife pick up on more serious things like anaemia that should have been tested for and should also have been noticed in her appearance. This is what she had to say about the period immediately after the birth: 'Afterwards I thought that someone is going to come and show me how to change a nappy. Someone is going to come and show me how to breastfeed, show me how to bottle feed and everything. No one'.

Shurma was left on her own after giving birth, and felt as if she was being prompted to do things she did not know how to do.

L.G.: And did you think that you had postnatal depression at the time?
SHURMA: No, I didn't even know what it was. All I … I thought I was just tired, and I just got fed up. I didn't want a baby any more. I just wanted to be on my own. I wanted to be single again, not married and all that. Yeah.
L.G.: So was it [your health visitor who] suggested that's what you might have?
SHURMA: Yeah.
L.G.: How did you first sort of, like, think [about it]?
SHURMA: I remember I was talking to one of my friends after I saw [my health visitor], and she was like, 'Oh, have you heard of postnatal depression? I think you might have that'. I think [my health visitor] spoke to me about that too – about postnatal depression.

At this point I asked her whether she knew about postnatal depression as a concept and whether she knew of it existing in Bangladesh:

I'm not sure, but I think, you know, Bengali ladies who grew up in Bangladesh, I don't think they believe in postnatal depression. Because when I was living with my mother-in-law and my sister-in-law and them, they saw me crying and they kept saying, 'Why are you crying?' 'I don't know, I don't know'. And my mother-in-law would say, 'Oh you stupid girl, she doesn't know why she is crying'. My older sister-in-law, she's got kids, and she was like, for the first time she was being nice, and she got me a cup of tea, and I was like thinking, 'Oh my god, she's normally so nasty to me'. And the little one, the little sister-in-law, she was like, really nasty, and she was like, 'Oh, why's she crying, she's so stupid'. Later, I was asking her about postnatal check and she was suddenly like, 'Postnatal depression, that's a load of crap. That's not true'. And I was like, 'Okay'.

Shurma's complaints about what happened afterwards were directed at some, but not all, of the midwives, but they were also clearly directed at the female members of her in-laws' family. She talked about having no space in the house, having to dress in a *shari* to receive visitors, having to deal with her mother and sister-in-law by herself as her husband was absent working night shifts. When I first knew Shurma, she often looked tired and complained about the sheer amount of household labour she was involved in. Shurma's story was a familiar one; I heard from many women throughout my fieldwork of women feeling unsupported and tired, whilst also being reprimanded. The people 'telling her off' in Shurma's case were the midwives at the hospital, who instructed her to get her own food, and then also her mother-in-law and sister-in-law at home because she did not know the 'little things' – for example, how to prepare formula milk. Importantly, she did not speak so much about the Caesarean, the pain during labour, the stitches she received or anything to do with the major procedures I knew that she had undergone, but more about the humiliation of feeling stupid and isolated.

At this point in the interview Shurma talked of a time when she began to feel better and more confident. She talked here of her family in ways similar to those in which she frames the midwives at 'Hamlets' hospital:

> And they expect you to know everything. It's like, I remember little things I used to ask. I didn't know nothing about babies. You have boil water for the milk and so many things. They used to say, 'Oh you stupid girl. You don't know this and that'. I remember my health visitor came to see me [and] I burst out crying, I couldn't stop crying. I just kept telling her, 'I want to go to my mum. I want to see my mum'. She was like, 'Why don't you go to your mum's then? Say you are going to hospital and just go and see your mum'. My health visitor was really nice.

It is at the point when the health visitor suggested something seemingly minor at a crucial stage that Shurma felt grateful for the support. At the time of interview, she lived in newer accommodation with her husband and had just had her second baby. She commented:

> This time round it was much better. When [my first baby] was born I didn't know how I was going to feel, what I was going to go through. But this time after [my second baby] was born I was, before he was born I told my husband, 'Look, I am going to need help. If I get mad at you, or if I tell you off for some reason, just be patient – because I'm really sorry and I don't mean it'. So he's been really helpful.

Mibi

Mibi's case highlights the need to collapse, or at least complicate, the bifurcation between modernity and tradition, and in addition the apparent divide between Islamic practice and biomedicine. Anthropologists have sometimes critiqued the gendered distribution of knowledge in Islam, arguing that 'orthodox' practices and scriptural knowledge are in effect denied to women, whereas informal, localized practices that are performed mainly by women are marginalized (Holy 1991; Inhorn 1994). I investigate how Islamic beliefs and knowledge were used, considered and sometimes sidelined. Jolly writes, 'The embodied maternal subject is pervaded by a profound tension, perhaps even a split, as the mother is sundered in contexts between "tradition" and "modernity"' (Jolly 1998: 1). The following analysis seeks to ground discussions of religious knowledge and identity located within accounts of motherhood.

Mibi was in her early thirties, and had been born in Bangladesh; she came to the UK when she was only one year old and has always lived in Tower Hamlets. Mibi was a subject of great interest to the other mothers in the centre, and also to Bangladeshi co-workers, because she had married a *ghora* (white man). Mibi felt herself to be deeply religious and made a point of aligning herself with the East London Mosque and, for associated reasons, with the home-education movement. She thought of her duties as a crèche worker, a mother and a home educator as religious in nature. Mibi also had many points of reference in her life other than religion. As a second-generation Bangladeshi, she referred to Bangladesh as 'back home', a practice common even amongst Bangladeshis who had never been to Bangladesh (Gavron 1997). Although she self-consciously did not conform to many of the negative stereotypes of Islamic women that she perceived to be currently held in Britain – such as being 'demure' or 'unopinionated' – she considered the roles of wives being to bring up children, perform domestic duties and undertake work outside the home primarily with children. This seemingly 'passive' identity was far from an ascribed one, but rather one that Mibi actively worked to achieve. Her identity was also anti-authoritarian in respect of the state. I asked her about what she thought about becoming a mother when she first got married:

> I think our religion, our faith, has a lot to do with it, so we don't go into a marriage thinking, 'Shall we have children?' It's just like, 'Yes'. You know, like you always try for children, children are like blessings for us. Hard work but, yeah. So we never sat down and said, 'Shall we have children?' It wasn't like that at all. We get to know each other. Because, obviously, our marriage, after – we get to know each other – not before. Love comes afterwards. First, you just get to know this guy you know. Then once things settle down, well, we didn't anyway, just got to know each other and then I was pregnant and that was it. But we're very happy with it. We were very excited when I got pregnant so. But, yeah.[2]

When talking to Mibi I was presented with a number of what I interpreted as being deliberately self-conscious statements about Islam and family life. Mibi always offered me this 'alternative', the alternative being an Islamic lifestyle. Mibi portrayed the Islam that she espoused as a unique way of creating a community, not a community composed of Bangladeshis necessarily but rather of Muslim sisters. Mibi proudly spoke to me of her Algerian, French and American friends. This community has been one that has supported her throughout motherhood, and during her more controversial efforts to educate her children at home.

When speaking about the actual process of having a child, Mibi only remembers being very excited. She was sick (she had extended and acute nausea for the first three months of her pregnancy, during which time she actually had a net weight loss) and remembered being very excited by choosing names, and also by the reaction of her husband's family. It was to be his parents' first grandchild:

> M: I've got an older brother, so he's married, and they already had a grandchild from him. It wasn't such a big novelty for them [her own parents].
> L.G.: Still, I bet they were pleased?
> M: Actually I think in Bengali families it was just so normal as well. Whereas, I find with his side of the family, it's like, 'Wow', because it's not something common, you know. It's like, we've not been brought up with little kids around, but most Bengali families have. But for me, it was like, right, I'm going to have a baby, get on with it.

Mibi saw the differences between herself and her husband arising from different upbringings and different communities, rather than from their different genders. Mibi saw herself as a 'rarity' in mainstream British society, a society that she thought viewed childbearing as something out of the ordinary. The difference in approaching children is seen in cultural and experiential terms. Mibi clearly recognized these categories of perception as they applied to her, and went beyond being 'only a mother' to understand motherhood as an occupation which she felt defied the institution of the state. She had a home birth in defiance of a state institution for a variety of complex reasons. In her narrative, Mibi sometimes pre-empted a view of motherhood that she assumed I might take, and reconfigured it.

Mibi carefully and self-consciously negotiated her way through a web of religious obligations, medical advice (that she sometimes saw as controlling and inhibiting) and various practical constraints. When Mibi had been younger, she had had personal experience of acting as a translator when she went to the hospital to see her aunts, and this had clearly left her with a bad impression of the hospital. She felt it was more convenient for her to have her child at home – in terms of her having her friends round, being able to walk around and not being bothered by a male presence. She continued:

> Yeah, it was my children, my health you're talking about. I think a lot of the time, because a lot of Bengali women can't, you know, tell straight out like that to a lot of people in the profession, they kind of like … whereas me, because I kind of speak out, I get what I want. Whereas, I find a lot of

Bengali people, they don't have the language. For instance, someone who is having their first baby, and says, 'I want a homebirth', and the doctor will say, 'Oh no, no, it's the first baby'. They will probably be like, 'Okay', whereas me, I am just like, 'No, [my] pregnancy is fine, I'm fine, I don't see why not'. Whereas, I know people won't argue, and a lot of people will say, 'The doctor says it's not wise to, I'm gonna stick to that'. I'm like, 'No, I don't want to go in there. No thank you'. Same with home education.

Mibi felt that it was her confidence in her decision to have a home birth that was, to her, unusual in comparison to the rest of the Bengali population. In her opinion, new migrants and those who couldn't speak English were not confident with doctors and would accept the medical advice that Mibi saw as unnecessary intervention. However, in my experience the reasons for Bangladeshi women not having a home birth were highly varied.

Mibi had varied opinions about the Bangladeshi population of Tower Hamlets. She was very sympathetic in respect of the powerless position that women sometimes found themselves in, where they were unable to communicate and unable to resist what she saw as biomedical domination. However, she was also dismissive of the Bangladeshi population because she regarded some 'superstitious practices' as un-Islamic. When I was shown pictures of her daughter as a small baby, I could see that the little girl had clearly had her hair shaved off. I asked Mibi if this was because 'birth hair' (*jonmo sool*) needed to be cut off as it was 'impure' (*napak*), and she looked disapproving. I asked:

L.G.: So it's both boys and girls that have their hair cut off?
M: On the seventh day, yeah, they have their head shaved, both boys and girls, yeah.
L.G.: *Jonmo sool*? Birth hair, yeah?
M: It's not the same as the things you might have heard. When they have their *aqiqah* on the seventh day, they finalize the name; the *aqiqah* is Muslim's day, they go and sacrifice a sheep ... And you do it on the seventh day. If you can do it, you do it on the seventh day; if you can't, then you can delay it, but it's ... yeah, the seventh day is when the names are confirmed, 'I'm not changing it anymore' sort of thing.

Mibi made a distinction between 'the things I might have heard' in my fieldwork and the proper Islamic form of events. Cutting the 'birth hair', like many practices, was considered to be Islamic by some people, and not Islamic by others. At other times, I asked her about adverts I had seen in East London Bengali newspapers for *tabiz* (an amulet) against all sorts of aliments; she was extremely disparaging, and saw poorly educated women as the victims of such adverts. *Tabiz* were not dismissed out of hand by all Muslims that I knew, and

I was advised of their 'proper' use, as opposed to their commercial use. The debate about what constitutes Islamic orthodoxy and what is heresy is complex, and goes beyond the limits of this chapter.

Mibi presented Islam to me as an effective grand narrative that was an all-encompassing guide to motherhood. Mibi's tendency to resist both state education for her children and state medical practices arose for many reasons: these are viewed by her as secular institutions, and also for a host of other causes, such as the bad treatment experienced by her relatives and her own personal convenience. She represented Islam as a practical religion, one that did not restrict medical treatment, and she directed her narrative to me as a Western woman interested in Islam. Mibi relished her identity and occupation as a mother, despite the hard work it involved, and did not view this as a 'sacrifice' or a 'compromise', but rather as an alternative lifestyle that was available for Bangladeshi and non-Bangladeshi Muslims. She had great sympathy for the Bangladeshi mothers she saw around her that were badly treated, and dismissed the hospital as both racist and uncaring. Despite her engagement with Islam being perceived as a radical set of beliefs in the current climate in Britain, she held what she regarded as orthodox beliefs.

Discussion

Khanum and Sharma, in their study of Bangladeshi women in Manchester, found that young mothers often 'exercise[d] ... personal agency within a political nexus in which the power of both family elders and medical personnel are crucial factors' (Khanum and Sharma 2003: 2). However, they stress that the body of work on South Asian women has lacked subtlety when dealing with the specific configurations of these power relations. This results in the denial of agency to the women involved, who may be subtly resisting these power relations. The support Shurma found came from a number of different sources: sometimes from health workers, and sometimes from family members, including her mother and husband. It is also questionable to what extent this story could be seen as only a story about a Bangladeshi woman in Tower Hamlets, and to what extent one about young women in Tower Hamlets in general, who may feel isolated and lack the key skills and knowledge to cope with the post-partum period. Here is scope for comparative work. Fox and Worts argue:

> Many factors shape the social context in which women mother – from their material resources and the nature of their relationship to the child's father to the social services available in their communities and the helpfulness of their partners, extended family, and friends. Because the essence of

motherhood is responsibility, however, the privatization of that responsibility seems especially significant. (Fox and Worts 1999: 330)

Shurma battled with both the hospital and her family, and it was a third party, the community health services, that provided help. There is considerable debate around the nature of specialist services for minority ethnic groups, and it would seem important to consider that Shurma did not seem to want a service that was aimed specifically at Bangladeshi women, but rather a service that could provide her with kindness, help and advice.

Shurma's story shows that, even in one woman's story, many competing sets of knowledge about motherhood can be unearthed. Work on gender and ethnicity sometimes has a tendency to portray ethnic minority women either as powerful strategizing agents or as helplessly burdened and 'passive victims of patriarchal institutions' (Greenhalgh 1995: 25). Shurma could be seen to be positioning herself somewhere in between. Whilst it is true that she found strategies for finding formula milk, or sneaking out to see her mother, it cannot be argued that she enjoyed a high level of choice. As Khanum and Sharma argue: 'a stress on agency should not lead us to overestimate the scope for choice which women enjoy[. W]hat needs to be recognized is that action taken within narrow limits of dependence is still action, and that decisions made within a very tight range of options still constitute decision making' (Khanum and Sharma 2003: 4). Indeed, Ram warns against the depiction of 'competing meanings and strategies [being] perceived as benign "pluralism" of medical options and choices', where in reality the 'cultural experience of maternity and birth [is] a site of considerable tension for women who have to mediate between discourses' (Ram 1998: 137). Too commonly, 'agency' is connected to autonomy, action and resistance. Shurma, although she did resist some practices, has also chosen to accept certain realities and compromises. As Madhok writes, 'there are thorny questions of … what constitutes [a] conformist choice' (Madhok 2004: 227). At the time of the interview, Shurma represented herself as more able to deal with motherhood, but only in the light of her previous struggles.

In much anthropological literature, discussions about 'agency' become, by a series of discursive practices, discussions of 'resistance'. However, this is increasingly being challenged. Mahmood has suggested that the moral practices of submission are, in fact, agentic (Mahmood 2005). Elsewhere, Mahmood suggests, 'The vexed relationship between feminism and religious traditions is perhaps most manifest in discussions on Islam' (Mahmood 2001: 202). Mibi would appear to have pursued practices and ideals ensconced in a tradition that, according to some versions of feminism, has historically accorded women a subordinate and passive status (ibid.: 205).

However, Mibi defended her choices to me as ones that were pious; she was practising religious submission that at the same time also subverted the expectations of the state and of certain biomedical practices. Mibi was keen to speak to me, a British woman, of the pleasures of this lifestyle as well as its duties.

As with Mahmood, it is essential to question the 'normative subject of ... feminist theory' that is still based on ideas of liberty, so that women's 'agency [is] largely conceptualized in terms of resistance to social norms' (ibid.: 208). Some feminists sometimes question why women are actively involved in practices that they see as oppressive. Metcalf asks the question, 'Why do contemporary women participate in religious movements?' (Metcalf 1999: 107), to which Ahmed-Ghosh replies from her work with Ahmadi women that they initiate the participation themselves and are: 'willing to "compromise" their own needs for autonomy in an endeavour to fulfil spiritual needs. They look upon their submission to the hierarchy as their duty to [G]od with the conviction that this hierarchy has a significant purpose in the lives of all believers' (Ahmed Ghosh 2004: 77).

Mibi did not wish to subvert religious practices, but rather she wanted to challenge the norms of 'mainstream' society as she perceived them. It is also this apparent (but complex) 'submission' that is read by some feminists as anti-feminist. A comparison can be made with feminist ideas about notions of agency and resistance to medicalized childbirth. Shurma did not necessarily want to resist the medicalization of birth, but rather she wanted more help and advice. Fox and Worts suggest that the valid criticism of medicalized childbirth can have some unintended consequences:

> Besides ignoring women's agency, there is an *implication* in the work of some writers who have developed the critique of medicalization that women *should* assume control over their labors and deliveries ... Interestingly, hospitals' responses to the critique – the provision of birthing rooms and allowing newborns to room-in with their mothers – encourage women to assume more responsibility for the birth and care of their babies, while at the same time failing to challenge medicine's control. (Fox and Worts 1999: 330, original emphasis)

In Shurma's story, being 'Bangladeshi' was not theorized in a self-conscious manner. This was despite the fact that some of her complaints were about having to meet relatives, attending to the needs of her in-laws' family or receiving advice from predominantly non-Bangladeshi health workers. In her own words, 'What mattered is that they helped'. Shurma's identities as a Bangladeshi woman, and as a Muslim woman, were not given primacy when she presented to me what had happened.

These two tales, from a narrative point of view, could be seen to focus on childbirth, but their narrative reach is, in fact, much wider. Birth narratives are never 'simple' stories, but are accounts which are barely able to contain the multiplicity of meanings that are held within them. As Pollock says: 'Understood as performance, birth stories dramatize the convergence of multiple stories on the birth experience. They undermine the presumed neutrality of medical procedures and the apparent transparency of birth experiences with the pressure of their own reflexivity' (Pollock 1999: 8).

Shurma and Mibi told me their stories at a particular point in time, and yet those stories appeared to reach their narrative conclusion neatly at the present day. Shurma's story could be seen to be about the realization that she was suffering from postnatal depression and the causes of her distress, and Mibi's could be said to focus on a series of self-conscious choices about birth, family life and identity. However, these narratives, like all narratives, contain within themselves interesting tensions and complexities. The ways in which both women sometimes appealed to notions of 'universally' held beliefs – for example, about homebirth, breast feeding, hygiene practices or the need for support – can in fact highlight the ways in which the specific configuration of practices are not, in fact, universal at all. 'Common sense' is not common to all cultures, and can be particularly revealing about the ideology of the person referring to it. A particularly eloquent definition of the concept of authoritative knowledge is the following: 'Authoritative knowledge is persuasive because it seems natural, reasonable, and consensually constructed ... Generally ... people not only accept authoritative knowledge (which is thereby validated and reinforced), but are actively and unselfconsciously engaged in its routine production and reproduction' (Jordan and Davis Floyd 1993: 152). Such stories can be seen to help construct authoritative knowledge to some extent. As the mothers rationalize their experiences, they provide an overall sense of logic.

Knowledges, although plural and changing, exist in powerful hierarchies. In any analysis of discourse that involves public health, patients and practitioners, there is usually a distinction between knowledge and beliefs as contrasting terms. As medical anthropology highlights, knowledge often refers to 'knowing about biomedical facts' and beliefs regarding 'traditional ideas' or 'folk models' (Good 1994; Pelto and Pelto 1997). In my analysis, this distinction becomes somewhat less clear as 'beliefs', as framed by religion, are offered by narrators as fact, and it is biomedical knowledge that is heavily and openly challenged as an independent or reliable source. It is these competing hierarchies and the women's narrative responses to them that are of interest in this chapter.

What people were actually keen to tell me about was living conditions, familial relations, living in the UK and their work, all in connection with –

and not in isolation from – their emotional experience of becoming a mother. This eventually resulted in much richer pictures of the way in which people embody their experience, and tell it in narrative form. As Ginsburg and Rapp write:

> it has been anthropology's longstanding contribution that social reproduction entails much more than literal procreation, as children are born into complex social arrangements through which legacies of property, positions, rights, and values are negotiated over time. In this sense, reproduction, in its biological and social senses, is inextricably bound up with the production of culture. (Ginsburg and Rapp 1995: 2)

From a methodological standpoint, narratives and ethnographic approaches provide a good basis through which to investigate the ways in which gender, ethnicity, class and health intersect. The effects of all of these dimensions are not simply 'additive', but rather it is 'their specific combinations [that] reflect unique historical experience forged by the social realities of life' (Krieger et al. 1993: 99). The nature of this intersectionality is brought into sharp focus by the analysis of the narratives of these individual women. Shurma complained:

> I was just left with a baby, and I can remember that I asked the midwife, 'Excuse me, can you show me how to put a nappy on?' And she said, I remember she said to me, 'Why have a baby if you don't know what to do?' Just like, 'Why have a baby if you don't know what to do?' I felt so bad.

Shurma's case demonstrates how powerfully authoritative and highly moralized knowledge can be used to diminish rather than support new mothers.

Notes

1. Interview with Shurma, 29 September 2003.
2. Interview with Mibi, 28 July 2003.

References

Ahmed, N. 2005. 'Tower Hamlets: Insulation in Isolation', in T. Abbas (ed.), *Muslim Britain: Communities Under Pressure*. London: Zed Books, pp.194–207.
Ahmed-Ghosh, H. 2004. 'Portraits of Believers: Ahmadi Women Performing Faith in the Diaspora', *Journal of International Women's Studies* 6: 73–92.

Eade, J. 1989. *The Politics of Community: The Bangladeshi Community in East London.* Aldershot: Avebury.

———— 1990. 'Bangladeshi Community Organisation and Leadership in Tower Hamlets, East London', in C. Clarke, C. Peach and S. Vertovec (eds), *South Asians Overseas.* Oxford: Oxford University Press, pp.317–30.

Fox, B., and D. Worts. 1999. 'Revisiting the Critique of Medicalized Childbirth: A Contribution to the Sociology of Birth', *Gender and Society* 13: 326–46.

Gardner, K. 2002. *Age, Narrative, and Migration: The Life Course and Life Histories of Bengali Elders in London.* Oxford: Berg.

Gavron, K. 1997. 'Migrants to Citizens: Changing Orientations among Bangladeshis of Tower Hamlets'. Ph.D. diss. London: London School of Economics.

Ginsburg, F., and R. Rapp. 1995. 'Introduction: Conceiving the New World Order', in F. Ginsburg and R. Rapp (eds), *Conceiving the New World Order: The Global Politics of Reproduction.* Berkeley: University of California Press, pp.1–17.

Good, B. 1994. *Medicine, Rationality, and Experience: An Anthropological Perspective.* Cambridge: Cambridge University Press.

Greenhalgh, S. 1995. *Situating Fertility: Anthropology and Demographic Inquiry.* Cambridge: Cambridge University Press.

Holy, L. 1991. *Religion and Custom in a Muslim Society: The Berti of Sudan.* Cambridge: Cambridge University Press.

Inhorn, M. 1994. *Quest for Conception: Gender, Infertility, and Egyptian Medical Traditions.* Philadelphia: University of Pennsylvania Press.

Jolly, M. 1998. 'Colonial and Postcolonial Plots in Histories of Maternities and Modernities', in M. Jolly and K. Ram (eds), *Maternities and Modernities: Colonial and Postcolonial Experiences in Asia and the Pacific.* Cambridge: Cambridge University Press, pp.1–25.

Jordan, B., and R.E. Davis-Floyd. 1993. *Birth in Four Cultures: A Crosscultural Investigation of Childbirth in Yucatan, Holland, Sweden, and the United States.* Prospect Heights, NJ: Waveland Press.

Khanum, S., and U. Sharma. 2003. 'Penetrating Roots and Encountering Barriers: The Politics of Pregnancy for Bangladeshi Women in Britain', unpublished paper presented at the ASA decennial conference 'Anthropology and Science', Manchester University.

Krieger, N., et al. 1993. 'Racism, Sexism, and Social Class: Implications for Studies of Health, Disease, and Well-being', *American Journal of Preventive Medicine* 9(6): S82–S122.

Madhok, S. 2004. 'Heteronomous Women? Hidden Assumptions in the Demography of Women', in M. Unnithan-Kumar (eds), *Reproductive Change, Agency and the State: Cultural Transformations in Childbearing.* Oxford: Berghahn, pp.223–44.

Mahmood, S. 2001. 'Feminist Theory, Embodiment, and the Docile Agent: Some Reflections on the Egyptian Islamic Revival', *Cultural Anthropology* 16: 202–36.

———— 2005. *The Politics of Piety: The Islamic Revival and the Feminist Subject.* Princeton: Princeton University Press.

Metcalf, B. 1999. 'Women and Men in Contemporary Pietist Movement: The Case of the Tablighi Jamaat.', in P. Jeffrey and A. Basu (eds.), *Resisting the Sacred and the*

Secular: Women's Activism and Politicized Religion in South Asia. New Delhi: Kali for Women, pp.107–22.

Pelto, P., and G. Pelto. 1997. 'Studying Knowledge, Culture and Behavior in Applied Medical Anthropology', *Medical Anthropology Quarterly* 11: 147–63.

Pollock, D. 1999. *Telling Bodies, Performing Birth: Everyday Narratives of Childbirth*. New York: Columbia University Press.

Ram, K. 1998. 'Maternity and the Story of Enlightenment in the Colonies: Tamil Coastal Women, South India', in M. Jolly and K. Ram (eds), *Maternities and Modernities: Colonial and Postcolonial Experiences in Asia and the Pacific*. Cambridge: Cambridge University Press, pp.114–43.

CHAPTER 5

Health Inequalities and Perceptions of Place

Migrant Mothers' Accounts of Birth and Loss in North-West India

Maya Unnithan-Kumar

In his focus on the health of North African immigrants in France, anthropologist Didier Fassin (2004) makes the important point that, despite being among the most equitable of health and social protection systems in the world, immigrants in France suffer poor health as a result of invisible processes which produce and sustain health inequalities. It is not so much that there are well resourced health systems or legal and social policies ensuring universal health coverage that determine immigrant well-being, he argues, but equally whether migrants perceive they have a legitimate claim to them, which is a key factor in understanding their continued health vulnerabilities. Drawing on the idea of migrant perceptions as influencing health-seeking behaviour and outcomes, in this chapter I examine a very different context of migration: the internal movement of poor labour migrants in Rajasthan, north-west India. My aim is to show how migrant perceptions of place in a social, embodied and 'therapeutic' sense (cf. Gesler 1992) – play an important role in the way women address healthcare inequalities and experience motherhood.

The chapter is especially concerned with understanding the subjective experiences of poor migrant women, their vulnerabilities and self-perceptions, as well as their productive, reproductive and nurturing capabilities and agency. It examines the consequences of internal migration for women's reproductive experiences and for their children's health, and is based on fieldwork in two urban slums in Jaipur city, the capital of Rajasthan.[1] It draws on the collaborative quantitative work I have done with Kirsty McNay and Adriana Castaldo, in which we focus on the migration experiences of approximately 100 women from their birth (rather than from their last move, as is common in migration literature), their experiences of giving birth and the loss of their children (Unnithan et al. 2008). It also draws on an ethnographic study completed in 2002 on poor rural women's reproductive health choices in Jaipur, where the increased potential for access to health services as a result of migration was both realized as well as rejected, indicative of women's reproductive agency as well as their subjection to new types of biomedical control (Unnithan-Kumar 2004).

A key though tentative argument of the chapter is that migrant health inequalities are produced through the interaction of two kinds of perception: on the one hand, those of migrants themselves about places as therapeutic, 'clean', safe, one's own, embodying self and constituted through webs of caring social relationships; on the other hand, those of health providers and the state which reflect more general public perceptions of migrants as poor, illiterate, ignorant, unimportant, unworthy of healthcare provision, and as constitutive of the wider processes of exclusion and discrimination which the poor in general face. As Fassin powerfully argues in the case of North African immigrants, health inequalities are actively produced in the space *between* the perception that immigrants have of their illegitimate claims on state health services and those of health providers keen to stress the migrants' illegitimate status. These may be directly manifest in terms of restricted access to healthcare, or indirectly produced through inequalities in working, housing and living conditions, all of which have an effect on health but which the healthcare system itself is unable to recognize or remedy.

Through its focus on the bodily experiences of childbearing, loss and anxieties of infertility, the chapter provides a critical understanding of migration as an embodied and gendered process. In addition, it considers the role of place or 'emplacement' – the process through which places are actively sensed and invested with meaning (Feld and Basso 1996) – to be central to decisions regarding the choice of birthplace and evaluation of healthcare interventions. It suggests that for migrant women birth is experienced as occurring across a range of socially supportive contexts called 'home' (the marital home in the slum, the natal and affinal homes in the village), highlighting how motherhood is constructed in relation to place. An examination of migrant perceptions of place reveals their evaluation of the best places to give birth in, the best places to nurture and be good mothers and their knowledge of places as therapeutic (including where efficacious remedies for infertility and child loss are dispensed).

It is important to note that in the context of the poverty-related migration in Rajasthan, health was not a major reason to undertake migration. Health and physical well-being were in fact regarded as a consequence of economic well-being (cf. Sinha 2005). Migration was undertaken, or indeed forced upon, individuals and families as a means to gain employment, income and related economic well-being and security. In the words of one respondent, migration is about physical labour (*mazdoori*) and lack of choice, or compulsion (*majboori*). The lack of an explicit connection to health in migrant narratives is also reflected in the invisibility of migrant health in health policy and planning.

The first section of the chapter describes the specificities of internal migration in India – its scale, its connection with poverty and the gendered nature of such movement. It describes how movement among poor communities is experienced as continuous, regular as well as circular (back and forth between rural and urban spaces). Movement among the urban and rural poor is routinized with different implications for women and men. That women and men experience migration differently is rooted in wider gender patterns of mobility in rural North India where a woman moves to her husband's home at the time of marriage. This pattern is further enhanced for migrant women who move several times including at the time of their marriage. As we see in the stories recounted below, migrant women maintain an ambivalence with regard to the benefits of such movement for the health and well-being of their families. The focus on perceptions of place, and the embodied experiences of migrant women in this chapter, contribute to the limited knowledge of migrant maternal and infant well-being in India, including their recourse to state healthcare services.

The Context of Internal Migration

The movement of poor labour migrants within India occurs on a large scale.[2] It is estimated that there are approximately 100 million unskilled labour migrants (GoI 2001; Chatterjee 2006) on the move in the country, with cities over 1 million having nearly a third of their population made up of migrants (Stephenson et al. 2003). The Indian state of Rajasthan, on which this study is based, itself has 4 million unskilled labour migrants out of a population of approximately 60 million people (GoI 2011). A fifth of its urban population lives below the poverty line and in slums (UHRC 2006).

Statistics on internal migration are important in understanding the scale at which India's poor are on the move, but information regarding the effects of this movement are still emerging. Understanding how migration is experienced as a gendered phenomenon has evolved considerably over the last decade, and particularly so in the context of transnational migration (e.g., Chant 1992; Mills 1997; Parrenas 2001; Jolly et al. 2003; Christou and King

2011). More recent trends within anthropology have also focused on gendered experiences within transnational migration (e.g. Bledsoe 2004; Bledsoe and Sow 2011; Browner and Sargent 2011), although within anthropology and sociology, as Bledsoe (2004) suggests, the area of reproduction has drawn little attention. There is less of an explicit focus on migration between countries of the global South (Goldade 2011), and on rural to urban, internal migration within those countries. In South Asia, with the exception of a few studies (notably Breman 1985), anthropological and sociological interest in rural–urban migration suffered neglect after the 1960s and 1970s, when urbanization and social mobility were first addressed (e.g., Beteille 1965; Srinivas 1966; Vatuk 1972; Gardner and Osella 2004). Since then, apart from the work of demographers, geographers and urban planners, there has been 'silence' on internal migration, despite its increasing centrality in people's lives (Gardner and Osella 2004; Deshingkar 2006). The gendered aspects of labour migration, particularly in terms of women and men's bodily and affective experiences of displacement, have consequentially also been neglected.[3]

Migration for labourers and other unskilled workers in Rajasthan, as elsewhere in India, is routinized in the sense that, for most of the rural poor, movement is a part of their life course. Most rural families would expect their men and women to undertake migration at some point in their early to mid life, whether at marriage for women or by young adult men and couples in search of employment. Rural to urban migration in this context is rarely a one-off phenomenon, and very often involves most of the poor population in some phase of movement in a wider trajectory of mobility. Rajasthani labour migrants, including those who are not categorized as seasonal migrants, often engage in circular or cyclical patterns of migration (GoI 2001; Gidwani and Sivaramakrishnan 2004; Chatterjee 2006; Deshingkar 2006; Deshingkar et al. 2008; Deshingkar and Akter 2009). As Vimlesh explains to me:

I grew up in Delhi as my father had gone there for construction work (*mazdoori*) from our village in Tonk district, Rajasthan. But I got married in the natal village itself when I was 12 years [old] – although I actually went to my affinal place (*sasural*) after a year. Their village was just two to three kilometres away. Both Goga [her husband] and I spent five years there engaged in farming-related work (*kheti-bari*), but then [we] went to my parents in Delhi to work with them … [T]his was when I gave birth to my twins. When work dried up after three years or so, we went back to his village in Tonk for a year or two, and then decided to try for work in Jaipur. We finally came to KN *basti* [a slum in Jaipur] in 1997 for stone quarrying work; the girls were then six years old. Sometimes people leave their older children in the village itself, only bringing their very small ones with them … Where you give birth and where you leave your children, it all depends on the people who look after them (*sambhalne vale*).[4]

A key social consequence of this continuous movement is that the rural and the urban become linked through migration rather than being experienced as separate settings dividing out migrant identities and social relationships. The spatial and social connections, as I suggest below, are particularly embodied in the birth and child-rearing experiences of poor migrant women. In terms of conceptualizing migrant identities and senses of self, Gidwani and Sivaramakrishnan's (2004) concept of rural cosmopolitanism, developed in the context of internal labour migration, is particularly useful in overcoming binary ways of thinking about the rural and the urban. According to Gidwani and Sivaramakrishnan, rural cosmopolitanism characterizes a condition where, as a rural–urban migrant, one can be global, cosmopolitan and modern at the same time as being embedded in the local. One can experience the global in the local context, and as they suggest, 'participate in multiple cultural worlds with a sense of belonging and adeptness in each' (ibid.: 343). The concept of rural cosmopolitanism is especially helpful, I find, in thinking about the non-linear constitution of migrant experiences. It emerged in the context of fieldwork, in the ways in which life in the *basti* was permeated with a sense of 'rural-ness', as clearly reflected in the domain of childbirth, birth-related healing and child nurture documented in the following lines.

Internal migration within Rajasthan occurs within a social and economic context characterized by a dominantly poor agrarian economy, strict social rules that define women's marital and reproductive roles and relationships, great social pressure for producing children, and a high infant and maternal mortality rate. In gender terms, women experience migration differently from men, and almost universally at the time of their marriage. Migrant women in Rajasthan often move greater distances at marriage or shortly thereafter compared to non-migrant women. The economic roles of migrant women change, and so does their relationship with members of their immediate and extended families. The relationship with women outside those defined by kinship expands, and, combined with a change in the access to health services, alters the social and medical setting in which migrant women experience childbirth and motherhood.

The movement of women from rural contexts to urban slums (*basti*) has significant implications for the quality of life their children will experience and how motherhood itself comes to be defined. The shift to women's work as domestic servants outside the household and the poor environmental conditions of the *basti* to which they move, are perhaps the two most important migration-related factors to impact on the health and survival of their infants and children. Overall, there seems to be a greater tendency towards increased child mortality and poorer use of preventive health services among more recently migrated women than longer term residents.[5] These findings complement the work of Brockerhoff (1994) and Stephenson et al. (2003), which suggest that the rate of child mortality experienced by rural migrants lies between that of rural and urban non-migrants. Fieldwork accounts from Rajasthan below suggest reasons why this may be the case.

Childbirth and Loss: Understanding 'Safe' Places for Birth in the Life-worlds of Migrant Mothers

Kanchan and Shajida, were two mothers from amongst a group of approximately 100 women in the slum of KN *basti*, whose lives we documented as part of a larger study of urban migrants. Shajida belonged to the Sayyid Muslim community, and Kanchan was Harijan, a low-caste Hindu. Shajida was unemployed and among the poorest of the 100 women interviewed.

MU: When did you come to KN *basti*?
Kanchan: I was born in Soda village near Diggi about three hours away from Jaipur by bus. I got married when I was 14 years [old] and left my village to join my husband in Amirpur village. We stayed there for seven years before we came to Jaipur in search of employment. We first rented a room in the GG *basti* in the north-west part of the city, where my grandparents had migrated to. After two or three years we moved to KN *basti* where we were able to have our own place for 2,200 rupees.

MU: Where did you give birth to your children and who helped you?
Kanchan: I had five children before I came to Jaipur, and one child, a son, now 10 years old, was born here. I had the operation [i.e., sterilization] about eight years back. Only three of my children are still alive. After my oldest boy was born [now aged 18 years], two boys and a girl after him died: they became sick, 'dried up' and died. All my births took place at home. The first four were in Amirpur, where a local midwife helped deliver them. For the fourth child, we called a nurse [an employee of the local clinic] to assist because the previous two had died when attended by the midwife. But the nurse too could not do anything to save the child. Then for the fifth child I went back to my parent's village. Here we again called a nurse. This time the child, my daughter, survived.[6]

Shajida: I was first married at nineteen years to a man who lived in Madhopur [a small town approximately three-and-a-half hours' drive from Jaipur]. Madhopur is about two hours away from the village where I was born. I stayed for seven years with my first husband and had four sons by him there. Then he left me and I had a divorce and returned to the village, leaving the children with him. Then after a year, my family married me off to my father's grandmother's son's son. This was when I came to KN *basti*. I had two daughters by my second husband here. I had my operation [female sterilisation] five years ago after my youngest girl Gulabsha was born. My sons were born in the government hospital in Madhopur, but my daughters have been born here in the *basti* itself: at the childcare centre (*anganwadi*). My second son died, he 'dried up' when he was four months old, back in Madhopur.[7]

As Kanchan's account above emphasizes, most of her children were born at 'home' – in her affinal and natal home – and not in the basti. In general, there was a stated preference for childbirth in the natal village because of the birth-related expertise associated with kinswomen and local midwives, rather than biomedical personnel. Local 'nurses' and 'doctors' (often gaining biomedical legitimacy through their degree of association with clinics and hospitals rather than on the basis of technical qualifications) are often called upon for assistance, such as in augmenting the labour process (by administering oxytocin injections) or to help with emergencies beyond the control of the family and other local midwives. Even where it is clear that the emergency services of a 'nurse' are regarded as necessary, it may often not be considered as wholly or primarily effective.

Kanchan's and Shajida's accounts also reveal wider patterns of the young age at which migration begins, its central association with marriage and the trauma that experiences of giving birth and migration entail. Their experiences were among those of three categories of migrant women interviewed during fieldwork: those who had come to KN *basti* from a rural context at different stages in their lives (either before, at or after marriage, such as Shajida); those who had arrived elsewhere in the city first, and then come to settle in the *basti* (such as Kanchan); and those who had been long associated with city life and were born or grew up in the *basti*, classified as non-migrant women. The women were all between 30 and 35 years of age in 2004, an age by which, according to the prevalent social norms, most women are approaching the end of their childbearing years (and as we were to find out subsequently, a time by which most women had also experienced child mortality).

KN *basti*, believed to have been populated since the 1950s, was among the smaller slums in Jaipur, with 300 households compared to the 4,000 households in Darana *basti*, one of the larger slums on the outskirts of the city. Residents of KN were in the process of undergoing forcible resettlement at the time of fieldwork in 2004, and had been part of a larger group of 1,500 households until a few years back – resettlement signifying their marginal political status within the city (see, e.g., Tarlo 2000). Muslims and Harijans constituted the main social groups in the *basti*.

What rural migrant women find different about living in the *basti* is the availability of a range of medical care in the city, from public hospitals and health centres to private clinics and medical institutions. However, in terms of women's preferences for giving birth, most first-order births continue to take place in the natal village with little recourse to biomedical expertise unless in emergency situations, with subsequent births more likely to be in the slum (especially for longer-term residents) or even in private hospitals, and much less frequently in government run hospitals, which are supposedly free of cost (but in reality involve a number of hidden costs, discussed below).[8] (The introduction of the recent scheme of cash incentives by the government as a means to promote institutional birth in the cities as part of its National Health Mission is set to change this pattern of seeking birth in the village; fieldwork observations, 2010.)

Two points are important to note here: firstly, the preference for first-order births to take place at home with subsequent births taking place in an institutional setting is a pattern which stands in inverse relation to the degree of risk associated with childbirth as conceptualized by biomedicine – that is, first-order births are considered to be times of greatest risk for mother and child, and where the provision of institutionally based emergency care can be essential. Secondly, it is worth noting here that for *basti* residents, as for women in the villages, clinics and hospitals were regarded as relevant only when a birth was construed as requiring emergency biomedical attention when it 'goes wrong', or when a birth is predicted to be difficult by a local midwife, and not in routine circumstances. These perceptions are manifest in the limited recourse to state antenatal services (IIPS 2005, NFHS-3). Biomedical attention in most of rural Rajasthan was more often sought when births 'went wrong'. It was only under emergency conditions when women experienced problems during their pregnancies (with bleeding, or when breech positions were revealed through a scan, for instance) or at birth (in cases of overly delayed labour, delayed presentation of the placenta) that the antenatal or delivery services were sought. In most cases the choice of institution was based on previous experience, the relationship with a particular doctor and through the contacts of a relative or friend (Unnithan-Kumar 2001).

The *basti* women who gave birth in hospitals were usually those who had relatives working there as sweepers or cleaners, and usually these were the longer-term residents of the *basti*. Public hospitals were places identified with 'problems', such as the hidden cost of services, and with discrimination (Ram 1998; Van Hollen 2002). Although professional services are free, ward and other cleaning staff charge for their services in arbitrary ways, often exploiting the vulnerability of their patients. Alongside this, public hospitals are feared because of the anxiety of being mistreated and sterilized during birth. As one woman put it, these are places where doctors carry out 'two kinds of work' (*ek hi bihoshi mein do kaam*) during one bout of unconsciousness; that is, there is the fear that a woman may give birth and then be sterilized while under anaesthetic. Hospitals were conceptualized as 'good places for sterilization and not birth'. The decision to give birth at home is thus a decision to remain free from caste and class-based discrimination and retain control over one's own body, a desire placed above the care which could be provided by a professionally trained birth attendant, or in biomedical terms what is regarded as a 'safe' childbirth.[9]

The statistics on birth as well as the accounts of women like Kanchan and Shajida are particularly striking for the extent of mortality and child loss that they reveal. Overall, there seemed to be a greater tendency for more recently migrated women to experience increased child mortality and make poorer use of preventive health services than longer term residents. The high rate of child mortality among poor families in rural and urban areas in Rajasthan is widely known. According to a family health survey conducted in Rajasthan in the late 1990s, one in every twelve children in Rajasthan dies in the first year of life (neonatal mortality), and one in every nine children born dies before they reach their fifth birthday (child mortality, IIPS 2001: 119). Most infant deaths take place just after birth and are related to the health status of the mother and the conditions of the birth, such as the presence of a skilled or trained attendant.[10]

While to a certain extent migrant women expected infant death and miscarriages to occur and took this in their stride, in much the same way that the poor Brazilian women described by Scheper-Hughes (1997) do, these were equally occasions for the expression of anxiety and grief. Following the death of their young children, no biomedical explanations were sought, and neither midwives nor medical personnel were consulted because it was believed they had little to offer; this was simply something that was 'up to God' (*bhagwan ki den*). It was faith healers to whom women turned for explanations and comfort following the death of their children. As a resident of Darana *basti* explained:

> in Darana there is lot of faith healing (*bhopa bhav*). In my narrow street (*gali*), there is Sita who gets possessed by a female spirit (Mata). Then there is Khataram, who lives just behind Sita. He gets possessed (*bhav aana*) by Syyed Baba [a Muslim spirit]. *Bhav* (state of possession) comes to those who are pure – that means they do not eat meat or drink alcohol … I only identified the spirit (*devta*) last year when I went to see a Muslim healer who has settled in the village nearby. He explained that the trouble I have of not being able to conceive another child for over nine years was because

I had not paid attention to the demands of this spirit. The trouble in the family – my husband's elder brother (*jeth*) had three operations, and then my husband's younger brother could not beget children, are all related to this.[11]

Faith healers also deflected the 'blame' associated with infertility away from women such as Vimlesh who were regarded as barren (*banjhdi*), unable to fulfil the cultural expectations of childbearing. The term applied equally to women who miscarried, or were otherwise unable to carry children to term. These women in particular experience the village and slum as interconnected therapeutic and social places, and bring the rural into the urban (inverting what Gidwani and Sivaramakrishnan call 'rural cosmopolitanism'). Living in the *basti* compared to the village had increased the range and access to faith healers for women and men.

In addition to the increase in recourse to faith healers enabled through migration, a number of women talked about the reproductive benefits of migration in terms of the economic gains they experienced from employment. This was especially the case when payment for their services was made in kind rather than cash, enabling them to provide food for their children. The *basti* was seen as better than the village because it enabled mothers to feed their children regularly on cooked food procured from the houses where they worked as domestic servants. Women's ability to be effective mothers was linked to the ways in which their migration had changed their ability to nurture, and their relationship to paid work, food and living conditions.

'Good Mothering Happens in Healthy Places': Place and Nurture in Migrant Accounts

During discussions, Kanchan and Shajida were clear about the respective benefits and drawbacks of living in the *bastis* of Jaipur.

> Kanchen: The *basti* is a much better place than the village. Here there is employment and I can feed the children. My husband works as a daily wage labourer and I work as a sweeper in about thirty houses. My oldest son works in a factory from 8 AM till 8 PM and brings back 1,800 rupees per month. I bring back some money, but also get a lot of cooked food. I am back by lunch time and love watching TV after that. The children are not so ill either. The doctors are good. I first go to Doctor Tank and then to Doctor Shekhawat if I need to.[12]

Shajida: The *basti* is worse than the village, it is much dirtier here. Also, you may have the doctors but you can't afford the medicines. So what is the use? Gulabsha is very ill all the time. Her whole body is swollen as you see, especially her stomach. The doctor says her liver is big. I have taken her to JK Hospital [Jay Kaylon, a mother and child government hospital] and to Doctor Shekhawat [a private doctor near the slum], but to no avail. I can't afford to keep giving her medicines. I don't work and my husband runs a glass-crushing mill – I don't know how much he earns. His sons from his previous marriage live with us. The older boy sorts rubbish and brings in 50 to 60 rupees per day. The younger boy repairs bicycles and gets 20 rupees per day.[13]

The ambivalent position of migrant women with regard to their migration was based on the positive and negative aspects they perceived regarding the *basti*. These self-perceptions also clearly showed that the connections between migration and health were not straightforward; indeed, they were more complex than we had imagined at the start of the study. Kanchan's ability to work as a domestic help, and thereby have access to cooked food, enables her to feel more empowered compared to her counterparts in the village. But Shajida, being a Muslim, is unable to undertake employment outside the house. Women like Shajida, who did not have independent earnings or access to cooked food, were also the ones who felt their children were worse off in the *basti* as compared to the village, where women had fewer opportunities to work and earn food. The migrant women who experienced child loss had especially negative views about their ability to nurture and care for their children, views connected to an overwhelming sense of their failure to be 'good mothers'. Women like Shajida, who were among the poorer Muslim residents and also the more recent migrants, acutely sensed their lack of control over where they lived and worked, and over their children's health.

From the perspective of the health of migrants' children, the data collected during fieldwork show a complex combination of factors, which included the mother's work and her independent income in cash and kind, the father and his relatives' support for the mother, the willingness and financial ability of the parents to access emergency care, their awareness of health risks and use of local aetiologies, the availability of perceived good curative services for the children, and a safe social and physical environment, including clean drinking water, a proper drainage system and rodent- and pest-free conditions of living.

A number of migrants viewed the *basti* as a place where their children could have access to a greater amount and range of food. Yet most children of the women in our qualitative survey (which charted the daily and weekly intake of foods) drank half a cup of tea in the mornings (made from milk used for tea for the whole family), and either had 'toast' (rusk) or *roti* (flatbread).

A further main meal of a *roti* with a 'small portion' (*aadha katori*) of lentils or spicy vegetables was usually all that they consumed in the day. Very few children drank milk or consumed curd, eggs or fresh fruit. Goat meat or chicken were occasionally eaten, but the portions were small as the dish was shared amongst a number of family members. From our limited survey, it was clear that children did not have a nutritious diet by biomedical standards (in the sense of calorie and protein intake), even though access to food on a daily basis was seen as an advantage of living in the *basti*.[14]

The positive aspect of the *basti* in relation to the feeding of children was a connection particularly made by the women who worked as domestic helpers and whose earnings were either in cash or in kind (cooked food, such as rice and curry; clothes). Women who did not have independent earnings and access to cooked food were also women who felt their children were worse off in the *basti* as compared to the village. This finding supports the findings of the national survey, which states that the children of mothers who are self employed are less likely to have moderate or severe levels of anaemia (IIPS 2001: xxx). There were also perceived to be negative effects of women's employment on infant health. In terms of breastfeeding, there was a tendency for women who were employed to give this up much earlier and switch to other kinds of milk (goat, cow, tinned) compared to women who did not work. This was further reinforced by the fact that women who worked shifted much of the childcare and household chores onto their older children, especially their older daughters.

The access to food gained by the move to the *basti* was offset in local perception by the view of the *basti* as a dirty, rodent- and mosquito-infested environment. The *basti* also had more hazardous chemical waste sites. The lack of proper sewerage and toilet facilities meant that there was a high incidence of diarrhoea. Nearly 77 of the 100 households in our survey did not have running water or a toilet facility, and used water from the public piped water tap. The nearby open drain (*nallah*) and open field at the back of the *basti* were used for defecation. Younger children defecated near the doorstep, and this was then thrown into the open drain, while older children and adults relieved themselves in front of the *basti* on the main road. Most households had an open sewer and sewage collected in a hole dug in front of the house. I was told that this was emptied into the open drain when it got full.

In terms of the prevalence of children's illnesses in the *basti*, 43 of our household questionnaires indicated that the most common self-reported cases of illness in the four weeks prior to the survey were to do with pneumonia, diarrhoea, fever, cough, colds and vomiting. In the second order of occurrences were tuberculosis, skin rashes, itches, typhoid, shortness of breath, malaria and chickenpox. Single cases of jaundice, liver condition, worms, gas, body pain and broken limbs due to accident were also reported. Diarrhoea, respiratory and skin infections were the main 'everyday' illness conditions, which were also linked to child mortality. Diarrhoea (*dusth* or *tutti lagna*) was, however, not regarded as an illness, and seen instead to be a result simply of what one ate or drank (*khana-peena*). It was also not regarded as something for which medicines were sought or a doctor consulted. The insignificance attributed to diarrhoea and related underreporting is very likely to contribute significantly to child morbidity and death in the *basti*. The effects of dehydration or *sookhna*, a common reason given by parents for the unexplained death of their infants, were not linked to diarrhoea in local perception. The inability to distinguish between diarrhoea and dysentery, for example, is a common cause of infant death elsewhere in South Asia (Nichter and Nichter 1996).

Fevers on the other hand were regarded by *basti* residents as signalling serious illness, and were treated with greater concern. I was told by the mothers whom I met that a fever was a serious matter, and that doctors have to be consulted when a child had a fever. Both migrant and longer term residents sought out private doctors rather than public ones to treat their children's fevers, as these doctors tended to be near the slum. Curative services for children were keenly sought by migrants and non-migrants alike, and were mainly from private doctors who were established in the locality of the *basti*, such as the doctors Tank and Shekhawat mentioned above, and in nearly all the accounts of *basti* residents. Migrants sought a greater range of private services, often going back to the natal and affinal village and previous places of residence to access local healers. Long-term residents were more likely to make use of hospital services in the city, which was a function of their greater social capital in the form of relatives and friends.

Access to medical services was seen as better in the *basti* compared to rural areas, but the question of cost and finances to cover especially chronic illness made them inaccessible to a number of residents, often recent migrants. A number of longer-term residents also had a low uptake of services because they were poor. This observation points to the levelling factor of socio-economic variables on the affects of migration.[15]

While it is easy in such cases to blame child deaths on parental ignorance or neglect, it is often the case such as with diarrhoea that health workers in these contexts are themselves ill-trained to distinguish it from the more dangerous condition of dysentery (Finnerman 1995) as signalled by blood in the stool – a point also absent in the report by IIPS (2001: 146). More generally, there was a dearth of public sector health providers within the *basti*, despite the fact that the state had set up several schemes to provide free medical care and services to the urban poor – including the medicare relief card system in 1999, free childbirth facilities through the Janani Suraksha Yojana in 2005, free provision of generic medicines in 2011, as well as more general schemes which address housing, sanitation, employment and food security needs

(UHRC 2006). Government services for maternal and child health in KN *basti* were administered through the child crèche (*anganwadi*) centre where Shajida was a frequent visitor. Here again, despite the underlying rationale that such centres should provide integrated maternal and child health services, it merely functioned as an outpost for the distribution of a limited, daily amount of cooked food for children under six years of age.

Conclusion

Migration has specific implications for women in terms of how they experience birth and how their changed work and domestic roles and relationships impact on the survival chances of their children, as well as their own sense of self and agency. Migrant women's accounts provide an insight into the systemic and institutional structures and processes through which they are rendered vulnerable, and which they in turn negotiate, especially for the well-being of their children and in accordance with their ideas of appropriate motherhood. Both patriarchal expectations and gender inequality are manifest in the obligation of poor migrant women in Rajasthan to participate in frequent cycles of movement, often initiated at marriage, to work, to sustain the household economy and to bear and nurture children at appropriate times, places and in appropriate ways.

Concerns for maternal and infant health per se remain submerged within a wider quest for economic betterment in migrant women's own accounts of their lives: employment generates a context 'where the food and drink is good' (*khaana-peena accha hota hai*), and thereby good health is achieved. Good health, especially for pregnant mothers and infants, rather 'sits in places' (Basso 1996) where relations of good care exist (*sambhalne vale*), and where one can afford the cost of medicines. Implicit in such understandings is a total absence of any right to make claims on the state, while present is the idea that health is a matter of individual and familial concern, a factor dependent on social capital and a 'good' acquired through economic wealth procured through movement.

Social networks primarily determined by kin ties in the widest sense (in a context of classificatory kinship), so significant for the survival of the poor in India, are also critical for poor migrants. Within urban healthcare contexts, these connections tend to work in favour of longer-term residents in the *basti*. For more recent migrants, being closer to a range of maternal health facilities does not in itself ensure a successful birth or the survival of one's children, with most women returning to give birth in their village 'home'. On the other hand, recent migrants, like other residents of the *basti*, have an advantage over their rural counterparts when it comes to the termination of their fertility and childbearing. It is the access to sterilization services and emergency care which sets the *basti* apart from the village. While migrant women make greater use of contraceptive services than rural women, they are also more able to resist the state's control of their fertility due to their movement between 'homes'. It is in their exploitation of this liminal position (following Van Gennep 1965) that women such as Kanchan and Vimlesh experience a degree of autonomy and power. The routine movement between village and *basti* also enables them to maintain a cosmopolitan identity in the rural context, and equally be associated with village-based practices (such as using faith healers) in the urban *basti*.

Migrant self-perceptions are critical to understanding what may appear to be inconsistent health-seeking patterns in relation to childbirth, child loss and contraception, at times following biomedical expertise, at other times ignoring it, irrespective of the severity of illness. It is only through a close analysis of the stories of migrant mothers that we can more clearly understand when their experiences and agency regarding giving birth and nurturing are disempowering or empowering, and in what way the resulting measures undertaken are strategic, pragmatic, tactical or a mixture of all three. While national figures on migrants and studies based on them are a useful guide to understanding the scale of mortality and poverty-related trends which define the region of Rajasthan, they are often insufficient in explaining the reasons underlying the statistics (Bose 2006), or the direction of causality.

Such national studies of family health are also unable to convey a sense of scale regarding morbidity (illnesses that have the potential of resulting in death) and how it is perceived, experienced and negotiated by migrants. The ethnographic observations offered in this chapter, by contrast have placed migrant women's maternal and child-health concerns and actions in their lived, everyday worlds, to focus on three aspects in particular: their recourse to faith healers and kin-defined relations of care; in relation to their palpable cynicism of state healthcare services; and with regard to their therapeutic assessments of place, both rural and urban. Unlike the existing documentation of internal migrants in Rajasthan, accounts presented in this chapter capture the inter-subjective processes through which health inequalities, as experienced by migrant families, are produced and sustained. While 'place' is a site whose social and moral value is keenly sensed and constituted through migration, it is also a context in which health inequalities are co-produced by migrants who seek or reject healthcare services and those who provide the services. As social and politically constructed sites, places actively determine the degree to which migrants can fully participate in social reproduction and women can self-identify as good mothers.

Notes

1. The fieldwork on which this chapter is based was carried out between 2002 and 2004 in two *basti* or slum areas in Jaipur city: KN *basti* and Darana *basti*. In Darana *basti*, information was collected in 2002 from approximately thirty women of lower to middle caste status on their changed access to healthcare as a result of their migration to the city. Fieldwork in KN *basti* was carried out in 2004, with a specific focus on understanding the implications of women's migration on their children's health. In this case a more detailed history was conducted on women's migratory histories from birth, followed by the birth experience for each of their children (including information on antenatal care, place of birth, birth attendant, birth outcomes, breastfeeding patterns, illness, health provider sought, immunization) and their health status four weeks prior to the survey. The research in KN *basti* was based at a school run by a popular and established voluntary organization in the slum, and all women were initially approached as parents of children in the school. Neighbours also became interested in the project, several of whom became willing respondents. In total, more than 100 women, mainly from lower Hindu castes and Muslim families (representing the dominant population in the slum), participated in a wider survey, with approximately fifty women providing more detailed information in Hindi on their birthing experiences and health-seeking practices. The field research was jointly conducted by the author and two research assistants, all experienced in using Hindi and each with independent contacts in the school and in the slum. Information relating to the school children was fed back to the school in terms of some useful preliminary observations on children's household circumstances, history of childhood illness and access to nutrition.

2. The migration of human populations has existed throughout human history, but its scale and magnitude, especially in the context of the growth of urban cities, has increased phenomenally in the present century. It is estimated that over half the human population of 3.3 billion, most of whom are poor, now live in such urban contexts (UNFPA 2007).

3. There are, however, some exceptions, e.g., Shah (2006).

4. Remarks by Vimlesh, 41 years old, Raigar caste, resident of Darana, autumn 2004.

5. While short birth intervals are connected to higher child loss, it is not clear whether they act as cause or effect. In fact, as Dasgupta (1997) shows for rural Punjab, and the material in this chapter also suggests, short birth intervals are caused by child loss rather than being a reason for their occurrence. As Dasgupta points out, this is because 'those who have lost children are pushed into more stressful reproductive cycles of shorter birth intervals and higher fertility' (Dasgupta 1997: 201).

6. Remarks by Kanchan, approximately 30 years, Harijan caste, resident of KN *basti* (autumn 2004).

7. Remarks by Shajida, approximately 30 to 35 years old, Muslim resident of KN *basti* (autumn 2004).

8. This pattern is likely to have changed following the more recent introduction of a cash incentive scheme to promote institutional births, especially among rural women, under the National Rural Health Mission promoted in 2009.
9. While such ideas of bodily control bring poor migrant women closer in their reproductive practices to those of Euro-American middle-class families who are increasingly opting for home births, they stand in stark contrast to the child-birth practices of middle-class Indian women, where hospital births and even Caesarean births are highly sought after (e.g., Donner 2004).
10. Post-neonatal deaths occur from the first to twelfth month of life, and child mortality as defined in the NFHS occurs between 1 and 5 years (IIPS 2001: 119).
11. Remarks by Vimlesh, low-caste resident of Darana basti. As I discuss elsewhere (Unnithan-Kumar 2002, 2010), whereas both men and women resort to healers, women consult healers for maternal and child-health matters while men consult healers for employment, land and money matters.
12. Remarks by Kanchan during a discussion in KN *basti*, summer 2004.
13. Remarks by Shajida, a Muslim resident of KN *basti* and a recent migrant, summer 2004.
14. The data presented in IIPS (2001) points to high levels of maternal and child-hood anaemia and its close relation to maternal and infant mortality. See Bose (2006) for the reliability of NFHS-3 findings on anaemia.
15. A similar observation has been made by Stephenson et al. (2003) in their study of the relationship between child mortality in under-twos and migration using 1991/92 data for a group of approximately 90,000 women aged 13 to 49 in all states in India. They suggest that, when controlling for socio-economic factors and health utilization variables, the effects of rural to urban migration on the survival rate of children disappear, meaning that migration makes no difference. This observation is further supported in the IIPS report, which states that rates of infant and child mortality in poorer households are twice as high as those of households with higher economic standards (IIPS 2001: 122). In general, child mortality is found to be inversely related to socio-economic status (e.g., Dasgupta 1997).

References

Beteille, A. 1965. *Caste, Class and Power: Changing Patterns of Stratification in a Tanjore Village*. Berkeley: University of California Press.

Bledsoe, C. 2004. 'Reproduction at the Margins: Migration and Legitimacy in the New Europe', *Demographic Research*, Special collection 3, article 4: 87–116.

Bledsoe, C., and P. Sow. 2011. 'Family Reunification Ideals and the Practice of Transnational Reproductive Life among Africans in Europe', in C.H. Browner and C.F. Sargent (eds), *Reproduction, Globalisation and the State: New Theoretical and Ethnographic Perspectives*. Durham, NC: Duke University Press, pp.175–92.

Bose, A. 2006. 'Falling Fertility and Rising Anaemia', *Economic and Political Weekly of India* XLI(37): 3923–26.

Breman, J. 1985. *Of Peasants, Migrants and Paupers: Rural Labour and Capitalist Production in West India*. Delhi: Oxford University Press.

Brockerhoff, M. 1994. 'The Impact of Rural–Urban Migration on Child Survival', *Health Transition Review* 4(2): 127–49.

Browner, C., and C. Sargeant (eds). 2011. *Reproduction, Globalisation and the State: New Theoretical and Ethnographic Perspectives*. Durham, NC: Duke University Press.

Chant, S. (ed.). 1992. *Gender and Migration in Developing Countries*. London: Belhaven.

Chatterjee, C. 2006. *Identities in Motion: Migration and Health in India*. Mumbai: Cehat Publications.

Christou, A., and R. King. 2011. 'Gendering Counter Diasporic Migration: Second Generation Greek American and Greek Germans Narrate Their Home-coming to Greece', *Journal of Mediterranean Studies* 20(2): 1–32.

Dasgupta, M. 1997. 'Socio Economic Status and Clustering of Child Deaths in Rural Punjab', *Population Studies* 51(2): 191–202.

Deshingkar, P. 2006. 'Internal Migration, Poverty and Development in Asia: Including the Excluded', *Institute of Development Studies Bulletin* 37(3): 88–100.

Deshingkar, P. and S. Akter. 2009. 'Migration and Human Development in India', Human Development Report, Research Paper 13. Geneva: United Nations Development Programme.

Deshingkar, P., P. Sharma, S. Kumar, S. Akter and J. Farrington. 2008. 'Circular Migration in Madhya Pradesh: Changing Patterns and Social Protection Needs', *European Journal of Development Research* 20(4): 612–18.

Donner, H. 2004. 'Labour, Privatisation and Class: Middle Class Women's Experience of Changing Hospital Birth in Calcutta', in M. Unnithan-Kumar (ed.), *Reproductive Agency, Medicine and the State: Cultural Transformations in Childbearing*. Oxford: Berghahn, pp.113–37.

Fassin, D. 2004. 'Social Illegitimacy as a Foundation of Health Inequality: How the Political Treatment of Immigrants Illuminates a French Paradox' in A. Castro and M. Singer (eds), *Unhealthy Health Policy: A Critical Anthropological Examination*. Lanham, MD: Altamira Press, pp.203–15.

Feld, S., and K. Basso (eds). 1996. *Senses of Place*. Santa Fe, NM: School of American Research Press.

Finnerman, R. 1995. 'Parental Competence' and Selective Neglect: Blaming the Victim in Child Survival', *Social Science and Medicine* 40(1): 5–13.

Gardner, K., and F. Osella. 2004. 'Introduction', in F. Osella and K. Gardner (eds), *Migration, Modernity and Social Transformation in South Asia*. Delhi: Sage, pp.xi–xlviii.

Gesler, W. 1992. 'Therapeutic Landscapes: Medical Issues in Light of the New Cultural Geography', *Social Science and Medicine* 34(7): 735–46.

Gidwani, V., and K. Sivaramakrishnan. 2004. 'Circular Migration and Rural Cosmopolitanism in India', in F. Osella and K. Gardner (eds), *Migration, Modernity and Social Transformation in South Asia*. Delhi: Sage, pp.339–68.

GoI. 2005. 'Mission Document (2005–2012)', National Rural Health Mission, Ministry of Health and Family Welfare. Retrieved 11 November 2010 from: www. mohfw.nic.in/NRHM/Documents/Mission_Document.pdf.

——— 2011. 'Census of India: D-series – migration tables'. Retrieved from: www. censusindia.gov.in/Tables_Published/D-series/Tables_on Migration_census_of_ India_2001.aspx.

Goldade, K. 2011. 'Babies and Belonging: Reproduction, Citizenship and Undocumented Nicaraguan Labor Migrant Women in Costa Rica', *Medical Anthropology* 30(5): 545–68.

Hulton, L., Z. Mathews and R. Stone. 1999. *A Framework for the Evaluation of the Quality of Care in Maternity Services*. Southampton: Southampton University.

IIPS. 2001. 'National Family Health Survey (NFHS 2), India, 1998–99: Rajasthan'. Mumbai: International Institute for Population Sciences and ORC Macro.

IIPS, 2005. 'National Family Health Survey (NFHS 3), India, 2005-06'. Mumbai: International Institute for Population Sciences and ORC Macro.

Jolly, S., E. Bell and K. Narayanswamy. 2003. *Gender and Migration in Asia: An Overview*. Brighton: Institute of Development Studies, University of Sussex.

Mills, M.B. 1997. 'Contesting the Margins of Modernity: Women, Migration and Consumption in Thailand', *American Ethnologist* 24(1): 37–61.

Nichter, M., and M. Nichter. 1996. 'Social Science Lessons from Diarrhoea Research and Their Application to ARI', in M. Nichter and M. Nichter (eds), *Anthropology and International Health*. London: Gordon and Breach, pp.135–73.

Parrenas, R. 2001. *Servants of Globalisation: Women, Migration and Domestic Work*. Stanford: Stanford University Press.

Ram, K. 1998. 'Maternity and the Story of Enlightenment in the Colonies: Tamil Coastal Women, South India', in K. Ram and M. Jolly (eds), *Maternities and Modernities: Colonial and Postcolonial Experiences in Asia and the Pacific*. Cambridge: Cambridge University Press, pp.114–44.

Scheper-Hughes, N. 1997. 'Demography without Numbers', in D. Kertzer and T. Fricke (eds), *Anthropological Demography*. Chicago: University of Chicago Press, pp.201–23.

Shah, A. 2001. 'The Labour of Love: Seasonal Migration from Jharkhand to the Brick Kilns in Other States of India', *Contributions to Indian Sociology* 40(1): 91–118.

Sinha, A. 2005. *India, Democracy and Wellbeing: An Enquiry into the Persistence of Poverty in a Dynamic Democracy*. New Delhi: Rupa Publishers.

Srinivas, M.N. 1966. *Social Change in Modern India*. Delhi: Orient Longman.

Stephenson, R., Z. Mathews and J.W. McDonald. 2003. 'The Impact of Rural–Urban Migration on Under Two Child Mortality in India', *Journal of Biosocial Science* 35: 15–31.

Tarlo, E. 2000. 'Body and Space in a Time of Crisis: Sterilisation and Resettlement during the Emergency in Delhi', in V. Das, A. Kleinman, M. Ramphele and P. Reynolds (eds), *Violence and Subjectivity*. Berkeley: University of California Press, pp.242–71.

UHRC. 2006. 'State of Urban Health in Rajasthan'. Report by the Urban Health Resource New Delhi: Centre for the Ministry of Health and Family Welfare, Government of India.

UNFPA. 2007. 'State of the World Population: Unleashing the Potential of Urban Growth'. New York: United Nations Fund for Population.

Unnithan-Kumar, M. 2001. 'Emotion, Agency and Access to Healthcare: Women's Experiences of Reproduction in Jaipur', in S. Tremayne (ed.), *Managing Reproductive Life*. Oxford: Berghahn, pp.27–52.

———— 2002. 'Midwives among Others: Knowledges of Healing and the Politics of Emotions in Rajasthan, North-West India', in S. Rozario and G. Samuel (eds), *The Daughters of Hariti: Childbirth and Female Healers in South and Southeast Asia*. London: Routledge, pp. 109–30.

———— 2004. 'Spirits of the Womb: Migration, Reproductive Choice and Healing in Rajasthan' in F. Osella and K. Gardner (eds), *Migration, Modernity and Social Transformation in South Asia*. Delhi: Sage, pp.163–89.

———— 2010. 'Learning from Infertility', *South Asian History and Culture* (special issue) 1(2): 315–28.

Unnithan-Kumar, M., K. McNay and A. Castaldo. 2008. 'Women's Migration, Urban Poverty and Child Health in Rajasthan'. Working Paper T–26. Brighton: Centre for Migration Research, University of Sussex.

Van Gennep, A. 1965[1909]. *The Rites of Passage*. London: Routledge and Kegan Paul.

Van Hollen, C. 2002. *Birth on the Threshold: Childbirth and Modernity in South India*. Berkeley: University of California Press.

Vatuk, S. 1972. *Kinship and Urbanisation: White Collar Migrants in North India*. Berkeley: University of California Press.

Chapter 6

Acculturation and Experiences of Post-partum Depression amongst Immigrant Mothers

Cultural Competency in Medicine

Mirabelle E. Fernandes-Paul

Studies conducted by major organizational bodies have shown that racial and ethnic health disparities are significant in the United States (Nelson 2002). The American Medical Association and medical schools have acknowledged the serious consequences of such disparities (Misra-Herbert 2003). To increase the quality of an immigrant's healthcare experience, experts have focused on making the healthcare system more culturally competent. 'Cultural competency' is a model designed to help healthcare professionals and organizations provide better care to immigrants (Nunez 2000). According to this model, organizations hire multicultural staff, use interpreters, provide brochures, signs and educational material in different languages and provide their staff with cultural competency training (Anderson et al. 2003).

Many have criticized the use of cultural competency, suggesting it be changed to cultural efficacy or cultural humility, thus infusing the issue with empathy and care (Nunez 2000; Taylor 2003). Currently, most cultural competency training is about providing a list of culture-based characteristics about specific groups (Taylor 2003). Wear has called cultural competency training 'reductionist, add-a-lecture; test-for-knowledge' (Wear 2003: 550), suggesting it encouraged an ethnocentric way of framing the dominant culture as the norm. Her scepticism is grounded in the premise of such training: mostly educated, middle- and upper-class, white physicians need to be educated about their patients, who might be uneducated, poor and belong to racial/ethnic/religious minorities. Such a simplistic approach is problematic because people are lumped into stereotypical one-dimensional groups (for example, Asian), thus ignoring other facets of their identity, such as gender, class, ethnicity, age, religion and sexual orientation (ibid.). Additionally, as immigrants acclimatize themselves and assimilate in the dominant society, they are transformed by the local culture and vice versa (Turner 2001; Kagawa-Singer and Kassim-Lakha 2003). Hence teaching anyone about the characteristics of a specific immigrant group is like studying something that is always in a state of flux.

Immigrant Women and Childbirth

Immigrant women are one such immigrant group. Traditionally, these women have done well in finding employment in the United States. As one white male production manager and hiring supervisor for a Silicon Valley assembly shop puts it: 'Just three things I look for in hiring [entry-level, high-tech manufacturing operatives]: small, foreign, and female. You find those three things and you're pretty much automatically guaranteed the right kind of workforce. Those little foreign gals are grateful to be hired – very, very grateful – no matter what' (Hossfeld 1994: 65).

Women often find themselves at the intersection of gender, race and class. Zinn and Dill have coined the term 'multicultural feminism' to describe the experiences of a variety of women, while treating racial inequality as an important factor in their experience as a minority group. 'It charges us to look beyond those women who supposedly "have it all" to those who "have none of it"' (Zinn and Dill 1994: 11). My research provides a snapshot of those who create meaning out of new motherhood while at the same time facing the challenges of living between two cultures and countries, challenges which include the racism they experience in their adopted land. In light of the work of multicultural feminists, this chapter highlights the urgent need for global feminists to understand and embrace the complexity and diversity that is an integral part of women's lives, and which must be incorporated into feminist perspectives.

Research on post-partum depression among immigrants has revealed a high incidence of childbirth-related depression among immigrants, as well as the importance of the socio-cultural context of new motherhood in an adopted country (Morrow et al. 2008). Taniguchi and Baruffi (2007) observed that language barriers, distance from social support networks and ethno-medical beliefs and practices about childbirth collectively increase the incidence of post-partum depression among immigrant women. Researchers have identified poor socio-economic standing, residence in inner-city environments, exposure to violence and discrimination/racism as stress factors in the post-partum period (Beeghly et al. 2003; Brown et al. 2003; Rosenfield

2006). In a recent study, Davila et al. (2009) reported that higher accultura-tion, pregnancy and single status increased the chances of depression among post-partum Latinas. However, Beck et al. (2005) found no consistent rela-tionship between acculturation and post-partum depression in a sample of Hispanic mothers.

Methodology

I focused on the complex web of interactions that constitute immigrant obstetrics in the hope of understanding how immigrants and healthcare pro-viders make meaning of their interactions with each other. Since the inter-views were structured around people's lived experiences, this qualifies as a phenomenological study, which is a research methodology that portrays phe-nomena from the context of those who experience it. In other words, it is the philosophy of experience (Smith and Thomasson 2005). Its researchers seek to better understand the lived experience of others (Sartre 1956). On the basis of its disciplinary orientation, this research can be called a phenomenological study, and a case study on the basis of its form. A case study is qualitative in nature and hypothesis-generating rather than hypothesis-testing (Merriam 1998). The method of case-study research enables us to get as close to the heart of a bounded sociological research question as we possibly can, due to its access to subjective factors like people's thoughts, feelings and desires (Bromley 1986).

My research involved a case study of immigrant obstetrics in the com-munity of Tranquillity, Minnesota, and its surrounding area from 2006 to 2008. I spoke to women who had experienced childbirth at Tranquillity Clinic or St Augustine Clinic and Hospital – the two locations that provide obstetric care in the area. To limit my sample collection, I set a time limit of ten years. Hence, to participate in the study a woman should have delivered on or after November 1996.

The public relations department at Tranquillity Clinic sent out invitations to potential subjects. Some of the subjects were recommended by people that agreed to be interviewed and volunteered to connect me with other subjects. I interviewed thirty women and six men, between 25 and 61 years of age. Participant names (changed to protect the identity of participants), countries and occupations are given in the Appendix.

All of the mothers I interviewed had lived in the US for less than twelve years, and had given birth at St Augustine Hospital at least once in the past three years. Five of the immigrant mothers requested interpretation services for the interview. Of those who requested interpreter services, all had studied up to age thirteen. They all qualified for and were using county services like

WIC. WIC is a special supplemental nutrition programme for women, infants and children that provides federal grants to states for supplemental foods, healthcare referrals and nutrition education for low-income pregnant, breastfeeding and non-breastfeeding mothers, and to infants and children up to age five. Of the women who did not request interpreter services, Julia had completed a doctorate in the US, Karen was about to enrol in a doctoral programme, Kim and Ayesha had Master's degrees in public health, Vanessa was about to enrol in a Master's programme in a healthcare-related field and Salma had attended school until age sixteen in Somalia.

I interviewed three Spanish-language interpreters (Lisa, Janice and Laura) one Somali interpreter (Zaynab) and one Vietnamese interpreter (Rose). All the nurses I interviewed were white. Elizabeth and Andrea were nurses at Tranquillity Clinic. Carole worked as an obstetrics nurse at St Augustine Hospital. Michelle also worked for St Augustine Hospital as a lactation specialist. Linda and Lynn ran the WIC programmes for the two counties that fed into the Tranquillity community. Eleanor, a public health nurse, visited new mothers in their homes providing education and support for parenting, safety and nutrition. Midwives Teresa and Helen, both white, had worked as midwives for many years. Licensed social workers, Trixie and Kristy, both white, had Master's degrees in social work. I interviewed six physicians, two female and four male; of these, five were white. Allison is the only obstetrics and gynaecology physician at Tranquillity Clinic. Diane, a family physician, was born and raised in Africa. Brad, Peter, Andrew and Lindon were physicians in the Obstetrics and Gynaecology Department.

On average, I interviewed each person for 90 minutes at a time and place that was convenient for the participant. In order to triangulate my data, I interviewed healthcare providers, patients and interpreters to collect different points of view of immigrant obstetrics in Tranquillity. Triangulation entails confirming events and phenomenon using different sources of information (Wolcott 1988). Not all immigrants in Tranquillity are in the US legally, and I was cognizant of the fact that identifying their legal status (or lack of it) for my study might cause them problems. Hence, I reminded them in the consent form that they were not to mention their citizenship/visa status at any time. The two dominant issues with regards to ethics in research are avoiding any harm to participants and informed consent (Bogdan and Biklen 1992). Hence, I drafted a consent form, and before the start of each interview I asked them to read and sign it. For interviews with non-English speakers, I drafted a separate form in which interpreters signed a note promising not to reveal any details of the interview to anyone else.

Results and Discussion: Straddling Two Cultures

A prominent theme that emerged from my data was a figurative act of 'straddling' that many of the immigrant women described. They described this straddling mostly as a feeling of being trapped between two cultures, one in which they were taught the rules of life and socialization, and the other in which they sought to earn a place. Seeking membership and feeling loyal to both worlds often became the source of their anguish. In Julia's words: 'I felt I am not here nor there. But I want to be both'. This straddling was intensified for the women who had gone through higher education in the United States and when family members from back home came to help. Julia has a doctorate and works as a statistician: 'I read a lot of books from here, American books. Actually, my mind is nurtured in the American way. But then my mom came and we had a lot of conflict because we do things differently'. It is possible that the completion of terminal educational degrees in the US increases the desire of a woman to assimilate and become more 'American'. Yet nostalgia and continued connections with a home left behind tethers them to their home countries. Hence, these women experience a high intensity of anguish created by straddling the two worlds they long to fit into.

The phenomenon of straddling played out in discussions of breastfeeding choices among immigrants. In the Western world, infant feeding has been debated using several different frames, mostly drawing the battle lines between breastfeeding and bottle feeding methods with very little overlap. Breast or bottle, women have to choose and they are judged on their choice. My research shows that such a clear demarcation might not exist in other cultures. In the US, it is feared that once the baby uses the bottle they will not accept the breast (Newman and Wilmott 1990). When asked about the breast and bottle combination strategy, healthcare providers spoke of noticing it in many of their African and Asian patients. As Dr Nixon put it: 'The African women breast and bottle feed instantly. Cracks me up! You give them a bottle and they will have no problems taking the breast. And I am like, "You know you really need to breastfeed. At least try to let the milk come in." And they say, "Oh yeah, breast and bottle!"'

As a physician, Dr Morton spoke of the implications of such stereotyping. An immigrant herself, she spoke of straddling the two worlds of being a healthcare provider and an immigrant woman. Hence, she defined breastfeeding through the lenses of overlapping loyalties to native and acquired cultures: 'There is a misconception on the obstetrics floor that immigrant women don't know how to nurse properly. They don't know how to do it right, or it is not in their culture to nurse. And I don't want them to give the impression to American people that it is not a cultural thing to nurse'. She blamed Western formula milk companies for their misleading advertising in the 1960s, which has been responsible for reducing breastfeeding by African women: 'Among the middle-class people, it became popular, "Oh Lactogen babies!" For many of the African women, bottle feeding is the cool thing. It is also a civilized thing to do. That's how it was in Africa for years because it was the rich who had access to bottle feeding. When you bottle feed, you're civilized; when you breastfeed you're uncivilized'.

The oppositional construction of breast and bottle in the West becomes problematic when analysing the choices immigrant women make when straddling the two worlds. Julia said she combined the use of the bottle, a breast pump and breastfeeding. After reading numerous American books and attending breastfeeding classes, Julia decided to go the 'American way' and only breastfeed. However, breastfeeding her son was not as smooth as she thought it would be in the days following his birth. This became a source of bitter conflict between her and her mother, because her mother wanted her to do it the Chinese way. She wanted her to, 'feed the baby formula for the first 24 hours. After that you can nurse the baby. Not all the time'. Julia's son fell asleep when put to her breast, probably because of his jaundice. The lactation specialists would then strip him of his clothes, and wipe him with a cold cloth to wake him up. Neither Julia nor her mother liked this, and feared he might catch a cold. Then her mother forcefully suggested, 'now you have to listen to my way'. Julia saw herself as straddling two cultures, two schools of thought and two worlds in her initial breastfeeding experience. She had wanted to breastfeed just like other American women do, but in her mother's presence she was reminded of her strong ties to China. Finally, she had to pick a side: 'In the end my mother was right', she admitted, almost grudgingly.

Having lived in the US for a few years and familiarized herself with the language, food and values of Americans, Julia felt justified in identifying with the American way of life. However, with her mother visiting from China, she was also afforded post-partum constructs from Chinese culture. At first, she wanted to do everything like an American woman would. She read books about woman-centred childbirth without the hegemony of patriarchal constraints, represented by male obstetricians; she chose to be under the care of a midwife, and regularly attended childbirth classes. However, in the end, Julia saw her plans crumble. She ended up needing a Caesarean section, and breastfeeding turned out be much harder than expected, devoid of the romance of baby's first gentle suckle. Her nipples were sore and cracked, she was exhausted and the lactation specialists mercilessly badgered her to keep letting the baby suck on her wounds. Betrayed by the American way, Julia felt vulnerable and too weak to protest when her mother took over with the Chinese way.

For Kim, doing things the way American women do was a way to assimilate and be less of a stranger. 'I went to the childbirth class. My husband and I decided that we will do all the things that people do here when they get pregnant'. Vanessa, Julia, Ayesha and Karen registered for the classes, and believed they would help them have an easier birth. However, the childbirth classes, even though intended to empower women like Kim, did not seem to help her. 'In the end, the childbirth class, my husband and I thought was just a way for the midwives to get some names. It really doesn't help anything'. Just as Julia faced conflict with her mother for wanting to do things the American way, Kim had to put up with resistance from her husband about going to the classes. He did not want to go and was sarcastic about it: 'Why do we need that?' Later on, when her labour did not progress and she had to have a Caesarean section, she regretted going to the classes.

Kim and her husband belong to similar communities in Bangladesh. If they had never left, Kim said she would probably have been a mother and full time homemaker. 'Back home we could afford a maid, or we could afford for me to stay home. In fact in our society women are encouraged to not have careers'. In the US, she is expected to be a liberated American woman who holds a job and brings home a salary. However, behind closed doors, her husband maintains the patriarchal domination that he witnessed while growing up. Kim said he watched his father take minimal part in household chores and parenting tasks, and that is what he practises. Hence, because of her immigrant identity, Kim found herself marginalized in more ways than one:

> It's better to be on either side than being in between. If I were back home, my relationships would have been different. I would have people to take care of things. I would have a social life and wouldn't feel so lonely. I am doing the same things as someone who was raised here does, but at the same time he wants to keep some things like they were back home. It's more work, it's a lot more work for me.

This hardship became worse when family visited from home. They still perceived and treated her as they would if she were a daughter and daughter-in-law back in Bangladesh. They expected her to abide by the constructs of a docile and dutiful woman. Kim's first few months after the birth produced some painful memories. She had to go back to work while struggling to fit in with the patriarchal model of her husband, all the while battling post-partum depression. 'It was not at all how I thought it would be. It was not supposed to be so difficult'. She said that as a child in Bangladesh she watched her mother do nothing during her pregnancies. Grandparents, servants and family members helped take care of the children, and run the home smoothly.

Besides Kim, many other women in my study spoke about the different ways that pregnancy and childbirth are constructed in cultures other than that of the US. As Karen told me, 'If the woman is working, she gets up to a year of paid maternity leave. So they can rest'. Vanessa, meanwhile, reported:

> I thought it was just so simple; you get pregnant and have a baby. A special time. They're treated as special. They aren't supposed to do anything. You're supposed to eat good food and make sure you eat healthy foods and stuff, rest all the time…you have a lot of relatives around you to take care of you and so you feel special.

Julia said that in China whole families rally around a pregnant woman, and continue to support her a great deal after the birth. For these women, pregnancy was a time to relax and be pampered. Vanessa said she was taking classes during her pregnancy, and had to often sprint out of class because of feeling nauseous. Kim was trying to get a legal work permit, so she was required to work full time. Karen was on a graduate assistantship that paid for her tuition, but it required her to register for nine hours of classes per week. Therefore, she had a full course load even during the last part of her pregnancy: 'I had the baby on Monday noon, and so I missed that day's class. But I went to class on Wednesday. My husband had class at the same time. So I was discharged on Wednesday morning, and then my friend gave me a ride to class and took care of my baby in the meantime'.

All of the women above were told by their physicians that their psychological and physical symptoms pointed towards varying levels of post-partum depression. The women said they felt angry about how things did not turn out the way they had envisioned. However, they were all sure that if it were not for their unique position as women who are 'half here, half there' (as Julia put it), their experiences would have been more pleasant.

One can use Goffman's concept of a 'moral career' (Goffman 1959: 128) to understand how immigrant women make sense of their dual identities during pregnancy, birth and after. He described moral career as a set of phases through which a person's identity and status develop. My data show that the moral careers of immigrant mothers are largely determined by the extent of their involvement in broader American culture, and the extent of their institutionalized membership of the American education system and workforce.

Goffman spoke of a 'home world' in which an individual has previously lived in and has established their self-identity (Goffman 1961: 12). When immigrants arrive in the US, they bring with them their conception of self, which is based on social arrangements in their home world. Goffman defined home world as a way of life and activities that are so habitual that they are taken for granted. It is only when a person leaves their home world that they begin to make meaning of that way of life. As Goffman explained: 'The recruit comes into the establishment with a conception of himself made possible by certain stable social arrangements in his home world. Upon entrance he is immediately striped of the support provided by these arrangements' (ibid.: 24). Upon entering her adopted culture, an immigrant woman may be expected to systematically strip herself of those beliefs, and often she may even want to do so as a way of feeling more American. Attending childbirth classes is one way to gain membership. A visit to the bookstore, online resources and journal writing are other ways of stripping themselves of home-world beliefs and being assimilated by the dominant culture.

All these resources and classes are unheard of in other cultures, where women receive such education from family and friends. Through the reference group of family and friends, these women have developed a certain sense of identity and self-expectations. Members of their reference groups constantly remind them of their responsibilities, and the cultural constraints that their roles entail. However, in the US, immigrant women find that the resources that went along with those responsibilities are missing. Understandably, many of the immigrant women I interviewed experienced shock and disappointment when their experiences of pregnancy and childbirth in the US were nothing like those that they had expected. Many of them worked long hours during pregnancy, and their days following the birth were marked with conflict with spouses and family members, those who were supposed to be of assistance during that time.

In her research on the intersection of identities among Southeast Asian immigrant mothers in Australia, Liamputtong (2006) showed that immigrant women have to understand competing discourses to make sense of their new identities in a new land. Their identities are defined by their gender, ethnicity, immigrant status and constructs of motherhood. Similarly, I have used Goffman's idea of a moral career to understand how immigrant women in my research make sense of the disconnection they experience between what they thought pregnancy should be like, and what it turned out to be in actuality.

My research corroborates Liamputtong's (2006) findings, but connects them with post-partum depression in immigrant women who felt that they were depressed for a temporary period following childbirth. Many immigrant women in my study expressed resentment and disillusionment over the friction caused between complying with cultural demands of their home culture and the lack of resources offered by their new culture. Possibly this resentment greatly contributes to or even causes post-partum depression among immigrant women. Goffman (1961) predicted that people who are in a transitional state while being socialized into a new identity often feel resentful. He termed this state of transition, which is marked by frustration and disillusionment, as rebirth. A person emerges from their rebirth with a new identity and beliefs, which are a confluence of the beliefs of their home world and their new world. The immigrant women in my study found themselves confused because of the stark contrast between what they thought pregnancy should have been, and what it turned out to be for them. Eventually, however, they renegotiated their identity as new mothers, which required surrendering some beliefs from their home culture, and adopting some ways of American culture.

Such renegotiation can be seen in the unique method of infant feeding that immigrant women in my study spoke of employing. As a possible coping strategy for stressful 'straddling', they used a combination of infant feeding habits from both their home and host countries. Such a strategy was unheard of among new American mothers at the hospital in Tranquillity. Therefore, backstage among healthcare providers there was an assumption that immigrant women tend not to breastfeed, even though they were continuing to breastfeed. Dr Morton, a physician and an immigrant mother, had access to the backstage banter, and felt personally offended by the stereotyping that went on. Hence, she encouraged immigrants to breastfeed: 'I don't want them to give the impression to American people that it is not a cultural thing to nurse. It is a cultural thing to nurse'.

When Goffman's theory of impression management is applied here, we see how Dr Morton felt like she lost face as an immigrant woman. Here, the nurses are the audience and immigrant women are the actors on stage. Goffman (1959) described face as a public self-image, or a group's reputation. Hence losing face would be perceived as a threat to this public image, which is what Dr Morton perceived when she heard nurses assume that the refusal or inability to nurse is cultural. By encouraging immigrant women to breastfeed, Dr Morton engaged in face-saving techniques, in that she tried to get her team-mates to perform, in order to impress the audience and restore the team's face. Additionally, healthcare providers reported that African babies who are fed both breast milk and infant formula are bigger, which is a symbol of health and prosperity in many African countries battling malnutrition. Hence, we see how bottle feeding and breastfeeding symbolize stage props that can be used to increase or decrease the status of one's group. If the bottle is considered a mark of a health and wealth, then it makes sense that an immigrant woman who is trying to establish a credible identity in America would choose to bottle feed in addition to breastfeeding.

The use of Goffman's notion of impression management here emphasizes cultural hegemony (Giroux 1981). My study suggests that immigrants find themselves playing the role of the actor on stage. However, American healthcare providers most often make up the audience. In the analysis in which I have used the lens of cultural hegemony, as well as the analysis in which I have used the lens of dramaturgy, it is perceived to be the responsibility of immigrants to alter their behaviours to fit in and earn a place in American society.

The last subset of findings that sheds light on a unique pattern of communication among immigrant women emerged among the highly educated group of women. This pattern was expressed in their interactions with their healthcare providers. First, the women spoke of the process of choosing an obstetrician. They set the bar high, and ruthlessly compared minute differences in the credentials of one physician with the other. Long before they even became pregnant, they sought references from friends and colleagues about the reputations of local obstetricians. This is clear in the following remarks by Kim:

> When I chose Dr Truman, I did … research to find out who is who. But I looked at other options – [such as] the only female they had. For her, it did not say 'Board Certified'; it said 'Board Eligible'. Not that it matters, but I thought he took the time to go for the test, and she just started practice without certification. I know from my experience that what I hear is a big deal. So I put a lot of preliminary research into it. I looked at all options even after I chose Dr Truman.

The women spoke of comparing their physicians' advice to the advice on medical websites like WebMD and in books like *What to Expect When You're Expecting* (Eisenberg and Murkoff 1984). They talked about going to every one of their antenatal appointments on time, prepared with handwritten or typed questions and concerns that they wanted to bring up in the consulting room. Some of the women even spoke of reminding the physician about a blood test or tetanus shot that they had forgotten to request. Later on, when it came close to the time of birth, the women talked of writing out elaborate birth plans in which they detailed specific requests for the different stages of their stay in the hospital: Kim specified who she wanted in the birthing room; Vanessa made sure to write down that she did not want any painkillers. Healthcare providers also spoke about some immigrants who resist Caesarean section, even if their physician elects to schedule one.

In this way, immigrant women employ unique modes of communication in their interactions with American healthcare providers. These forms of communication point to complex power dynamics between immigrant women and American healthcare providers. As a function of their gender, race or class, these women usually found themselves to be the less powerful member of the dyadic interaction. However, the women who had received higher education attempted to alter their position of powerlessness by using numerous unique forms of communication. Presumably, their education empowered them to resist the unequal distribution of power.

Conclusion

In spite of their numerous educational qualifications, groups like women and racial minorities often feel like they have to work harder than their male and white colleagues to prove themselves (Dryburgh 1999). Overt and covert forms of race- and ethnicity-related bullying have been reported in a wide variety of work settings (Fox and Stallworth 2005). Perhaps when people endure such disillusionment at work, they look for other arenas where they can engage in more favourable impression management. For many women in my study, the clinic functioned as the front stage where they engaged in performances in order to take back the power and validation that they struggled to establish in the outside world. By appearing prepared, confident and informed, the women attempted to impress upon the physician and nurses that they are forces to be reckoned with. It is also possible that these front-stage performances also function as proactive steps that the women (as a group experiencing multiple layers of 'isms') take in order to protect themselves from, or cope with, any forms of racism or discrimination that might be directed towards their foreignness.

Whether it be mourning a death or celebrating a birth, the experience of any life-changing event increases in complexity for an immigrant. Based on the desire or opportunity of adopting the host country's culture or retaining attachment to one's roots, the immigrant can feel quite torn and conflicted. In the case of childbirth, several cultural norms, rituals, beliefs and practices are woven into the experience of a new mother. For immigrant women, what could be a time to celebrate new life can sometimes be a time filled with conflict and confusion. My research shows that this conflict is intensified among those women who have had opportunities to obtain higher educational qualifications in the US and who have a desire to assimilate into American culture.

Appendix
Interviewees and Interview Dates

Julia, 7 May 2008
Karen, 13 April 2007
Kim, 27 March 2007
Dr Morton, 6 June 2007
Dr Nixon, 26 June 2007
Vanessa, 9 April 2007

References

Anderson, L., et al. 2003. 'Culturally Competent Healthcare Systems: A Systematic Review', *American Journal of Preventive Medicine* 24: 68–79.

Beck, C.T., R. Froman and H. Bernal. 2005. 'Acculturation Level and Post-partum Depression in Hispanic Mothers', *American Journal of Maternal Child Nursing* 30: 299–304.

Beeghly, M., et al. 2003. 'Prevalence, Stability and Sociodemographic Correlates of Depressive Symptoms in Black Mothers During the First Eighteen Months Post-partum', *Maternal and Child Health Journal* 7: 157–68.

Bogdan, R. and S.K. Biklen. 1992. *Qualitative Research for Education*. Boston: Allyn and Bacon.

Bromley, D. 1986. *The Case Study Method in Psychology and Related Disciplines*. New York: Wiley.

Brown, C., J. Abe-Kim and C. Barrio. 2003. 'Depression in Ethnically Diverse Women: Implications for Treatment in Primary Care Settings', *Professional Psychology: Research and Practice* 34: 10–19.

Davila, M., S.L. Mcfall and D. Cheng. 2009. 'Acculturation and Depressive Symptoms Among Pregnant and Post-partum Latinas', *Maternal and Child Health Journal* 13(3): 318–25.

Dryburgh, H. 1999. 'Work Hard, Play Hard: Women and Professionalization in Engineering – Adapting to the Culture', *Gender and Society* 13: 664–82.

Eisenberg, A., and H. Murkoff. 1984. *What to Expect When You're Expecting*. New York: Workman Publishing.

Fox, S., and L.E. Stalworth. 2005. 'Racial/Ethnic Bullying: Exploring Links Between Bullying and Racism in the US Workplace', *Journal of Vocational Behaviour* 66: 438–56.

Giroux, H.A. 1981. *Ideology, Culture, and the Processes of Schooling*. Philadelphia: Temple University Press.

Goffman, E. 1959. *The Presentation of Self in Everyday Life*. New York: Doubleday.

Goffman, E. 1961. *Asylums: Essays on the Social Situation of Mental Patients and Other Inmates*. New York: Anchor Books/Doubleday.

Hossfeld, K. 1994. 'Hiring Immigrant Women: Silicon Valley's "Simple Formula"', in M.B. Zinn and B.T. Dill (eds), *Women of Color in US Society*. Philadelphia: Temple University Press.

Kagawa-Singer, M., and S. Kassim-Lakha. 2003'.A Strategy to Reduce Cross-cultural Miscommunication and Increase the Likelihood of Improving Health Outcomes', *Academic Medicine* 78: 577–87.

Liamputtong, P. 2006. 'Motherhood and "Moral Career": Discourses of Good Motherhood among Southeast Asian Immigrant Women in Australia', *Qualitative Sociology* 29: 25–53.

Merriam, S. 1998. *Qualitative Research and Case Study Applications in Education*. San Francisco: Jossey-Bass.

Misra-Herbert, A. 2003. 'Physician Cultural Competence: Cross-cultural Communication Improves Care', *Cleveland Clinic Journal of Medicine* 70: 289–303.

Morrow, M.S., et al. 2008. 'Shifting Landscapes: Immigrant Women and Post-partum Depression', *Healthcare for Women International* 29: 593–617.

Nelson, A. 2002. 'Unequal Treatment: Confronting Racial and Ethnic Disparities in Healthcare', *Journal of National Medical Association* 94: 666–68.

Newman, J., and B. Wilmott. 1990. 'Breast Rejection: A Little-appreciated Cause of Lactation Failure', *Canadian Family Physician* 36: 449–53.

Nunez, A.E. 2000. 'Transforming Cultural Competence into Cross-cultural Efficacy in Women's Health Education', *Academic Medicine* 75: 1071–80.

Rosenfield, A. 2006. *New Research on Post-partum Depression*. New York: Nova Science.

Sartre, J.P. 1956. *Being and Nothingness*. New York: Philosophical Library.

Smith, D.W., and A.L. Thomasson. 2005. *Phenomenology and Philosophy of Mind*. New York: Oxford University Press.

Taniguchi, H., and G. Baruffi. 2007. 'Childbirth Overseas: The Experience of Japanese Women in Hawaii', *Nursing and Health Sciences* 9: 90–95.

Taylor, J.S. 2003. 'Confronting "Culture" in Medicine's "Culture of No Culture"', *Academic Medicine* 78: 555–59.

Wear, D. 2003. 'Insurgent Multiculturalism: Rethinking How and Why We Teach Culture', *Academic Medicine* 78: 549–54.

Wolcott, H. 1988. 'Ethnographic Research in Education', in R. Jaegger (ed.), *Complementary Methods for Research in Art Education*. Washington, DC: American Education Research Association, pp.187–206.

CHAPTER 7

'A Mother Who Stays but Cannot Provide Is Not as Good'

Migrant Mothers in Hanoi, Vietnam

Catherine Locke, Nguyen Thi Ngan Hoa
and Nguyen Thi Thanh Tam

Vietnam embarked on a reform process in the mid to late 1980s that has transformed the nation's centrally planned communism to a form of 'market socialism'. This transition process, known locally as *doi moi*, has been defined by the state as primarily economic in nature, involving very limited political change. However, the economic changes have also entailed fundamental shifts in the relation between citizens and the state, notably, for the purposes of this chapter, the rolling back of social provisioning, the relaxation of restrictions on internal migration and the promotion of new ideologies of womanhood. The concentration of new income-earning opportunities in the cities, the withdrawal of public provisioning and the long-standing expectation that women make productive contributions to the household mean that newly married women are no longer necessarily 'left behind' or 'tied to the bamboo grove' to give birth to and raise children (Kabeer and Thi Van Anh 2002). Today, large numbers of married women, like married men, migrate to the cities for work to sustain their families (GSO 2005). Newly married women in low-income households are increasingly likely to find themselves 'going home' to give birth, leaving behind young infants in the care of others, and/ or giving birth to and raising babies in the city. This shift implies a radical break with conventional expectations of young married women as new daughters-in-law and as the mothers of young children. How do married women negotiate these conflicting expectations in confined economic circumstances? What does this mean for the construction of their identities as migrant mothers?

In this chapter we use the qualitative life histories of female migrants to Hanoi to explore their strategies for reproduction and parenting. We focus on childbearing and early parenting strategies, with some reference to maternal health choices, and ask how migrant mothers, in particular, craft strategies of childbearing and childrearing, and what this means for their construction of their own parenting identities.

We utilize a social relations of reproduction perspective that emphasizes gendered power relations across the life course. Reproductive strategies are embedded in wider social relations and processes, and reproductive outcomes are shaped and given meaning by men's and women's attempts to 'manage' their reproductive lives (see Bledsoe 1994; Greenhalgh 1995; Tremayne 2001). Reproductive strategies not only mediate access to a productive livelihood (see, e.g., Chant 1992; Murphy 2002), but they are intrinsically meaningful and, like decisions about employment and migration, constitute 'strategic life choices' (Santillan et al. 2004). Further, creating and maintaining meaningful familial relationships is a key source of belonging, achievement and emotional satisfaction for poor women (and men) (Cornwall 2001; Le Grand et al. 2003), and as such is central to their construction of identity. The motivation for migration may involve both marital aspirations and sacrifices as well as the desire to make a better life for one's children (Davin 1996; Zhang 1999). From this perspective, for married women, migrating in order to engage in productive work may be centrally *about* as well as *in tension with* being good mothers (and wives). A social relations of reproduction framework facilitates the exploration of migrant mothers' reproductive agency, the challenges they face in managing complex social identities and the inevitable ambiguities of their lived experiences. Moreover, a social relational analysis of reproduction situates individual agency within an analysis of power through paying close attention to institutional and structural factors. In this balancing act, contemporary gender norms and expectations represent the unequal resources and constraints within which individual women negotiate for the interests that they value and which influence how they experience different outcomes of their strategic life choices.

Mothering in the Transitional Era

Mothering is central to women's identity in Vietnam. Marriage within the context of a patrilineal kinship system is virilocal, virtually universal and remains primarily about reproduction: both in the sense of having children and in the sense of ensuring the continuity of the lineage. In this context, women's primary identities are as daughter-in-law and mother, rather than as wife (Pham Van Bich 1999; Werner 2004; Klingberg-Allvin et al. 2008).

Traditional expectations imply that the new wife's first duty is towards her mother-in-law and childbearing, particularly the bearing of sons, and early childrearing (Pham Van Bich 1999; Rydstrom 2006). However, socialist attempts to improve family relations, including addressing gender inequality and gerontocratic control, have somewhat strengthened conjugality, as reflected in the shift away from arranged marriages and in the decline in the duration of newly-weds' co-residence with the husband's parents (Goodkind 1996; Summerfield 1997; Hirschman and Minh 2002). Although spouses usually choose their marriage partners today, there are strong continuities with arranged marriage in the importance placed on parental approval and in the moral characteristics valued in a future husband or wife (Locke et al. 2008). The centrality of having children as part of marriage, the belief that love grows within marriage as children arrive and the perception that marriage and childbearing are about reproducing the lineage remain highly distinctive (Pham Van Bich 1999).

Male heirs play a vital role in continuing the lineage, and women face a 'reproductive dilemma' (Johansson 1998: 2) as they are caught between the state's desire to limit childbearing and the family's desire for sons. Population policy in Vietnam has never been as strict as in China, and it has a two- rather than a one-child policy (Summerfield 1997: 203), as well as an increasingly strong official line that all family planning decisions are voluntary (GoV 2002; UNFPA 2004). Nevertheless, 'rates of IUD use, as well as induced abortion, are among the highest in the world' (Santillan et al. 2004: 544). Family planning decisions are strongly influenced by both the husband and his close relatives, particularly his mother and father. Pressure on having the first child after marriage – within the first two years – is very strong, especially in the north, and the desire for a son remains strong, a desire that is in some cases sharpened by lower fertility.

Parenting in Vietnam is closely tied to the responsibility for bringing up children to be morally upright, and it is strongly gendered with normatively distinctive roles for fathers and mothers. The moral socialization of children is a strong theme in both traditional familialism and in socialism, albeit with rather different emphases on filial piety and good citizenship respectively. Fathers are seen as the 'pillar' of the family, responsible for discipline and guidance, particularly that of sons, while mothers are perceived to play an important role in keeping harmony in the family and in raising healthy children to take on adult responsibilities. Social norms of traditional familialism suggest that the mother must be the primary care-giver for an infant under two or three years, but that the father's care-giving is less important during infancy as he is perceived as not knowing how to look after a baby. Gendered parenting responsibilities are particularly significant during adolescence. At this time, a mothers' socialization of a girl is vital for teaching her how to behave appropriately and how to become a good wife and mother. Fathers are highly valued during adolescence for providing discipline to the family,[1] being both stricter with adolescent girls than mothers, and playing a special role in guiding sons (with respect to occupation, the transition to becoming a man and, vitally for the lineage, ensuring that a son 'follows' his father).

The shift during the mid 1980s away from a centrally planned economy to market socialism under *doi moi* has seen a reduced commitment to gender equality and a renewed emphasis on femininity, including motherhood. The restructuring of the social sector has seen social reproduction pushed back to the family sphere; related to this, a new nostalgia for, and resurgence of, traditional family and religious values about femininity and women's family roles has emerged (Goodkind 1996; Wisensale 1999; Rydstrom and Drummond 2004). Specifically, Phinney (2008) argues that the 1986 Marriage Law and the Happy Family Campaign together define a woman's primary identity as a mother, and define a successful marriage in terms of its economic stability and the fulfilment of family obligations around social reproduction. This builds on a long history whereby family formation is construed as playing a key role in nation-building. In this ideology, married women have both productive responsibilities to contribute to their family's economic stability as well as reproductive responsibilities to bring up their children to be responsible citizens. As part of their reproductive role, mothers have special responsibility for the moral socialization of their children, including their avoidance of 'social evils' (Rydstrom 2006). Feminist commentators have observed that these dual roles in both family-making and nation-building are highly problematic for women's gender identities (Pettus 2003).

In short, while the state is withdrawing from social-sector investment, it continues to have high expectations for the family, and the role of mothers in particular (Rydstrom 2006; Phinney 2008). However, for many low-income rural women, migration away from home is an increasing phenomenon. How, then, do low-income migrant mothers manage their childbearing and early parenting, and what does this mean for their identities as mothers?

Mothering across the Rural–Urban Divide

Migrant women's strategies for pregnancy, giving birth and infant care are shaped by evolving trends in the gendered nature of migration flows, and related changes in gender discourses about migration, as well as by the structuring of maternal and child health and education entitlements across rural and urban contexts.

Cultural expectations offer more support to a father's absences than to a mother's,[2] but women too are increasingly migrating before and immediately after marriage, and between childbearing. By 2004, as with men, around half of women migrants to Hanoi were married, and, as with men, around 30 per cent of women migrants who had moved in the past five years were already married when they first moved (GSO 2005). National estimates of migrant behaviour indicate that of those who are married when the first migration is made, 82 per cent already have at least one child. Of those who are married at the time but who do not already have a child, 66 per cent go on to have children after moving, as do 21 per cent of those who already have one child when they first move (GSO 2006a: 38).[3] These figures may indicate, as Hoy (1999) found in China, that success in reproduction, particularly the production of a son, makes it easier for married women to migrate because they are perceived as having fulfilled their obligations to their mothers-in-law. The study by Jensen et al. (2008: 18–19) of women roving street vendors in Hanoi also suggests that married women are increasingly migrating before and during peak childbearing years. Of those in their sample migrating between 2006 and 2008, 28 per cent migrated before they had their first child, 14 per cent between the birth of the first and second child and 58 per cent after their childbearing was 'complete'.

Despite conventional opposition to the migration of newly married women, particularly with young children (Lan Anh Hoang 2008), newer norms are emerging that are more supportive of women's migration, and they are more evident in locations with longer histories of women's migration. Whilst there remains anxiety over the protection of women, it is also commonly argued that: female migrants are 'safe' and under effective surveillance since they live with fellow women villagers; women migrants can, more easily than men, earn a living in the city without either capital or physical strength; and that women are more likely than men to save more of their earnings and bring them 'home' (Resurreccion and Khanh 2007; Jensen et al. 2008). These newer norms build on older and widespread concerns that male migrants will be tempted into social evils (drinking, using drugs, visiting commercial sex workers or having affairs), which potentially jeopardise not only their remittances but also the health and continuity of their family (Resurreccion and Khanh 2007).[4] There is then increasing flexibility for the creative construction of cases for and against the migration of wives and mothers that are intimately tied to fulfilling their sexual and reproductive responsibilities.

Migrants' choices about pregnancy care, delivery and early childrearing are influenced by the structuring of maternal and child health and education entitlements across rural and urban contexts. Socialist legacies of control over mobility require migrants to maintain ties to their home areas, and the household registration system has been used to structure social entitlements to discourage spontaneous migration, to deter settlement and accompanying dependants. There is a direct parallel with international migration where,

Parrenas argues, the host society, in this case the city, 'neither wants the responsibility for the reproductive costs of these workers nor grants them the membership accorded by the contributions of their labour to the economic growth of receiving nations' (Parrenas 2001: 368). Most migrants to Hanoi are registered as temporary residents, but, despite some important reforms, permanent residents retain privileged access to urban entitlements creating difficulties for migrants in accessing health and education in the city (Locke et al. 2008). Despite recent shifts of attitude in national policy in the direction of greater recognition of migrants' needs, the attitude of the Hanoi authorities and much popular opinion about 'free' migrants remains negative, and is reflected in the discriminatory attitudes and behaviour that rural migrants experience every day.

Aside from the difficulties related to the household registration system, migrants also have to negotiate the inequalities that exist in the provision of maternal and child health, childcare and education services between rural and urban situations. However, around 70 per cent of migrants to Hanoi come from the nearby Red River Delta (Guest 1998; GSO 2005), and the maternal and child health, childcare and education 'gap' between the Red River Delta and Hanoi is relatively lower than between other provinces and the main cities (CPFC 2003).[5] The availability of relatives in the countryside to support the new mother and care for her children, the relatively lower cost and absence of discriminatory attitudes towards rural people in rural services and the relative proximity of the Red River Delta sending areas to Hanoi encourage migrant women in Hanoi to go 'home to birth' and the practice of 'leaving children behind' when they migrate for work.

Mothers on the Move

This chapter uses detailed life history data collected in 2008 from married female migrants in their peak childbearing years to explore these strategies, and to examine what they mean for identities of motherhood in Vietnam. We focus here on twenty low-income rural-to-urban female migrants to Hanoi who have at least one child under eight years of age. This sub-sample is drawn from a larger data set that includes 17 married male migrants to Hanoi and a comparative sample of 20 married female and 19 male migrants to Ho Chi Minh City. The sub-sample includes women who were migrating with their husbands, leaving their husbands behind, who had husbands migrating elsewhere as well as single, divorced or widowed mothers (see Table 7.1).[6]

Migrants in these purposive categories were identified from localized sites with a very high incidence of migrants (from a single ward in Hanoi, and from two such wards in Ho Chi Minh City) using a combination of gatekeep-

Table 7.1: Purposive sample of low-income
rural–urban female migrants in Hanoi

Marital Status and Spousal Residential Arrangements at Time of Interview	Female Migrants in Hanoi with at least one child under 8 years old
Co-resident with spouse	Sam, Thao, Le, Thuy, Linh (n=5)
Spouse 'left behind'	Ha, Hang, Nhan, Binh, Hien (n=5)
Spouse migrating separately	Chau, Que, Mai, Dieu, Giang (n=5)
Separated from spouse/single/widowed	Cuc, Anh, Hai, Nga, Tran (n=5)
Total	20

ers, usually local women's officers, but also migrant guesthouse owners, as well as snowballing sampling methods to identify migrants in these categories. The life histories involved a two-part interview, often conducted consecutively following the preference of the migrants, consisting of a semi-structured questionnaire and a more narrative-based informal interview that was tape recorded, transcribed and translated. Hoa and Tam conducted the overwhelming majority of these interviews and verified every translation. In addition, the quality of translation was verified for two interviews by an independent Vietnamese researcher, and the researchers referred back to Vietnamese transcripts during data interpretation. Quotations from migrants below are verbatim translations from the in-depth interviews; with editorial additions inserted where necessary.

The data is primarily qualitative, but it is supported by structured information about informants', spouses' and children's moves, birthing choices, residence and schooling. However, the life histories need to be regarded as narrative data that express the migrants' subjectivities, which are inevitably influenced by their efforts at self-presentation, rather than as factual accounts. This data is supported by secondary data as well as interviews with researchers who have worked closely on migration in Vietnam. Ethical clearance was given by the University of East Anglia and by the Vietnamese Academy of Social Sciences, and all names used here are pseudonyms.

Low-income migration to Hanoi is circular: it is about investing in the rural homestead that has been left-behind, and typically 'migrant life' is perceived as a 'miserable life' and the city as an unsuitable place to raise one's rural children. Although there are differences in the distances between home village and Hanoi that structure the individual costs and difficulties of visiting, the vast majority of the women who come from the Red River Delta are able to negotiate these to visit for a few days every two weeks, or at most every month.[7] Although the 'leaving behind' of children and, until quite recently young wives too, is strongly institutionalized, family migration strategies are diverse and dynamic. Our purposive categories thus represent points on a more complex journey, and many at some point in their lives have been or will be 'left behind' or will 'leave behind' a husband or migrate separately from or together with their husbands.

Women's movements for work vary in relation to the labour migration of their husbands and in relation to the key reproductive events of marriage and childbearing (see Table 7.2).[8] Migrant mothers' experiences are not simply the inevitable consequence of having to go away for work; rather, their strategies of migration and reproduction are mutually interlinked in ways that illustrate their 'reproductive agency' (Unnithan-Kumar 2001), as well as the influence of gendered power relations with husbands and in-laws within the institutional context of prevailing social and cultural norms and economic conditions. At least five distinctive trajectories have been captured, and these reflect the fact that the timing and motivation for migration for these women was centrally about reproductive and family-building strategies. Whilst some women may migrate before and after marriage and between childbearing, almost all the women in our Hanoi sample were either at home or came home to give birth, and almost all remained at home until their baby was ready to be weaned and nearly walking. All women moved upon marriage to live with or near their in-laws. However, marriage is generally endogamous, so most women move a relatively short distance on marriage, often to the same or neighbouring commune, with important implications for the accessibility of natal kin when going or staying at home to give birth. As with fathers, a mother's migration was triggered most notably by the need to provide for a child (or children), to save (or pay back money borrowed), to buy land or build a house. However, it is evident that most women stayed at home until the birth of their first child, and this was so even in half the cases where they had migrated before marriage. Indeed, the start of childbearing and the planning of subsequent births are closely linked to women's (un)availability for migration.

The pressure to start having children as soon as possible after marriage is reflected in all the narratives, and generally militated against family planning at this stage. Newly married couples, and particularly wives, are usually co-resident with the husband's parents, and this represents a critical period for the new wife to develop relations of filial piety towards her mother-in-law. Although this did not in some cases prevent newly married women from migrating with husbands for work, producing a child takes precedence over establishing the economic basis for independent living at this stage. As Hien said: 'We [she and her husband] really wanted to have time to strengthen the household economy first. However, later, we discussed over and over, and then changed our minds. We wanted to have a child right away because a child

Table 7.2: Women's (and their husbands') migration for
work across the reproductive life course

Migrant (husband's status in brackets)	Ever migrated for work…..			
	before marriage?	after marriage and before childbearing?	after first child and before second child?	after second child?
Cuc	Y (Y)	Y (Y)	Y (Y)	Y (n/a)
Ha	Y (military service)	Y (N)	Y (N)	Y (N)
Chau	Y (Y)	Y (Y)	Y (Y)	Y (Y)
Sam	Y (Y)	Y (Y)	Y (Y)	Y (Y)
Anh	Y (military service)	N (N)	Y (N)	Y (N)
Thao	Y (Y)	N (N)	Y (Y)	n/a (n/a)
Le	Y (military service)	N (Y)	Y (Y)	Y (Y)
Thuy	Y (Y)	N (Y)	Y (Y)	n/a (n/a)
Hai	N (Y)	Y (Y)	Y (Y)	n/a (n/a)
Que	N (Y)	Y (Y)	Y (Y)	n/a (n/a)
Nga	N (N)	N (N)	Y (Y)	Y (n/a)
Hang	N (N)	N (N)	Y (N)	Y (N)
Nhan	N (N)	N (N)	Y (N)	n/a (n/a)
Mai	N (N)	N (N)	Y (Y)	Y (Y)
Dieu	N (N)	N (Y)	Y (Y)	Y (Y)
Giang	N (N)	N (N)	Y (Y)	Y (Y)
Tran	N (N)	N (Y)	N (Y)	Y (Y)
Binh	N (N)	N (N)	N (N)	Y (Y)
Hien	N (N)	N (N)	N (N)	Y (Y)
Linh	N (N)	N (N)	N (N)	Y (Y)

would cement the relationship between husband and wife, and the family would be happier'. The imperative for a wife to bear children, even in poverty, is illustrated by the pressure Hien received when she was unable to conceive for seven years after her marriage: 'My mother-in-law said that if I could not give birth to a child, she would even marry another wife for her son … [M]y father, when he was dying, told me, "Everything would be in vain"'.

However, once the first child is secured, in some cases the first son, there is more flexibility regarding delaying the birth of a second child and going away to work. In many cases in our sample, the mother-in-law allowed the young couple to 'eat separately' shortly after the birth of the first child. This first step to living independently enables the married couple to start managing their own finances and save up to build a room or a house for themselves. Although there is a strong feeling that children should be spaced at least two or three years apart for reasons of child and maternal health, in practice many migrant couples try to space children five to seven years apart so that mothers can go away to work and improve the stability of the family finances before another child arrives. As Mai said: 'We would not be able to make much money in one to two years'. Thao, who had one child, said: 'If I got pregnant now … I would have to stop working here and go home, and we have numerous problems to worry about … I could not earn any money at all … and consequently I could not concentrate on raising my child'.

Going Home to Give Birth

Despite the relatively small maternal healthcare 'gap' between Hanoi and the Red River Delta compared to other migrant-sending areas in Vietnam, the decision to give birth at home is strongly influenced by perceptions of cost, quality of care and inter-personal relations with providers, as well as cultural expectations that childbearing should occur in the mother-in-law's (or mother's) home place,[9] plus considerations about the availability of relatives to support and guide the new mother. Antenatal care at the rural Commune Health Station (CHS) is free, but pregnant women need to pay around 3,000 to 5,000 dong for medicine at each visit, and then around 100,000 to 200,000 dong for delivery and 'out of pocket' expenses (2008 prices).[10] The government also subsidises basic maternal healthcare in urban areas, but there are additional user fees for both migrants and non-migrants.[11] Urban CHS offer a 'free check', including to migrants registered as temporary residents, but are not as well equipped as rural CHS to support even normal deliveries, and most urban women get referred or go direct to the district hospital for maternal healthcare.

Maternal healthcare costs more at the level of the district hospital, and more sophisticated tests may be ordered, but the quality of doctors and availability of special clinics for expecting mothers is better. At public hospitals, there is a standard fee for normal service and normal delivery (up to 1 million dong), but superior service or more complex deliveries cost up to 2 million dong.[12] Although the larger private hospitals in Hanoi are out of reach of even most professionals, smaller private hospitals and clinics are more accessible and, despite higher costs than public hospitals, they are perceived to offer a faster service and better quality of care, particularly with respect to staff behaviour. Whilst 'free' migrants generally return to the village to give birth, 'workers' (formal employees) may be able to use the factory service, or they may have insurance and may be more able to choose to deliver in the city.

All but six women in our sample stayed at home after marriage and until their first child was born, and this included four of the eight women who had been migrating for work before marriage. Of the six who migrated as newly-weds, all came home to give birth apart from Cuc, who had begun an adulterous relationship in the city with a married man from her own commune and 'could not' return home. Of the fifteen mothers migrating after their first child, eleven have had a second child,[13] and all but two went home to give birth: Cuc was again unable to, and Nga's husband's family were residents in Hanoi.

The number of antenatal care visits our respondents reported – whether migrant or not when they first got pregnant (see Table 7.3) – seems to be in line with the more general situation in the Red River Delta, where antenatal coverage is at 98 per cent, and nationally, where the median number of antenatal consultations for those who did have antenatal care was 2.5 visits (CPFC 2003: 87).[14] Many respondents showed passive and compliant attitudes towards antenatal care rooted in part in the belief that pregnancy is not an illness, but also in the socialist style in which maternal health 'campaigns' are delivered, particularly in rural communes, by 'calling' pregnant women, often using a loud-speaker system, to the CHS for check-ups. For instance, Binh reported: 'In my village, women don't get any antenatal care', but that they were 'called' just once in the final months of pregnancy for an examination, to get iron tablets and an 'inoculation' (tetanus toxoid injection).[15] Variations in antenatal care in many cases may simply reflect variations in what the CHS in their home commune offered at the time of their births (over the period from 1994 to 2007).[16] In other cases it is clear that the decision to seek or neglect antenatal care was driven by initial ignorance at its benefits, such as Cuc, and by psycho-emotional factors, such as Hang, who was resentful at being 'pregnant against my will' because her IUD had failed.

In cases where women had migrated for work, their access to antenatal care when they got pregnant depended in part on when they decided to go back home for the birth. Some, like Anh, returned in the early months of pregnancy, particularly where morning sickness was so bad it made it difficult for them to work, but others returned only in the last month of pregnancy. Even those expectant mothers who were migrating and returned home early in the pregnancy report working 'until delivery'. However, several who returned later in pregnancy described their decision as one of avoiding excessively 'hard work', such as Anh, or environmental health hazards in the city that might damage their baby, such as Que, and they talked of going home 'to rest' (even though they resumed normal domestic and farm work duties until delivery). Almost all reported taking no special nutritional measures and

Table 7.3: Reported antenatal care for
first and second births by migration status

Migrant	Migrant before first birth?	Number of antenatal care visits first birth	Migrant before second birth?	Number of antenatal care visits second birth
Chau	Yes	Unknown	Yes	Unknown
Le	No	Unknown	Yes	Unknown
Binh	No	None	No	None
Cuc	Yes	None	Yes	None
Dieu	No	None	Yes	2 visits
Nhan	No	1 visits		
Mai	No	2 visits	Yes	2 visits
Tran	No	2 visits	No	3 visits
Nga	No	2 visits	Yes	3 visits
Thuy	No	2 visits		
Anh	No	2 visits	Yes	2 visits
Hai	Yes	2 visits		
Thao	No	3 visits		
Hien	No	3 visits	No	3 visits
Ha	Yes	3 visits	Yes	3 visits
Hang	No	3 visits	Yes	4 visits
Sam	Yes	3 visits	Yes	Unknown
Giang	No	3 visits	Yes	4 visits
Que	Yes	4 visits		
Linh	No	5+ visits	No	7 visits

some, like Nga, reported serious hardship. She said: 'We had no money then, it was difficult, and we had nothing. I had no pregnancy check-ups. I still don't understand how I could survive and live back then'.

Some of those who continued to work in Hanoi whilst pregnant, like Sam, combined urban and rural antenatal care. Some, like Ha, went home when they heard that pregnant women were being 'called' for the check-ups. Others, like Mai, delayed antenatal care until they returned home for delivery. Mai says that she didn't want to go for antenatal care in Hanoi because she was 'afraid that I was rural ... afraid to be looked down upon'. Despite the advice of development workers to use urban clinics, she added that, 'village women went home in the fourth or fifth month for examination'. Although many know or have been told by development workers, residents or other migrants that there are 'free' check-ups for expectant migrant mothers in the ward medical centre, a few migrants preferred to use private clinics that offer check-ups for between 50,000 and 100,000 dong. Chau explained that if you go for a check-up in the city 'without money' you get 'complained and grumbled at', but that in the countryside and in the private clinics you are treated better. The meaning of higher or lower usage of antenatal care needs to be interpreted with care. For instance, Hien did not have an ultrasound 'because I did not care whether it was a boy or a girl', whilst Linh's increased use of antenatal care for her second birth was to ensure that her second child was the son that she and her husband desired.

For these migrant mothers, giving birth in the city was not a realistic or attractive option. Aside from considerations of cost, fear of discrimination against rural people and the need for support from parents-in-law and parents during and after delivery, many live in extremely difficult conditions when they are working in the city, often sharing small rooms with several other migrants or migrant couples from the village. As a result, most low-income migrant mothers take it for granted that they will return to the countryside to give birth. All our respondents gave birth at a health facility[17] and had normal deliveries,[18] and none voiced any complaints about the service they received: sixteen of their first births were in a rural CHS, as were twelve of the fifteen second babies. Four respondents delivered in district or provincial hospitals for varying reasons,[19] and two had their babies in an urban setting. Nga had her second baby in Hanoi because that was where her husband's family lived. However, she went to their suburban CHS and did not, as most urban women do, go to the hospital, so as to avoid additional costs. Cuc had all her children in Hanoi, and by the time her third child was born her adulterous relationship with her 'husband' had fallen apart. Her resulting vulnerability was reflected in the fact that the doctors and her relatives put pressure on her to give her daughter up for adoption. For Cuc, giving birth 'alone' in Hanoi was not a choice but a product of her social exclusion.

For most migrant women, their preference for going home to give birth was reinforced by social expectations and the economic costs of urban childbirth. In contrast, in addition to social expectations, women's desire to remain with their children during their early childhood pulled against the economic incentive to return to migrant work in problematic ways. Below we explore what effect migrant women think leaving children behind has on their early parenting and identity as mothers.

Table 7.4: Mothers (and fathers) leaving children behind

	Age first child left behind or sent back by mother	Age first child left behind or sent back by father	Age second child left behind or sent back by mother	Age second child left behind or sent back by father
Chau	12 months; child dies at 2 years	Migrates over infancy; child dies aged 2 years	12 months	Migrates over infancy
Hang	I2 months	Father never migrates	15 months	Father never migrates
Nga	Infant taken to city at 3 months and 'sent back' at 12 months	Infant 'sent back' at 12 months	Infant born in city at mother-in-law's, taken to current residence when a few months old	Now separated from father
Giang	12 months	Father migrates when 9 months old	Child brought to city at 6 weeks, and at 1 year was still there	Father migrating over infancy
Thuy	13 months	Father migrates over infancy	n/a	n/a
Ha	14 months	Father never migrates	12 months	Father never migrates
Nhan	18 months	Father never migrates	n/a	n/a
Thao	18 months	Father migrates when child is newborn	n/a	n/a
Que	Infant taken to city at 4 months and 'sent back' at 19 months	Father migrates during birth, infant taken to city at 4 months, 'sent back' at 19 months	n/a	n/a
Hai	26 months	Father migrates over infancy, now divorced	n/a	n/a
Anh	3 years	Father never migrated, father now dead	18 months	Father never migrated, father now dead
Mai	3 years, 3 months	Father migrates 3 years 1 month	2 years	Father migrates when 3 months old
Dieu	Infant brought to city at 9 months old and then 'sent back' at 1 year	Father migrates during infancy, child brought to city at 9 months	Infant brought to city at 6 months, 'sent back' at 15 months	Father migrates during infancy, child brought to city at 9 months
Le	3 years, 8 months	Father migrates during infancy	11 months	Father migrates during infancy
Linh	4 years, 3 months	Father migrates when child is 3 years, 5 months	18 months	Father migrates when child is 8 months old
Hien	5 years	Father migrates when child is 4 years	3 years	Father migrates when child is 2 years old
Tran	5 years	Unclear: father migrating on and off during infancy	4 years	Unclear: father migrating on and off during infancy
Binh	7 years	Father migrates when child is 7 years old	2 years	Father migrates when child is 2 years old
Cuc	8 years	Child born and raised in Hanoi, 'sent back' to live with father at 8 years	7 years	Child born and raised in Hanoi, and 'sent back' to live with father at 8 years
Sam	Infant brought to city to live with father (and mother) and 'sent back' at 11 years	Infant brought to city to live with father (and mother), 'sent back' at 11 years	Infant brought to the city to live with father (and mother) at 18 months	Infant brought to city to live with father (and mother) at 18 months

Constructing Migrant Mothering

The timing of a mother's initial decision to migrate for work or her return to migration involved negotiation between her and her husband and her mother-in-law, as well as sometimes with her mother in cases where a woman's mother had taken on the care of the child. Whilst the consensus was that mothers should remain with infants during the key period of breastfeeding (at least six months), and ideally up until children began kindergarten at three years, some children were left once they reached twelve months (see Table 7.4) and all mothers resumed hard rural work around the village leaving infants in the daytime care of grandmother or other relatives within a few months of their birth.

Whilst 'free' migrants often remain at home with newborns for a year or more, 'workers' are tied to the provisions of maternity-leave entitlements (officially four months, but often only two months in private factories and small businesses), which cuts short the breastfeeding period and places them under pressure to return to work more quickly. However, some 'free' migrants and many 'workers' with babies who are too young to be weaned persuade mothers or mothers-in-law to come and live with them in the city, or access private childminders or nursery care to look after their child whilst they work (see Table 7.4). Que, Dieu, Giang and Sam all brought young infants too small to be weaned to the city,[20] and Cuc and Nga both raised children in the city. The difficulties migrant mothers face in raising very young children in the city vary in relation to the types of work they do, the security of their incomes and the support they have available to them.

Giang raised her first son at home to the age of one year, but brought her second son to Hanoi when he was six weeks old. She worked at night carrying goods in the market, whilst her mother stayed with her baby in their shared room. Whilst her first child was exclusively breastfed until four months, being fed when Giang went home or the baby was brought to the fields, her second child needed extra bottle feeds from six weeks because Giang worked throughout the night. She says that her second son is sickly, and she blames this on his inadequate early nutrition: 'he could not be well and regularly breastfed because I had to work at night'. Dieu too brought both her children to the city, but as somewhat older infants, from nine months and six months respectively, and as a fruit seller she was able to break off from work to come home and breastfeed at regular intervals. Sam says that she and her husband were the first couple from her commune to take a baby with them to Hanoi. They used a small private nursery (costing 200,000 dong a month), and she worked as a housemaid while her husband worked as a shoe cleaner, taking it in turn to drop and collect their child. Nga separated from her violent, gambling husband a year before our interview, and was deeply in debt. Her children (then eleven and eight years old) stayed in their room in the city alone while she worked running a chicken butcher's stall. She started work at midnight, and worked all day; the children had to 'look after one another'. Although they went to school, there was nobody to help them study, and 'they have to teach themselves'.

Strikingly, many migrant mothers who had left children behind justify their actions. They contrast the negligence of leaving young children alone in the city during working hours with the normality of being cared for by grandparents in the countryside, even when the migrant woman is co-resident with her mother. Although Mai (a porter) says that 'It [would be] better to stay home because my child was still young', she emphasized that she came to Hanoi when her child was only eighteen months old because she and her husband were 'still poor' and 'had nothing', and she presented her earning as 'for' her baby. Crucially, she stressed that she did not 'just wean and go', but invested considerable effort in socializing her baby into her mother-in-law's primary care.

Migrant mothers reported that they did not face any negative criticism from villagers for leaving their children because of widely recognized economic realities. For example, Mai feels that, as a migrant, 'our children do not have the same care like those kids whose parents stay at home', but she offered a justification common amongst Vietnam's migrants when she said that:

I think a mother who stays but cannot provide for her children is not as good as migrant people like us. We come here to work because the money is quick. We work in the morning and have money in the afternoon. We have money to pay school fees. That's better than those staying at home. That's what I think. Those mothers who carry bricks at home are not paid for months. They have no money to pay school fees, and the teacher sends their children home.

Patterns of chain migration mean that there have been substantial shifts in social norms within communes where female migration has become more established. Binh (a compact-disc seller in Hanoi) said:

In my home village there are many people migrating to Hanoi. We all understand that, because of the difficulties in life, people have to leave their children at home to go to big cities to earn a living. No mother or father wants to leave their children behind … [P]eople do not think mothers, like me, are bad mothers, because they leave their children at home to come here to earn a living [and] not to go wandering aimlessly around.

Narratives like those offered by Mai and Binh play well with the official ideology of the *doi moi* era, which selectively reinterprets traditional norms and promotes 'happy families' that are economically stable as a result of a wife's as well as a husband's productive income generation (Pham Van Bich 1999; Pettus 2003; Rydstrom 2006).

Despite the strong social expectation that parents should live with their children, in the context of economic transition migration offers the possibility for women and men to ensure their children's nutrition and continued education. As Linh (a porter in Hanoi) noted: 'I have to migrate for work when they are still young. I am worried about them. But I cannot do anything about that. If I want to provide for them, I have to migrate. But when I migrate, I cannot take care of them'. The implications of parental absence are constructed by migrants in ways that are strongly gendered, both in relation to children and parents, and in relation to children's age. Migrants attempt to manage their parenting from a distance in various ways that go beyond the sending of regular remittances and frequent visits home. Migrant mothers in Hanoi who have left young children at home commonly visit for a few days every two weeks, or at the very least every month, and more often if circumstances such as a child's illness require it. Strategies of maintaining parenting included fostering direct contacts with children's teachers through telephone conversations when away from the village, and personal visits when home. Many reported the poor quality of rural education, but the much greater cost and real difficulties of school admission for migrant children in urban areas (as a result of the household registration system) and the problems of out-of-school care prevented many from bringing their children to study in the city. It is notable that migrant mothers construct their visits home as being about 'taking care' of their children, whilst migrant fathers go home 'to visit'.

Migrants are deeply concerned that the long term emotional impact of parental absence on their children will lead to an absence of proper 'sentiments' between parents and children, both in terms of love but also in terms of attitudes of respect that are vital not only materially but also emotionally and spiritually to the continuity of lineages. Most hope their children will understand their absences, and mothers explain the necessity of their absences to older children. Dieu reports how her young child was distant from her during visits home until she reached three years of age and could understand better that Dieu was her mother. Despite the female migrants' efforts to portray their work as parenting, they all expressed strong feelings of grief and loss that they had to suppress to get on with their tasks. Tran openly said that she was a 'poor mother' because of her absences. Parental migration for work by mothers is constructed as a 'sacrifice' that is required of them as part of their obligations to their children.

For many migrant mothers in Hanoi, then, the period when their children are 'still young' and their mothers-in-law are 'not yet old' represents a window of opportunity to migrate to earn money so as to improve their family's financial position. As Linh said, 'we can't work here forever', and most hope to be able to return once children are further on with schooling and reach an age where they need close moral and social guidance. However, it is evident that despite this hope that many are unable to return home because of the lack of income-earning opportunities in rural areas. Others envisage having to return when their mother-in-law is no longer able or available to take care of their grandchildren. Although many fear being forced to return home because of the implications of increased family poverty, those migrant women who have become 'stranded in the city' are in the most vulnerable situation. This is reflected in various cases: Hai did not feel comfortable in her natal village after her divorce, Cuc had been driven out of her village after the disintegration of her adulterous relationship, and Le remained in the city because of the pro-longed mental illness of her husband, whilst her children (then thirteen and eight respectively) live alone in the countryside.[21]

Conclusion

For the mothers in this study, staying at home to conceive their first child was important in forging resilient bonds with their husband and their husband's family. The few who went away to work after marriage, and the many who subsequently went away to work after their first child was born, all returned home to give birth. Aside from differentiated entitlements in urban areas, poor urban living conditions and the absence of supportive relatives, the cultural convention of giving birth at one's mother-in-law's rural place meant that migrant mothers took it for granted that they would have their babies in the countryside. Mothers who were away from home during their pregnancy returned there when living or working in the city became too hard, and either delayed antenatal care until their return, visited home when they knew women were being 'called' to prenatal examinations in their communes, or used urban facilities. Despite generally passive attitudes towards antenatal care, migrant women expressed preferences for rural services or private clinics. The maternal healthcare 'gap' between Hanoi and the Red River Delta is relatively small, and 'going home to give birth' is strongly institutionalized.[22]

Migrant mothers use discursive strategies to justify leaving children behind and to represent their absence for income generation as important parenting work. At the same time, absent mothers actively manage their parenting roles through sending remittances, by visiting home and through various means of keeping in touch with their children's carers, teachers and the children them-selves. Nevertheless, migrant mothers remain extremely concerned with the emotional impact of their absence on their children, and many migrant mothers plan to return to their village (or for their husbands to do so) when the child enters school. Migrant strategies for managing raising young children involve struggles over family roles,[23] but, between three years and the early teenage years, children's parenting needs are perceived as being less complex. In contrast to public policy fears that parents' migration may endanger young children's health, nutrition and education, all the migrants stressed that it was only through migration that they could ensure that their children were properly nourished, got medicine when they were sick and were not sent home from school because fees were unpaid or they lacked school uniform.

Female migrants closely link their understandings of the meaning of their absences to the performance of their social identities as mothers, and they argue that it is better to be able to provide for their children than to stay at home and be unable to feed, clothe, educate or buy medicine for them. Nevertheless, mothers express grief at being separated from their children, revealing the importance of 'emotional and psychological struggles' entailed in leaving children behind (Toyota et al. 2007: 157). Migrant mothers' perspectives suggest that migration does improve the lives of their children, but it also entails a 'lack of sentiment' between children and mothers. The mothers' own 'miserable lives' involve 'accepting the sacrifice' of living separately from children, and whilst most hope that their absence will only be temporary, others cannot see how they can ever earn a sufficient living for their family in the countryside. Contemporary government policy in Vietnam builds on traditional expectations that wives 'help' their husbands through contributing to productive household income, and both support some mothers' desires to migrate as well as adding pressure on other mothers who wish to stay behind. In both cases, casting women's migration as parenting work obscures the contradictions between their parental obligations and their desire to provide everyday care for their children.

Acknowledgements

The research on which this chapter draws was funded by the Economic and Social Research Council (ESRC) and the Department for International Development of the UK (UKAid). Any errors or view expressed remain the responsibility of the authors.

Notes

1. Kuat Thu Huong, Institute for Social Development Studies, Hanoi (personal communication, 11 November 2008).
2. There is a long history of 'visiting marriages' (Pham Van Bich 1999; Kabeer and Thi Van Anh 2002; Resurreccion and Khanh 2007) in which the husband

migrated for work, leaving his wife and children behind, particularly in the north of the country.

3. These figures must be treated with caution as they represent all women surveyed in the 2004 migration survey (GSO 2005). Whilst they are reasonably representative of all migrants in Vietnam, they are not necessarily a good indicator of the behaviour of migrants to Hanoi and Ho Chi Minh City, for which no disaggregated figures are available.

4. The points in the previous two sentences were also made clear to us by Tran Thi Van Anh, Institute for Family and Gender Studies, Hanoi (personal communication, 10 March 2008).

5. Urban women are more likely to receive antenatal care from trained medical staff than rural women (96 per cent versus 84 per cent), and are more likely to get that care from a doctor as opposed to a nurse or a midwife. Whilst there is no data disaggregated by wealth difference, 48 per cent of those with no education receive no antenatal care, compared to 10 per cent of those who have completed primary school and 4 per cent of those who have completed lower secondary school (CPFC 2003: 86). Those who do not receive any antenatal care miss out on preventative measures that are important for protecting the health of mother and child (ibid.: 88). Although there are large regional differences, antenatal coverage is highest in the Red River Delta (at 98 per cent).

6. It must be remembered that our sample is extremely small and not representative, and that it does not capture women who migrated during their peak childbearing years and subsequently remained living in the countryside. Our attention is firmly on the experiences, strategies and representations of mothers who were migrating whilst they were bearing and rearing young children.

7. This is in contrast to the migrant mothers we interviewed from Ho Chi Minh City, many of whom migrated over long distances and were only able to visit home once a year for the Tet festival. The disruptive implications of this much greater distance for remote parenting strategies are discussed in detail in Locke et al. (2012).

8. Although not the subject of this chapter, it is worth emphasising the diversity of fathering strategies (see Table 7.2): whilst some men migrate across their entire working life, and continue to do so through the birth and early years of their children, others only start migrating when they are building a new family, and some find ways to be closer to home for their children's birth and early infancy. This evidence stands in contrast to the prevailing negative assumptions about migrant men and their fathering roles, and will be explored in depth in future publications.

9. It is quite common in northern Vietnam for a woman to have her baby, especially her first, at her mother's house, or at least to spend some of the early days with her, or for her mother to come and stay at her mother-in-law's house to look after her (Kuat Thu Huong, Institute for Social Development Studies, Hanoi, personal communication, 11 November 2008). There is some flexibility in this practice. For instance, Thuy stated that her husband and mother-in-law advised her to have her baby at her mother's house because her mother-in-law was old and her brother-in-law's family were young, so there was nobody to help and her mother's

house was closer to medical facilities. However, endogamy means that a woman's parents and in-laws often live nearby to one another, sometimes in the same commune, enabling strong access to natal kin.

10. Vietnam's Ministry of Health reports that more than half of maternal health clients do not pay for antenatal consultations, but that 80 per cent had to pay for delivery, and that for about 60 per cent of these clients delivery cost in excess of 100,000 dong (MoH 2003: 19).

11. Tran Hung Minh, Consultation of Investment in Health Promotion (CHIP), Hanoi (personal communication, 12 March 2008).

12. Tran Hung Minh, Consultation of Investment in Health Promotion (CHIP), Hanoi (personal communication, 12 March 2008). Although health insurance was opened up to non-government employees in 2008, low-income workers in the private sector cannot afford the contributions (around 200,000 to 400,000 dong a month, with varying proportions of medicine costs left uncovered), and thus are seldom covered.

13. The numbers of women in our sample with third children was very small, and we have not considered these births here.

14. This average falls well below the WHO recommendation of 4 antenatal care visits for 'normal' pregnancies (Abou-Zahr and Wardlow 2003).

15. This also suggests problems with reported numbers of visits. Binh told us she had no antenatal care, but it is clear from her interview that she did attend one antenatal visit for each birth. Table 7.3 shows women's self-reports.

16. Equity in antenatal care deteriorated seriously in Vietnam during the 1990s (Wagstaff and Nguyen 2004: 343). Overall uptake has improved since the late 1990s, but there remain marked inequalities.

17. Over 90 per cent of births in the Red River Delta occur in health facilities (as compared to 99 per cent of urban births), and physical proximity to facilities is not a problem. However, nationally only 63 per cent of district hospitals provide comprehensive obstetric services, and only 14.3 per cent of health facilities at district and provincial levels were capable of providing emergency obstetric services (MoH 2003: 20). However, the lifetime risk of maternal mortality for the Red River is relatively low.

18. However, there were two reported miscarriages (Giang and Thuy), an ectopic pregnancy (also Thuy) and a termination (Tran), and many women experienced worries and some received tests and treatment for delays in conceiving.

19. Cuc had all her births in a public hospital in Hanoi because she could not return to her home place; Que delivered her first baby in a provincial hospital because there was a high risk of needing a Caesarean, which her CHS could not handle; Chau delivered in a provincial hospital because she was afraid of a difficult labour and something happening; and Thao delivered in a provincial hospital because the CHS was cut off by heavy rains and the hospital was closer at land.

20. Although breastfeeding is very common in Vietnam (98 per cent of children are breastfed at some time), there is a trend towards early supplementation of breast milk with foodstuffs as well as water, and only 30 per cent of infants of one month old are still being exclusively breastfed. The initiation and duration of breastfeeding are important for maternal and infant health, with early initiation

recommended and exclusive breastfeeding for four to six months. Although 9 per cent of six-month-old babies are no longer breastfed, at 18 months over 50 per cent are not and by two years 90 per cent are not (CPFC 2003: 105). In line with this national picture, our respondents generally supplemented breast milk when they felt they did not have enough, children needed more food or they needed to be gone for longer hours for rural work; the children who were left behind at a younger age were obviously weaned before their mothers went away to work.

21. Although other relatives, neighbours and the teacher in the commune may keep a loose eye on them when their mother is away, none is appointed as their guardian. The children live on their own as an independent household (doing their own cooking, cleaning and washing, and managing their daily activities and school work themselves).

22. Whilst 24 per cent and 27 per cent of Vietnam's population was urban in 2000 and 2005 respectively (GSO 2001, 2006b), only 17 per cent of its births in 2002 were urban (WHO 2009: 1).

23. Kuat Thu Huong, Institute for Social Development Studies, Hanoi (personal communication, 11 November 2008).

References

Abou-Zahr, C.L., and T. Wardlow. 2003. *Antenatal Care in Developing Countries: Promises, Achievements and Missed Opportunities – An Analysis of Trends, Levels and Differentials, 1990–2001*. Geneva: World Health Organization.

Bledsoe, C. 1994. '"Children Are Like Young Bamboo Trees": Potentiality and Reproduction in Sub-Saharan Africa', in K.L. Keissling and H. Landberg (eds), *Population, Economic Development and Environment: The Making of Our Common Future*. Oxford: Oxford University Press, pp.105–38.

Chant, S. (ed.). 1992. *Gender and Migration in Developing Countries*. London: Belhaven Press.

Cornwall, A. 2001. 'Looking for a Child: Coping with Infertility in Ado-do, South-Western Nigeria', in S. Tremayne (ed.), *Managing Reproductive Life: Cross-cultural Themes in Fertility and Sexuality*. Oxford: Berghahn, pp.140–56.

CPFC. 2003. 'Vietnam: Demographic and Health Survey 2002'. Calverton, MD: Committee for Population, Family and Children and ORC Macro.

Davin, D. 1996. 'Gender and Rural–Urban Migration in China', *Gender and Development* 4(1): 24–30.

Goodkind, D. 1996. 'State Agendas, Local Sentiments: Vietnamese Wedding Practices amidst Socialist Transformations', *Social Forces* 75(2): 717–42.

GoV. 2002. 'Comprehensive Poverty Reduction and Growth Strategy'. Hanoi: Government of Vietnam.

Greenhalgh, S. 1995. 'Anthropology Theorizes Reproduction: Integrating Practice, Political Economic and Feminist Perspectives', in S. Greenhalgh (ed.), *Situating Fertility: Anthropology and Demographic Inquiry*. Cambridge: Cambridge University Press, pp.3–28.

GSO. 2001. 'Vietnam Statistical Yearbook'. Hanoi: Government Statistical Office.

———— 2005. 'The 2004 Migration Survey: Major Findings'. Hanoi: Government Statistical Office.

———— 2006a. 'The 2004 Migration Survey: Internal Migration and Related Life Course Events'. Hanoi: Government Statistical Office.

———— 2006b. 'Vietnam Statistical Yearbook'. Hanoi: Government Statistical Office.

Guest, P. 1998. 'The Dynamics of Internal Migration in Viet Nam', Discussion Paper 1. Hanoi: United Nations Development Programme.

Hirschman, C., and N.H. Minh. 2002. 'Tradition and Change in Vietnamese Family Structure in the Red River Delta', *Journal of Marriage and the Family* 64(4): 1063–79.

Hoy, C. 1999. 'Issues in the Fertility of Temporary Migrants to Beijing', in F. Pieke and H. Mallee (eds), *Internal and International Migration: Chinese Perspectives*. Richmond: Curzon Press, pp.134–56.

Jensen, R., D.M. Peppard and T.M.T. Vu. 2008. 'Women's Circular Migration in Vietnam: A Study of Hanoi's Roving Street Vendors', unpublished paper presented at the Vietnam Study Conference, National Convention Centre, Hanoi, 5–7 December.

Johansson, A. 1998. *Dreams and Dilemmas: Women and Family Planning in Rural Vietnam*. Stockholm: The Division of International Health (IHCAR), The Karolinska Institute.

Kabeer, N., and Thi Van Anh. 2002. 'Leaving the Rice Fields, but Not the Countryside', in S. Rasavi (ed.), *Shifting Burdens: Gender and Agrarian Change Under Neoliberalism*. Bloomfield, CT: Kumarian Press, pp.109–50.

Klingberg-Allvin, M., B. Nguyen, A. Johansson and V. Berggren. 2008. 'One Foot Wet and One Foot Dry: Transition into Motherhood among Married Adolescent Women in Rural Vietnam', *Journal of Transcultural Nursing* 19(4): 338–46.

Lan Anh Hoang. 2008. 'Social Structures and the Ability to Choose: Migration Decision-making in Rural Vietnam', PhD diss. Norwich: School of Development Studies, University of East Anglia.

Le Grand, T., T. Koppenhover, N. Mondian and S. Randall. 2003. 'Reassessing the Insurance Effect: A Qualitative Analysis of Fertility Behaviour in Senegal and Zimbabwe', *Population Development Review* 29(3): 375–403.

Locke, C., Nguyen Thi Ngan Hoa and Nguyen Thi Thanh Tam. 2008. 'The Institutional Context Influencing Rural–urban Migration Choices and Strategies for Young Married Women and Men in Vietnam', Research Report for the Project 'Linking Migration, Reproduction and Well-being'. Norwich: University of East Anglia.

————. 2012. 'Struggling to Sustain Marriages and Build Families: Mobile Husbands/Wives and Mothers/Fathers in Hanoi and Ho Chi Minh, *Journal of Vietnamese Studies* 7(4): 63–91.

MoH. 2003. 'National Plan on Safe Motherhood in Vietnam 2003–2010: An Implementation of National Strategy on Reproductive Healthcare 2001–2010'. Hanoi: Ministry of Health.

Murphy, R. 2002. *How Migrant Labour is Changing Rural China*. Cambridge: Cambridge University Press.

Parrenas, R.S. 2001. 'Mothering from a Distance: Emotions, Gender and Inter-generational Relations in Filipino Transnational Families', *Feminist Studies* 27(2): 361–90.

Pettus, A. 2003. *Between Sacrifice and Desire: National Identity and the Governing of Femininity in Vietnam*. London: Routledge.

Pham Van Bich. 1999. *The Vietnamese Family in Change: The Case of the Red River Delta*. Richmond: Curzon Press.

Phinney, H.M. 2008. '"Rice is Essential but Tiresome, You Should Get Some Noodles": Doi moi and the Political Economy of Men's Extramarital Sexual Relations and Marital HIV Risk in Hanoi, Vietnam', *American Journal of Public Health* 98(4): 650–60.

Resurreccion, B.P. and H.T.C. Khanh. 2007. 'Able to Come and Go: Reproducing Gender in Female Rural–Urban Migration in the Red River Delta', *Population, Space and Place* 13: 211–24.

Rydstrom, H. 2006. 'Sexual Desires and "Social Evils": Young Women in Rural Vietnam', *Gender, Place and Culture* 13(3): 283–301.

Rydstrom, H., and L. Drummond. 2004. 'Introduction', in L. Drummond and H. Rydstrom (eds), *Gender Practices in Contemporary Vietnam*. Singapore/Copenhagen: Singapore University Press/Nordic Institute of Asian Studies Press, pp.1–25.

Santillan, D., et al. 2004. 'Developing Indicators to Assess Women's Empowerment in Vietnam', *Development in Practice* 14(4): 534–49.

Summerfield, G. 1997. 'Economic Transition in China and Vietnam: Crossing the Poverty Line is Just the First Step for Women and Their Families', *Review of Social Economy* 55(2): 201–14.

Toyota, M., B.S.A. Yeoh and L. Nguyen. 2007. 'Bringing the "Left Behind" Back into View in Asia: A Framework for Understanding the "Migration-Left Behind Nexus"', *Population, Space and Place* 13: 157–61.

Tremayne, S. 2001. 'Introduction', in S. Tremayne (ed.), *Managing Reproductive Life: Cross-cultural Themes in Fertility and Sexuality*. Oxford: Berghahn, pp.1–24.

UNFPA. 2004. 'Mid-term Review: Viet Nam-UNFPA 6th Country Programme (2001–2005)'. Hanoi: United Nations Fund for Population Activities.

Unnithan-Kumar, M. 2001. 'Emotion, Agency and Access to Healthcare: Women's Experiences of Reproduction in Jaipur', in S. Tremayne (ed.), *Managing Reproductive Life: Cross-cultural Themes in Fertility and Sexuality*. Oxford: Berghahn, pp.27–51.

Wagstaff, A., and Nga Nguyet Nguyen. 2004. 'Poverty and Survival Prospects of Vietnamese Children under Doi Moi', in P. Glewwe, N. Agrawal and D. Dollar (eds), *Economic Growth, Poverty and Household Welfare in Vietnam*. Washington: World Bank, pp.313–50.

Werner, J. 2004. 'Managing Womanhoods in the Family: Gendered Subjectivities and the State in the Red River Delta', in L. Drummond and H. Rydstrom (eds), *Gender Practices in Contemporary Vietnam*. Singapore/Copenhagen: Singapore University Press/Nordic Institute of Asian Studies Press, pp.26–46.

WHO. 2009. 'Vietnam Country Profile'. Geneva: Department of Making Pregnancy Safer, World Health Organization.

Wisensale, S.K. 1999. 'Marriage and Family Law in a Changing Vietnam', *Journal of Family Issues* 20(5): 602–16.

Zhang, H.Q. 1999. 'Female Migration and Urban Labour Markets in Tianjin', *Development and Change* 30(1): 21–41.

CHAPTER 8

'A *City Walla* Prefers a Small Family'

Son Preference and Sex Selection among Punjabi Migrant Families in Urban India

Sunil K. Khanna

Although the relationship between culture and fertility is well established in scholarly literature (Basu 1992; Greenhalgh 1995; Sheker and Hatti 2010), only recently have scholars paid attention to the role of cultural factors in defining family building or family composition processes, especially among migrant groups (Bledsoe 2004; Carling 2008; Khanna 2010). Much of the work on examining the complex relationship between culture and fertility is in the broad area of anthropological demography – an interdisciplinary perspective that adopts explanatory models from both anthropology and demography to examine the complex relationship between culture and key demographic variables, namely fertility, mortality and migration (Kertzer and Fricke 1997; Basu and Aaby 1998; Coast et al. 2007; Johnson-Hanks 2007). In this chapter I adopt an interdisciplinary approach combining both anthropological and demographic methods of data collection and explanatory perspectives to examine the complex relationship between culture and reproductive outcomes in a community of internal migrants in India.

I draw on micro-demographic and ethnographic research in Punjab Vihar (a pseudonym) – a residential cluster or neighbourhood in New Delhi exclusively inhabited by first generation immigrant families from the north Indian state of Punjab – to examine the regulation of fertility and family composition in this community. Emphasizing their current urban residence, immigrant couples in this cluster identify themselves as 'urban people' or 'urbanites' (*city wallas*), thus distinguishing themselves from their rural roots. I focus on 'desired' and 'actual' family size and sex composition among immigrant

Punjabi married couples, particularly in relation to shifting notions of self and family brought about by migration experience, education, employment, and urban residence.[1] Finally, I discuss the extent to which an anthropological demographic approach, informed by ethnography, can be used to explain family-building behaviour in an internal migrant community experiencing rapid cultural transformation and globalization.

The region of Punjab is considered in the literature as representative of the larger northwestern area of India in terms of kinship organization, gender relations, women's decision-making power and levels of women's autonomy. Communities from this region practice patrilineal kinship, patrilocal residence after marriage, village exogamy and correspondingly a strong son preference (Dyson and Moore 1983; Oppenheim 1984; Rahman and Rao 2004). Scholars have used unique historical and cultural characteristics to explain demographic outcomes – fertility rates, family size, sex differentials in child morbidity and mortality, sex ratio and desired versus actual family size and sex composition in the region (Das Gupta 1987; Basu 1992; Agarwal 1994; Khanna 1997; Rustagi 2006; Fernandez and Fogli 2009).

Studies among groups of internal migrants in India and elsewhere suggest that, in comparison to their non-migrant counterparts, migrant women and families experience less negative reproductive outcomes, small family size, balanced family sex composition (equal numbers of daughters and sons) and increased parental investment of household resources in children (Khan and Raeside 1997; Cleland 2001; Mace 2008). These and several other studies point to an increase in women's level of education, overall household income and accessibility to and use of healthcare services as possible outcomes of migration and settlement, and support the observation that urban residence and improvement in household income are positively associated with a small family size, decline in son preference and a balanced family sex composition (Bhat and Zavier 2003; Chung and Das Gupta 2007). Nevertheless, only a few studies use an ethnographic perspective to examine preferences for family size and sex composition among married couples living in urban areas in India (Basu 1992; Wadley 1993; Khanna 1997).

In an effort to 'situate' demographic behaviour in its cultural context, scholars have proposed explanatory models in terms of a preference for sons, inheritance rules regarding family name, property and assets, marriage customs and practices, and women's education and participation in income-generating activities (Greenhalgh 1995; Kertzer and Fricke 1997; Khanna 2001; Sudha and Rajan 2003). Cultural explanations of demographic behaviour become especially relevant when one examines reproductive outcomes and family-building strategies among migrant communities (Basu 1992). Building on studies which examine the social 'location' of reproductive behaviour and demographic outcomes from a cross-cultural perspective (Greenhalgh

1995), this chapter examines family-building strategies – family size and sex composition – and the means undertaken to achieve these preferences by married couples living in Punjab Vihar.

Residential Clustering in New Delhi

New Delhi provides an ideal opportunity for documenting the experiences of migrants, especially decision-making processes related to family size and sex composition. For the past three decades, the city has been one of the most common destinations for internal migrants looking for employment and access to a growing urban environment. Tens of thousands of people move into the city annually, making it the fastest growing region in the country. Punjab Vihar is located in a recently developed neighbourhood characterized by a residential pattern that can be described as 'residential clustering' (Srinivas 1966) – a common characteristic observed among migrant communities living in New Delhi. By living in close proximity, families obtain benefits in terms of recreating residential and community characteristics that, to some extent, mimic their traditional cultural environment (Khandelwal 2002).

Couples in Punjab Vihar have maintained varied levels of contact with their relatives living in their native state of Punjab. During my research they described to me the benefits of living in close proximity with people who share their regional, linguistic and religious background, and expressed a sense of neighbourhood familiarity and security. A sense of shared community acts as a strong regulatory force on individual and family behaviour. However, some residents feel unduly pressured by the community's efforts to maintain an excessively parochial social network. They feel a sense of 'intrusion' by their neighbours in such matters as family size, child spacing, son preference, children's education and women's employment. Clearly, the discourse surrounding this dual adjustment process is far from homogeneous. While some families feel residential clustering as a way of maintaining their identity and culture, the critics have seized on the isolationist mindset of and attempts by conservative families to control the neighbourhood. This reveals how individuals construct their own views about the benefits and limitations of 'residential clustering', depending on their immediate personal and family circumstances.

Table 8.1: Demographic profile of Punjab Vihar

	Punjab Vihar (n=60)
Mean age at marriage for women	22.3
Mean family size	4.0
Child sex ratio (0 to 6 years)[1]	890
Mean annual family income[2]	$28,800
Number of single-income families (only husband employed)	10 (17 per cent)
Number of double-income families	50 (83 per cent)
Number of men with at least high-school degree	60 (100 per cent)
Number of women with at least high-school degree	54 (90 per cent)

Notes
1. Sex ratio is calculated as number of females per thousand males.
2. These figures are based on the 2009 currency exchange rate of $1 = 45 rupees.

Punjab Vihar: Socio-demographic Profiles

Twenty-two (approximately 37 per cent) of the women respondents I worked with in Punjab Vihar were between 25 and 29 years of age. The majority of couples is reproductively active, and has not yet achieved their desired family composition. Notwithstanding intra-community variation in household income, all sample families can be described as 'wealthy' by Indian income standards (see Table 8.1): most families either own their homes or make regular mortgage payments. More men than women are professionally qualified as doctors, engineers, government officers or university professors. The average family size in Punjab Vihar is 4.0, which is markedly lower than that reported for Delhi (5.0) and for India as a whole (5.3). Thirty families in Punjab Vihar have two children; eighteen families have three; and eight families have only one child. Boys outnumber girls in the 0 to 6 years age range in Punjab Vihar (sex ratio 890 girls per 1000 boys). The child sex ratio among respondent families is lower than India's national child sex ratio (927 girls per 1000 boys).

At 22.3 years, the average age at marriage among women in Punjab Vihar is slightly higher than that reported for Punjab (20.5 years) and India (18.3 years). Several women reported delaying their marriage by approximately one year so that they could complete their education, obtain a reliable job or achieve financial stability before getting married or having children. Punjabi women suggested that their participation in income-generating activities has increased their decision-making power over household matters, especially regarding decisions about family size and the education of children. This finding is consistent with evidence that suggests that educated and employed women, especially in urban areas, are more likely to postpone marriage, use contraceptive methods for child spacing or limiting family size, and seek balanced sex composition in the family (Dharmalingam and Morgan 1996; Jeffery and Basu 1998; Jejeeboy 1998; Nath et al. 1999).

Family Size in Punjab Vihar:
Balancing Career Goals and Family-building Preferences

Qualitative data collected during in-depth interviews with fifteen couples in Punjab Vihar forms the basis of the following discussion of family size and sex composition.[2] All the couples stated that household income and professional demands played a key role in determining their desired family size. According to a 28-year-old woman:

> When I got married, I wanted to have a large family – at least three children. After my second child, I decided that I simply could not manage my career and raising two kids. Another reason for not having a large family is the amount of money it takes to send children to good schools. Government (*sarkari*) schools are bad – run down buildings, incompetent teachers and crime. You have to send children to private schools, which is expensive.

For Punjab Vihar couples, small family size symbolizes being educated and urban. Most informants negatively portrayed a large family size as symbolic of illiteracy and ignorance on the part of the parents. Some suggested that a large family size reflects a lack of knowledge about contraceptives or a willingness to adapt to a modern and urban lifestyle. According to a 28-year-old woman:

> It is just not the modern thing to do. New Delhi is an urban place, and people who live here are well educated and professionally successful. Some parents forget that they are living in a city. They continue to believe what their parents believe and continue to live like them. As a result, they end up having large families and are unable to manage them. I am a *city walla*, and a *city walla* prefers a small family. What I mean is that people living in villages who have many children are not able to provide them with a good education and upbringing. A small family is good for both parents and children. Parents can take good care of their children. Well-educated children can become doctors, engineers, managers etc. These careers pay well.

When one examines the opinions and values of Punjab Vihar couples that underlie their family size preferences, the most common emergent theme is the incompatibility between a large family and urban living. Working couples believe that, relative to their financial situation and professional demands, a small family is a strong determinant of the future prosperity for their children and grandchildren. Couples are acutely aware of the economic advantages of a small family, and this awareness directly translates into their reproductive choices and behaviour. While some couples do not see any conflict between balancing family size and career demands, others feel a sense of contradiction between taking advantage of the available professional opportunities and their obligations to create a large family as traditionally defined by the wider Punjabi community. However, one gets a strong sense that the couples in the sample as a whole shared many common reasons for their own desired family size. These included a perceived need for educating and providing support to children, fear of being ridiculed by neighbours and friends for having a large family, adopting the behaviour expected from an educated and urban individual, and complying with the national interest to control India's growing population. These shared concerns primarily reflect how married Punjabi couples rationalize adjusting their family-building strategies to their urban experiences.

Sons and/or Daughters: Family Sex Composition in Punjab Vihar

A large body of literature suggests that son preference is strongly associated with fertility behaviour and family size in India and that, in comparison to communities in South India, son preference is stronger in communities in the North (Wadley 1994; Sudha and Rajan 2003; Pande and Astone 2007). Scholars have explained son preference among communities in Punjab, as evidenced in the form of a historically established masculine sex ratio, as being based on the region's peasant past and ethos, and a strict adherence to patrilineal kinship and patrilocal residence after marriage (Das Gupta 1987; Agnihotri 2000; Jha et al. 2006). While scholars have heavily focused on examining the reasons for and implications of son preference within its historical context, there is scant research that examines son preference and its implications for family size among migrant communities from Punjab (McCartney and Gill 2007). Little ethnographic information is available on how the migration and adjustment experience impacts upon cultural characteristics associated with son preference, daughter neglect and family-building strategies. Therefore, this study specifically tried to investigate son preference among Punjab Vihar couples. Learning about the desired number of sons and daughters and the reasons for the 'stated' desire are important for examining the possible relationship between son preference and family.

In rural communities, the preponderance of a large family size suggests that couples continue to have children in order to have a desired number of sons per family. However, in urban communities many aspects of modernization – education, employment, the availability of contraceptives and the easy accessibility of new reproductive technologies – not only temper son preference, but also provide the means to achieve a desired family composition without increasing family size (Khanna et al. 2009). An analysis of qualitative data collected during in-depth interviews revealed two broad patterns with regard to the 'desired' preference for family sex composition among Punjab Vihar couples.

The majority of couples (ten out of fifteen) in Punjab Vihar expressed a strong desire for a sex-balanced family. According to a 36-year-old woman:

> A small and balanced family shows that we are different. People stereotype our Punjabi community as having a large family and holding a strong discriminatory attitude towards daughters. My husband and I want to show that not all Punjabis are alike. There are differences between a rural Punjabi family and an urban one. We are city wallas and we are different. Because we live in this city, we have more income, better living standards and higher education than our relatives who live in Punjab. As a city family, we are modern, and we are open-minded. We want our children, whether sons or daughters, to be educated and have successful careers.

Other informants expressed similar views on 'desired' family sex composition. The couples strongly felt that a small and sex-balanced family size is adaptive to their urban lifestyle. It reflects their improved educated and economic status, and conforms to the new 'urban' values that they now perceive to be a core element of their identity. The results of the study show how expectations of family sex composition not only are transformed by urban residence, but reflect a newly adopted urban identity. Among Punjab Vihar couples, the reasons for desiring a sex-balanced family are multiple, but a major explanation for their desire reflects an admiration for and an eagerness to adapt to an urban style of living.

Notwithstanding the majority view on 'desired' family sex composition, five couples in Punjab Vihar reported a preference for two sons and one daughter. They cited financial reasons for not having more than one daughter, expressing concerns for wedding and dowry expenses. The couples justified their desire for at least two sons in terms of security in old age, financial stability, social prestige and the risk associated with raising a daughter in the city. The following words of a 35-year-old woman clearly express these views:

> We are a bit more traditional than other families in the locality. My husband and I wanted three children. Fortunately, we have two sons and a daughter. My youngest child is a girl. Of course, I did want one of my children to be a girl. That is why I did not stop after I had two sons. Having a

daughter is important for my sons and me. They are learning how to deal with a woman. I am sure this will help them later when they grow up. In our culture, giving a daughter in marriage (*kanyadan*) is an important duty of a father. My husband wants to perform that duty … [W]e did not want more than one daughter. The fact is that it may not be expensive to raise a daughter, but it is very expensive to get her married and pay for her dowry. I think we can afford to raise only one daughter. I also fear for the safety of my daughter in this city. Our village is a safe place. People know each other and neighbours look after neighbours. The situation is quite different here in this city. I only know two families in my neighbourhood. Most of my relatives live in Punjab, so they cannot help us. I do not work, so my full time job is to take care of my children. My sons are fine, but I fear for my growing daughter. I am happy I have only one daughter.

Although a few couples in Punjab Vihar expressed a preference for sons to daughters, all couples expressed a strong desire to have at least one daughter per family. It is important to note that none of the sample couples expressed the desire for just a daughter, two daughters and one son, or just two daughters.

For the majority of Punjab Vihar couples living in an urban environment, increased exposure to education and media and improvement in their economic status are important reasons for a small and sex-balanced family. However, some couples expressed concern about the high cost associated with dowries. At least for these couples, as the small family size norm has taken root, the experience of adapting to an urban environment itself has become a strong reason for son preference.

Contraception, Ultrasonography and Abortion: Achieving Desired Family Sex Composition

Punjab Vihar couples are knowledgeable about the possible medical and diagnostic uses of ultrasonography for pre-natal sex identification. They are also aware of the illegality surrounding the use of ultrasonography for the purpose of pre-natal sex identification (MHFW 2005). Notwithstanding the illegality of pre-natal sex determination, the proximity of Punjab Vihar to a variety of hospitals and clinics providing ultrasonography services makes it easy for couples to access and use this diagnostic technology for discovering the sex of the foetus. Punjab Vihar couples reported that several medical practitioners in the area offered a service to reveal the sex of the foetus. In some cases, extra payment was required for this service. The couples especially pointed out that this practice is quite common among physicians working at diagnostic centres in the area. Eight couples in Punjab Vihar reported that they had used ultrasonography or the selective abortion of females to achieve a desired number of sons. According to a 25-year-old woman from Punjab Vihar:

> I have a two-and-a-half-year-old daughter and I want to wait for a few more years to have my second child. My husband and I have very demanding jobs. I work for a private company and I cannot take leave for a long period. They would simply find someone else to replace me. Therefore, I have to plan my family in such a way that I can take a break from work to take care of the newborn. Then last year I found out that I was pregnant. I told my husband that I did not want another child now. We both decided to discontinue the pregnancy. When we went to the doctor, she performed an ultrasound exam. I found out that I was pregnant with a daughter. Since I already have a daughter, it was an easy decision for me to seek abortion. I feel blessed that we live in a city, which makes it easy for us to get this kind of care, and we do not have to tell anyone. We can maintain complete privacy about it. This city is so big; no one really knows or cares what the other family is doing.

Most agreed that it was appropriate for a couple to seek selective abortion of female foetuses if the goal is to achieve a sex-balanced family composition while keeping a small family size. The qualitative data did not reveal any gender-specific difference in this regard. Instead, the data suggests a similar pattern observed earlier, in which ethnic or regional congruity and a high level of trust between patient and provider becomes an important factor facilitating the transfer of knowledge and use of ultrasonography for pre-natal sex determination. According to a Punjab Vihar couple:

> I know a ... doctor who runs a maternity clinic in the area. She is from Punjab and understands the needs of a working family. She has helped me on many occasions, particularly when I was interested in delaying having a child. She has educated me about the latest medical technology and tests that can be useful if one plans to have a family of one's choice. What I like the most about her is that I can trust her with my secrets. Usually when people learn that you have used ultrasound to know if it is a boy or girl, they think it is bad ... [M]ost do not understand why a family needs to know the sex of the foetus for abortion. Each family's circumstances are unique. I am glad I live in this area and have access to good qualified and trusting doctors.

The study suggests that some doctors practising in the area, regardless of the illegality of using ultrasonography for pre-natal sex identification, do reveal the sex of the foetus to the expectant mother or family. This important finding is consistent with the literature on the involvement of the medical community in the misuse of pre-natal diagnostic technology in urban India (Khanna 1997; Malpani and Modi 2002; Patel 2007). Several respondents did report that, whilst they used ultrasonography as part of their routine pregnancy check-up, they did not seek information about the sex of the foetus during or after the procedure. In general, however, the findings of the study reinforce results already reported on the increasing use of pre-natal diagnostic technology and abortion for family balancing in India's urban communities (Croll 2000; Khanna 2010). This study suggests that regardless of an overall improvement in household economic status, and increase in women's education, participation in income-generating activities and intra-household decision-making power, son preference continues and plays and important role in Punjab Vihar parents' strategies for achieving a 'desired' family size and sex composition.

Achieving Desired Family Size: Urban Residence, Access to 'Modern' Medical Care and Patient–Provider Relationships

Punjab Vihar is located near two major private hospitals and several government-run and private clinics, health centres and dispensaries. The strategic location allows the residents of the community easy access to quality healthcare services, including family planning services. Several government-run health centres provide free advice to married couples and distribute free condoms. In addition, improvements in education, employment and household income have positively influenced the couples' access to and knowledge and use of the available health services in New Delhi.

Punjab Vihar couples exhibited a high level of knowledge, acceptance and use of temporary methods of contraception such as condoms and the intrauterine device (IUD) to avoid an unwanted pregnancy. The couples are well aware of the range of options available to avoid pregnancy. Eight couples in Punjab Vihar reported using contraceptive methods on a regular basis for child spacing. Five of the women said they had been satisfied with the choices they made regarding the timing of using contraception. Most users of temporary methods of contraception suggested that these options allowed them to regulate their family size by child spacing. Couples' opinions about the use of contraceptive methods show a deep concern for their own careers, the demands of urban life and a strong desire to be defined as 'modern' or 'urban'. As one 28-year-old woman said about contraceptive methods:

I got married when I was twenty-three years old. That year we moved in to our new apartment in Punjab Vihar. After two years of my marriage, my daughter was born. Of course, my husband and I want to have another child. As I began to think about having another child, I talked with my husband about our priorities. Do we want another child now; complete our family first before thinking about our careers? Alternatively, do we want to be stable in our professional lives before thinking about having another child? We decided to focus on our careers and opted for a temporary method of contraception. I went to a nearby private hospital to consult with a lady doctor who recommended that I use an IUD. I knew the doctor and trusted her opinion. She is a Punjabi woman, and I felt comfortable discussing my situation with her. I did not want to go to a government hospital because they do not have competent doctors or staff, and the facility is filthy. I did not mind paying for the procedure as long as the right doctor performed it.

The women I interviewed expressed a high level of trust and satisfaction with their healthcare providers. They describe trust in the context of what they perceived to be good qualities in the provider: private practice, participatory clinical experience and the provider's caring attitude. Most importantly, they emphasized the importance of regional affiliation as central to the continuity of their relationship with their doctor. A similar sense of satisfaction with the quality of available reproductive healthcare is further evident in the words of a recently married couple:

HUSBAND: A married doctor couple runs a private clinic near our locality. They provide the best healthcare in the area. I know the family very well because our parents and relatives live near each other in Punjab. You can say that the two families are very close. Unlike the kind of healthcare we used to get in our village, this clinic is cutting edge, and the doctors are well educated and certified.

WIFE: I cannot even imagine going to a doctor in Punjab to seek cure for reproductive health problems. Neither our village nor the district have a well-qualified specialist … [M]ost doctors were either MBBS [Bachelor of Medicine and Bachelor of Surgery] or RMPs [Registered Medical Practitioners] or traditional (*desi*) healers. I know that my mother and aunts advised each other about their health problems. Here, I do not have to deal with traditional (*desi*) doctors. I have access to the most recent medical care and diagnostic technology. I just have to go to this clinic and get professional advice and care.

Two couples in Punjab Vihar have opted for sterilization after achieving their desired family size. According to a 39-year-old man, who elected to undergo a vasectomy:

> Both my wife and I made this decision a year after the birth of our second child. We thought [that], since we are not going to have any more children, why not opt for a reliable method of contraception? My wife wanted to undergo tubectomy. When she consulted her OBGYN, the doctor told her that I should be the one undergoing the sterilization procedure. My doctor told me that it [a vasectomy] is an easy and safe procedure. I am happy with my decision. I know medical care in Delhi is expensive, but I am very satisfied with the quality of care we get here. The doctor who operated on me was an MD and had received advanced medical training in England. I do not think anyone could access this kind of care in Punjab.

The high acceptance and use of temporary and permanent methods of contraception is, in part, an outcome of couples' increased exposure to an urban environment and an overall improvement in their educational and economic status. Furthermore, qualitative data collected for this study confirms findings from other studies that among migrant communities easy access to reliable healthcare services, ethnic or regional congruence between the patient and provider, in addition to provider trust and competency, collectively improve utilization of care (Kao et al. 1998; Roter et al. 1999; Roberts and Aruguete 2000). Despite the potential difficulties of generalizing on the basis of such local-level evidence, the strikingly high level of acceptance and use of contraceptive methods among Punjab Vihar couples underscores the importance of increased access and improved patient–provider communication for providing healthcare to migrant communities.

Conclusion

This chapter supports the thesis that demographic outcomes ('desired' and 'actual' family size and sex composition) can be best explained in terms of their historical and cultural underpinning (Greenhalgh 1995). The analysis presented here examines how urban residence, improvements in household income, women's education and employment, and increased access to reliable health services influence parents' 'desired' and 'actual' family size and sex composition in an internally migrant community in India. An examination of the family-building strategies adopted by migrant groups thus suggests that the post-migration adjustment experience strongly influences parents' opinions surrounding 'adaptive' family size and sex composition as well as the means to achieve a desired family size and sex composition. The changes suggest how an internally immigrant community adapts to living in an urban environment not only in terms of responding to the economic demands of living in a city, but also in terms of adopting an urban identity and ethos in terms of their family-size preferences. Consequently, the emergent family-building strategies involve using temporary methods of contraception for child spacing; opting for permanent methods of contraception to keep a small family size; seeking medical care from providers who share regional and ethnic affiliation; and exploiting the available healthcare services, especially diagnostic services, for pre-natal sex identification and sex-selective abortion.

Although the study describes migrant couples as strategic in terms of achieving their desired family size and sex composition, the conflict between adapting to an urban environment and cultural beliefs is, at times, quite evident. However, the core of these family-building processes constitutes a set of complex and strategic steps – rejection, acceptance and adaptation – that prioritizes a selective investment of household resources and facilitates in the adoption of an urban identity. Women's education and participation in income-generating activities emerge as two reliable predictors of 'desired' and 'actual' fertility and decision-making power within the household. The key findings of this study suggest that urban residence and improvements in education, employment, household income and access to health services collectively and synergistically influence family size and sex composition (Basu 1992; Arnold et al. 1998; Khanna 2010). Both macro-level regional studies and micro-level community studies of demographic behaviour in urban areas indicate that urban exposure has the most positive influence on the use of contraception, decline in child mortality and fertility reduction (Lahiri 1974; Dreze and Murti 2001).

Based on macro-analysis of data from the National Family Health Survey (NFHS II), researchers have suggested that desire for a small family size in India is associated with a decline in a preference for sons and a desire to balance the sex ratio among children in the family (Bhat and Zavier 2003). Furthermore, the available evidence from South Korea points to a trend of gradual decrease in family size and a balancing of the sex ratio. This, in part, is attributable to the collective effect of an increase in women's education and employment levels, improved family income and living standards, urbanization and gradual changes in social norms leading to a decline in son preference (Chung and Das Gupta 2007).

The findings presented here support the above observations that a desire for family size is associated with an increased 'stated' preference for a sex-balanced family in an internally migrant community. Crucially, however, these results do not suggest a decline in son preference or an emergence of daughter preference in India. The results clearly show that migrant couples' desire for a small and sex-balanced family size means that they will use ultra-sonography for pre-natal sex determination and engage in the practice of sex-selective abortion of female foetuses. These findings lend urgency to understanding the complex relationship between urban residence and fertility patterns in migrant communities. Furthermore, the chapter calls for a more nuanced examination of the means used to achieve the ideals of a 'small family' and the long-term demographic consequences of emerging family-building strategies in urban communities in India and other parts of Asia.

Acknowledgements

The initial phase of this study was supported by a grant from the Wenner-Gren Foundation for Anthropological Research (grant number 5–56720). An expanded version of the results reported here are can be found in part in Khanna et al. (2009).

Notes

1. The analysis presented here is based on data collected through household surveys and in-depth interviews during an extended field study conducted during three visits between 2007 and 2009, which investigated the relationship between urban residence and family-building strategies among Punjabi immigrant families living in New Delhi. Study participants included first generation migrant married couples (between 20 and 49 years old) living in Punjab Vihar. The neighbour-hood is a multi-storey residential complex, with ninety-two families, located in the south-west part of New Delhi. A detailed family survey (with close-ended questions) was used for data collection on a purposive sample of sixty families. The sample exclusively represents nuclear families for two main reasons. First, only eight families in Punjab Vihar were joint or extended families at the time of data collection. Second, married couples in the 20 to 49 age range are most likely to make decisions regarding family size and sex composition. Additionally, in-depth open-ended individual interviews were used to collect opinions and experiences of fifteen married couples. The questions pertained to 'stated' desired family size and sex composition, son preference, knowledge and use of contraceptive methods, the use of ultrasonography for pre-natal sex determination and the practice of sex-selective abortion. Qualitative data analysis – performed by using QSR NVivo 7 – involved the systematic coding and organizing of data for identifying and interpreting recurrent themes.

2. Since a majority of couples lived in double-income families, for purposes of homogeneity and generalizability, the study focused on the subset of double-income couples. The informants made the decision if they wanted to be interviewed individually or as a couple. Spouses of twelve couples opted to be interviewed separately.

References

Agarwal, B. 1994. *A Field of One's Own: Gender and Land Rights in South Asia*. Delhi: Oxford University Press.

Agnihotri, S. 2000. *Sex Ratio Patters in the Indian Population: A Fresh Explanation*. New Delhi: Sage.

Arnold, F., M. Choe and T. Roy. 1998. 'Son Preference, Family Building Process and Child Mortality in India', *Population Studies* 52: 301–15.

Basu, A. 1992. *Culture, the Status of Women, and Demographic Behaviour: Illustrated with the Case of India*. Oxford: Clarendon Press.

Basu, A., and P. Aaby (eds). 1998. *The Method and Uses of Anthropological Demography*. Oxford: Clarendon Press.

Bhat, M., and F. Zavier. 2003. 'Fertility Decline and Gender Bias in Northern India', *Demography* 40(4): 637–57.

Bledsoe, C.H. 2004. 'Reproduction at the Margins: Migration and Legitimacy in the New Europe', *Demographic Research* 3: 88–116.

Carling, J. 2008. 'Toward a Demography of Immigrant Communities and Their Transnational Potential', *International Migration Review* 42(2): 449–75.

Chung, W., and M. Das Gupta. 2007. *Why Is Son Preference Declining in South Korea? The Role of Development and Public Policy, and the Implications for China and India*. Washington: World Bank.

Cleland, J. 2001. 'The Effects of Improved Survival on Fertility: A Reassessment', *Population and Development Review* 27: 60–92.

Coast, E.E., K.R. Hampshire and S.C. Randall. 2007. 'Disciplining Anthropological Demography', *Demographic Research* 16: 493–518.

Croll, E. 2000. *Endangered Daughters: Discrimination and Development in Asia*. London: Routledge.

Das Gupta, M.D. 1987. 'Selective Discrimination against Female Children in Rural Punjab, India', *Population and Development Review* 13: 77–100.

Dharmalingam, A., and S. Morgan. 1996. 'Women's Work, Autonomy, and Birth Control: Evidence from Two South Indian Villages', *Population Studies* 50(2): 187–201.

Dreze, J., and M. Murti. 2001. 'Fertility, Education, and Development: Evidence from India', *Population and Development Review* 27: 33–63.

Dyson, T., and M. Moore. 1983. 'On Kinship Structure, Female Autonomy, and Demographic Behaviour in India', *Population and Development Review* 9: 35–60.

Fernandez, R., and A. Fogli. 2009. 'Culture: An Empirical Investigation of Beliefs, Work, and Fertility', *American Economic Journal: Macroeconomics* 1(1): 146–77.

GoI. 2001. 'Census of India: Provisional Population Totals'. New Delhi: Office of the Registrar General, Government of India.

Greenhalgh, S. (ed.). 1995. *Situating Fertility: Anthropology and Demographic Inquiry*. Cambridge: Cambridge University Press.

Isaac, A., and T. Frank. 1999. 'Structural Assimilation and Ethnic Fertility in Ghana', *Journal of Comparative Family Studies* 30(3): 409–27.

Jeffery, P., and A. Basu (eds). 1998. *Appropriating Gender: Women's Activism and Politicized Religion in South Asia*. New York: Routledge.

Jejeebhoy, S. 1998. *Women's Education, Autonomy, and Reproductive Behaviour: Experience from Developing Countries.* Oxford: Clarendon Press.

Jha, P., et al. 2006. 'Male-to-female Sex Ratio of Children Born in India: National Survey of 1·1 Million Households', *Lancet* 367: 211–18.

Johnson-Hanks, J. 2007. 'What Kind of Theory for Anthropological Demography?' *Demographic Research* 16:1–26.

Kao, A.C., et al. 1998. 'Patients' Trust in their Physicians: Effects of Choice, Continuity, and Payment Method', *Journal of General Internal Medicine* 13: 681–86.

Kertzer, D., and T. Fricke (eds). 1997 *Anthropological Demography: Toward a New Synthesis.* Chicago: University of Chicago Press

Khan, H., and R. Raeside. 1997. 'Factors Affecting the Most Recent Fertility Rates in Urban-Rural Bangladesh', *Social Science and Medicine* 44(3): 279–89.

Khandelwal, M. 2002. *Becoming American, Being Indian: An Immigrant Community in New York City.* Ithaca, NY: Cornell University Press.

Khanna, S.K. 1997. 'Traditions and Reproductive Technology in an Urbanizing North Indian Village', *Social Science and Medicine* 44(2): 171–80.

——— 2001. '*Shahri Jat* and *Dehati Jatni*: The Indian Peasant Community in Transition', *Contemporary South Asia* 10: 37–53.

——— 2010. *Fetal/Fatal Knowledge: New Reproductive Technologies and Family Building Strategies in India.* Belmont, CA: Cengage/Wadsworth.

Khanna, S.K., S. Sudha and S. Irudaya Rajan. 2009. 'New Reproductive Technologies and Family Building Strategies in Urban India: Converging Trends in Two Culturally Distinct Communities', *Contemporary South Asia* 17(2): 141–58.

Lahiri, S. 1974. 'Preference for Sons and Ideal Family in Urban India', *Journal of Social Work* 34: 126–36.

McCartney, M., and A. Gill. 2007. 'From South Asian to Diaspora: Missing Women and Migration'. Working Paper No. 152. London: School of Oriental and African Studies.

Mace, R. 2008. 'Reproducing in Cities', *Science* 319: 764–66.

Malpani, A., and D. Modi. 2002. 'Preimplantation Sex Selection for Family Balancing in India', *Human Reproduction* 17(1): 11–12.

MHFW. 2005. 'Annual Report on Implementation of the Pre-conception and Pre-natal Diagnostic Techniques (Prohibition of Sex Selection) Act'. New Delhi: Ministry of Health and Family Welfare, Government of India.

Nath, C., C. Kenneth and G. Goswami. 1999. 'Effects of the Status of Women on the First-birth Interval in Indian Urban Society', *Journal of Biosocial Science* 31: 55–69.

Oppenheim, M.K. 1984. *The Status of Women: A Review of Its Relationship to Fertility and Mortality.* New York: Rockefeller Foundation.

Pande, R., and N. Astone. 2007. 'Explaining Son Preference in Rural India: The Independent Role of Structural versus Individual Factors', *Population Research and Policy Review* 26: 1–29.

Patel, T. (ed.). 2007. *Sex-selective Abortion in India: Gender, Society, and New Reproductive Technologies.* New Delhi: Sage.

Rahman, L., and V. Rao. 2004. 'The Determinants of Gender Equity in India: Examining Dyson and Moore's Thesis with New Data', *Population and Development Review* 30: 239–68.

Roberts, C.A., and M.S. Arguete. 2000. 'Tasks and Socioemotional Behaviours of Physicians: A Test of Reciprocity and Social Interaction Theories in Analogue Physician–Patient Encounters', *Social Science and Medicine* 50: 309–15.

Roter, D.L., et al. 1999. 'Effects of Obstetric Gender on Communication and Patient Satisfaction', *Obstetrics and Gynecology* 93: 635–41.

Rustagi, P. 2006. 'The Deprived, Discriminated, and Damned Girl Child: Story of Declining Child Sex Ratios in India', *Women's Health and Urban Life* 1: 6–26.

Sheker, T.V., and N. Hatti (eds). 2010. *Unwanted Daughters: Gender Discrimination in Modern India*. New Delhi: Rawat Publications.

Srinivas, M. 1966. *Social Change in Modern India*. Bombay: Allied Publishers.

Sudha, S., and I. Rajan. 2003. 'Persistent Daughter Disadvantage in India: What Do Estimated Sex Ratios at Birth and Sex Ratios of Child Mortality Risk Reveal?' *Economic and Political Weekly* 38: 115–36.

Wadley, S. 1993. 'Family Composition Strategies in Rural North India', *Social Science and Medicine* 37: 1367–76.

———— 1994. *Struggling with Destiny in Karimpur, 1925–1984*. Berkeley: University of California Press.

CHAPTER 9

Restoring the Connection

Aboriginal Midwifery and Relocation for Childbirth in First Nation Communities in Canada

Rachel Olson

I found that the word in our language for midwife – because midwife is a German word, it means 'with woman', *mit wif* – our word is *iewirokwas*. Of [all] the words we have that's the one I find to be the most beautiful. It means 'She's pulling the baby out of the water, or out of the earth, or a dark wet place'. And that certainly represents the perspective of reproductive ecology that our people have about integrating the natural world in the birth process.

Katsi Cook

In Canada, Aboriginal midwives are the symbol of returning childbirth practices to First Nation communities, as well as being politically engaged advocates of First Nation peoples and their rights to health and self-determination. In this chapter, the narratives of Aboriginal midwives are explored in order to understand the underlying notions of 'authoritative knowledge' and identity as it relates to the current practice of evacuating pregnant women from their home places in order to give birth in urban hospitals, often referred to as 'maternal evacuation' (Jordan 1997: 56). Framing this discussion is also the concept of maternal evacuation as a state enforced practice of displacement, focusing on the movement, or circulation, of women from one place to another as a result of government policy and procedure. These movements, or circulations, are viewed as 'cultural events rich in meaning for individuals, families, social groups, communities and nations' (McHugh 2000: 71). This notion of using displacement as the focal point in the study of maternal evacuation has yet to be explored in depth, and this chapter seeks to contribute to the ongoing discussion of maternal evacuation through this lens.

In order to do this properly, it is important to contextualize the practice of maternal evacuation within the historical and cultural context of Canada's indigenous peoples' relationship with the state and its medical institutions. As O'Neil and Kaufert point out in their work on obstetric care among Inuit women in the Canadian North, 'the politics of one woman's birth experiences and the politics of Inuit relationships with Western medical institutions and the larger Canadian society are inextricably linked' (O'Neil and Kaufert 1990: 53). In particular, this chapter will focus on a workshop of the National Aboriginal Council of Midwives held in October 2009 in Winnipeg, Manitoba, at their yearly gathering. During this meeting, they held a visioning session to try and articulate the goals and vision of their council. Through this workshop, the vision of the collective of Aboriginal midwives clearly articulates the historical place of midwifery in their communities, and relates this to the system of dislocation that has been perpetuated through state policy. They also collectively visualize a healthy community through notions of safety, support, knowledge and responsibility.

Alongside the government's practice of dislocation is a broader set of ideas that attempt to modernize indigenous peoples through reframing social, political and geographic structures through education and Western medical practice. Looking at evacuation within a larger discourse of modernization and development, we can see the ways in which authoritative Western medical knowledge about childbirth, and the power associated with this, becomes the normalizing structure from within which maternal child health policies operate (Kaufert and O'Neil 1990: 431; Van Hollen 2003: 167). This coincides directly with historical changes to childbearing practices across Canada. During the period from the mid nineteenth century until the middle of the twentieth century, major changes took place in the field of childbirth. There was a push to medicalize and modernize childbearing practices across Canada. Childbirth in a hospital setting, under the authority of physicians, grew steadily, and by the 1940s midwifery was 'no longer an option for the vast majority of Canadian women' (MacDonald 2006: 237).

The policy of maternal evacuation can be seen as legitimizing a certain set of ideas about pregnancy and the body, namely that it is primarily physiological and in need of active management by medical experts, while disregarding other views, including the social and cultural dimensions as important parts of reproduction. Integral to this was the idea that childbirth had to be redefined as a 'medical event, fraught with danger and in need of intervention by obstetricians' (ibid.: 239). Key to this is the understanding of the process of medicalization as not only 'the appropriation of women's bodies as a site for medical practice, but also the social arrangements and political forces that contribute to such experiences' (Lock and Kaufert 1998, cited in Unnithan Kumar 2004: 17). From this understanding, important themes emerge. Knowledge of childbirth – both who has it (for example, doctors, nurses, midwives, women) and where it is located (in hospitals, in clinics, in communities, in women's bodies) – becomes a central issue to the practice of maternal evacuation. Also central is the issue of identity as linked to childbearing and its connections to space and place. As one midwife commented, 'As many women have said, "Now our babies are born outside of our territory. Nobody is born on Cree land". Many women have said, "I want to be able to say that my child was born on Cree territory"'. The work of Aboriginal midwives becomes clearer in that it is not only about returning reproductive knowledge back to the communities from which it has been taken, but is also about the possibility of reframing identity through the practice of giving birth in one's home place, of pulling babies from the water, or from the earth, as indigenous peoples in Canada. The chapter looks at how aboriginal midwives characterize the difficulties that aboriginal families face in their communities, and how they envision future generations if birth is returned to home places. Notions of disconnection and reconnection are central to these descriptions. Through this, the narratives of midwives become important markers for understanding both the process of moving birth back into indigenous communities, as well as the implications of the current practice of dislocation.

Background

I think there is a responsibility there. As a native woman, who is on the front lines, looking after Aboriginal women every day, there is a responsibility of the federal government to pay attention to the fact that we have a very high morbidity and mortality rate in our communities. It is like a fourth world. Not quite, but Canada should not have morbidity and mortality like we do in our communities. Bottom line. And we need to develop leadership in this area of looking after women and children. To have a postcolonial vision of what our families could be. To bring back that memory. If I wanted to talk about ceremony or sacredness, all the things that make people feel good about who we are as native people, it should be that kind of vision. (NAHO 2008: 55)

This chapter follows the narratives of Aboriginal midwives, rather than focus on one specific community's experience of maternal evacuation. Because of this, it is important to state that there are regional differences in approaches to health, healing and tradition across Canada, and this chapter acknowledges these limitations. Adelson seeks to address this diversity by stating that the 'threads holding the definition of Aboriginal populations together is two-fold: first their "autochthonous status" on the land, and the subsequent "historical relationship since contact" that each Aboriginal person "continues to have to the nation-state"' (Adelson 2008: S47).

This being said, however, it is important to understand the context from which the practice of evacuation takes place, as it is stated in the national statistics of the Canadian government. The overall picture may be understood as the basic 'facts' about Canada's indigenous population, or it may also be seen as what Paul Farmer refers to as the 'biological expressions of social inequality' (Farmer 2005: 307). There are approximately 760,000 First Nation people in Canada, spread right across the country (Statistics Canada 2006). Of these, 68 per cent live on reserves, or 'a tract of land, the legal title to which is vested in Her Majesty, that has been set apart by Her Majesty for the use and benefit of a band', and the rest live in 'urban, rural, special access, or remote areas'.[1] There are currently 610 First Nation communities across Canada. The Aboriginal population is also young, with over half of it under the age of twenty-five. The population of Aboriginal peoples is also growing, and from 1996 to 2001, the population grew by 22 per cent, in contrast to Canada's national population growth of 3 per cent. This is attributed to a higher fertility rate, and also to the increasing self-identification of Aboriginal peoples within the survey data (Statistics Canada 2010).

According to the statistics, Aboriginal peoples do not share the same 'quality of life' as the rest of the population. The two biggest concerns have been identified as 'access to adequate housing and their overall health' (ibid.: 1). The percentage of Aboriginal peoples living in overcrowded housing is five to six times higher than the equivalent figure for the national population. In terms of disease and illness, rates of tuberculosis, diabetes, HIV/AIDS are also extremely high, compared to that of the national population (ibid.: 2). In the report of the Royal Commission of Aboriginal Peoples, it was stated that 'stillbirth and perinatal death rates among Indians are about double the Canadian average; among Inuit living in the Northwest Territories, they are about two and a half times the Canadian average' (RCAP 1996: 127). The Canadian Institute of Child Health compared the difference in Aboriginal post-neonatal mortality from 1979 to 1981 and 1991 to 1993, and found that the rates were three times higher than the national population (CICH 2000: 173). These statistics point to the need to understand the strengths and weaknesses of existing policies and practices that affect pregnancy and child-birth for First Nation women.

The topic of Aboriginal midwifery has also been addressed by a few authors. Carroll and Benoit focus on the colonial forces which have led to the destruction of Aboriginal midwifery and the rights of women to assist 'birth within their traditional territories' (Carroll and Benoit 2004: 264). Benoit et al. (2006: 14–15) provide an overview of the presence of Aboriginal midwifery by province, and they note the differences in legislation with regards to the practices of Aboriginal midwives. They note that the province of Manitoba has an 'independent Midwifery act', and midwifery has been regulated in the province since June 2000 by the College of Midwives of Manitoba. The college is 'mandated to operate a standing committee to provide advice and direction of issues related to midwifery care to Aboriginal women'. This committee, called Kagike Danikobidan, is 'committed to ensuring that traditional midwifery practices are respected and incorporated into care and ensuring that Aboriginal people have opportunities to become registered in Manitoba' (Benoit et al. 2006: 14–15).

Couchie and Nabigon explore the loss of Aboriginal midwifery care within the colonial context, and connect the 'healing and strengthening of contemporary Aboriginal communities with midwifery care' (Couchie and Nabigon 1997). This is done using the Annishabe concept of the four directions (north, south, east and west), and exploring Couchie's own experiences of becoming an Aboriginal midwife. This chapter attempts to bring Aboriginal midwifery to the centre of discussions of relocation for birth, and thus extend our understanding of the historical context of Aboriginal health, the current context of relocation and the possibilities that Aboriginal midwifery has for the future of Aboriginal communities in Canada.

This chapter draws on multiple sources. Fieldwork was carried out over fifteen months in Manitoba from spring 2009 to autumn 2010, during which my research was focused on the relocation of childbirth. This research included participant observation in various settings, such as an urban and rural hospitals, various inter-governmental meetings, and interviews and participant observations with women who had experienced, or were at the time experiencing, evacuation for childbirth. Individual and group interviews also took place and were recorded and transcribed. In particular, the chapter focuses on a visioning workshop of the National Aboriginal Council of Midwives (NACM) that took place in October 2009. The workshop was recorded and transcribed, and subsequently analysed. I also draw upon my previous research, undertaken while employed by the National Aboriginal Health Organization (NAHO). I contributed to the series Celebrating Birth, helping out with conducting interviews and the collaborative writing of, in collaboration with other NAHO staff members, a revised edition of a research paper (see NAHO 2008).

Authoritative Knowledge and Identity

This chapter focuses on the relocation of women from their communities to give birth. Along with the physical relocation of people, implicit in this movement is also the relocation of reproductive knowledge, and also its affect on the identity of Aboriginal peoples. Before we begin to unpack the history of First Nations in relation to the state, it is important to understand how these broader notions underlie most of the action of the state and its consequences.

Knowledge about childbirth exists in many different forms and places, and how some knowledge systems become authoritative over others is important. In the history of midwifery in Canada, the perception that authoritative knowledge of childbirth was resolutely taken away from Aboriginal peoples is clear. Through looking at narratives of Aboriginal midwives, we can see how this knowledge is being returned to communities through returning childbirth to communities, and this helps us understand what constitutes authoritative knowledge of childbirth in this context. The flip side of this is understanding how authoritative knowledge has been seen to have been taken away from communities; of import here is who has taken this knowledge, and where is it now located. In this section, we need to first understand the perception that in the discourse of returning birth, there is a claim to authoritative knowledge in the past. According to Jordan, the central observation of the construction of authoritative knowledge is that, 'for any particular domain, several knowledge systems exist, some of which, by consensus, come to carry more weight than others, either because they explain the state of the world better for the purposes at hand (efficacy), or because they are associated with a stronger power base (structural superiority), and usually both' (Jordan 1997: 56). Through Jordan's explanation, we can see how authoritative knowledge becomes unquestioned in its dominance, and how it is normalized through practice. As anthropologists, we can look at how authoritative knowledge is 'produced, displayed, resisted, and challenged in social, clinical, and political interactions' (Davis-Floyd and Sargent 1997: 21).

In the North American context, this is usually tied to the discrediting and virtual disappearance of the practice of midwifery. For indigenous populations, this link is made stronger through the wholesale disregard for indigenous knowledge systems in general. Also directly related to this loss of knowledge is the loss of identity of First Nations as indigenous peoples. For the purposes of this chapter, indigenous identity will be understood in terms of 'relatedness' (Carsten 2000). Drawing on Tim Ingold's discussion of 'indigenous', we seek to understand identity through a 'relational approach' in which 'both cultural knowledge and bodily substance are seen to undergo continuous generation in the context of an ongoing engagement with the land and with the beings – human and non-human – that dwell therein' (Ingold

2000: 133). The relational approach is very helpful in connecting identity and place. There is a need to develop the understanding that:

> to inhabit the land is to draw it to a particular focus, and in so doing to constitute a place. As a locus of personal growth and development ... every such place forms the centre of a sphere of nurture. Thus the generation of persons within spheres of nurture, and places of the land, are not separate processes but one in the same. (ibid.: 149)

In the context of this essay, we can then ask the question of how birth in home places for indigenous populations can constitute spheres of nurture, and how the displacement of people for childbirth is connected to the loss of nurturing places that 'constitute their identity, knowledgability, and the environments in which they live' (ibid.: 133). In relation to maternal evacuation for Inuit communities, Douglas points out:

> the controversy over evacuation was driven by Inuit dissatisfaction with medical services in general and with evacuation for childbirth in particular. An essential component of traditional Inuit health is their connection with the land which functions as an important part of Inuit identity. One of the most important components of this connection is birth within the community, and hence on the land itself ... Evacuation breaks this first connection between an Inuk and the land. (Douglas 2006: 125)

This point is made clear when women stated that the children they had at home were 'real Inuit, not the later ones' (Kaufert and O'Neil 1990: 33). In making this link to identity and the land, we can also understand how the concept of 'place' plays an important role in this discussion. In this context, it is important to stress that understandings of place must move from discussions which focus mainly on 'material land forms' and which do not take into account other communities who may 'have associations with such land forms as [being] instead fundamentally interpersonal in nature' (Gone 2008: 372). While this distinction will be discussed in further detail below, an example of the interpersonal relationship between places and peoples in the context of pregnancy and childbirth can illuminate and clarify this point. In discussing relocation for Navajo peoples in the United States, Schwarz quotes a Navajo woman who clarifies points to connection between birth and place:

> When you are pregnant, you are inside of your mother. You got your mother's breath, and it's the same with the Big Mountain, that way. It is my breath. See, I was born around the Big Mountain, and so that is my

mother too. So all of my life, I just will always be thinking of this place. My spirit is going to be here forever. (Schwarz 1997: 43)

This example displays how we must not be tied to the materiality of place, or think of place as sites, but rather understand the complex notion of relationships with places and the meanings attached to them, particularly ones that are embodied and inextricably linked to peoples senses of belonging and understandings of home.

Margaret McDonald questions the relationship between space and place when looking at new midwifery movements in Canada. According to her, 'midwives seem to use these words in opposite terms'. For a birth may occur in 'a physical setting of a hospital – a place – but the space they create within that room can be an entirely different matter'. In this way 'space can transcend place' (McDonald 2007: 130). It is with this in mind that she poses questions inspired by Gupta and Ferguson (1992): 'How are places, including clinics, homes and hospital rooms produced as midwifery spaces and rendered meaningful? Who contests this? What is at stake?' (McDonald 2007: 130).

The concept of 'home' is a 'powerful motif in the contemporary popular and academic project to (re)locate identity in a globalized world of movement' (Basu 2004: 27). Home can be understood as 'located in space but it is not necessarily a fixed space ... Home starts by bringing some space under control' (Douglas 1991: 287). According to Robertson, in her work with urban Aboriginal women in Vancouver, this idea of home resonates with what she refers to as 'taming space'; it involves 'active choice, acquiescence and negotiation, actions that highlight identity-constituting activities that are themselves shaped by spatial and representational regimes' (Robertson 2007: 528–29). Basu (2004: 28) contends that the term 'homeland' gives substance to this otherwise slippery concept. This is especially apt when discussing birth in indigenous communities. In Australia, the majority of indigenous groups experience the same policy and practice of maternal evacuation. The movement to return birth back to their communities is commonly referred to as 'birthing in the homelands'.

The Current State of Maternal Evacuation in First Nation Communities

Birth is the fundamental ceremony of our tribes. It is the most sacred ceremony that we have ... It just happens. So we have never lost it. It always happens, babies are always born, and women are always doing that, and they are caring for them. We don't have to get back birth because it has never left us, but we have to get back in control of that ceremony. We have handed over the control of that ceremony to other people, and it has to be brought back home to us. (NAHO 2008: 58)

As with most people who live in rural and remote settings, access to healthcare often means that a woman has to leave their community to give birth. In First Nation communities, accessing healthcare becomes more complex. In Canada, the provision of healthcare is the responsibility of the provincial government, whilst reserve land, as noted above, is considered federal, or for the use of 'her Majesty'. Thus healthcare provision for First Nations is delivered on the reserves by First Nations and Inuit Health, a branch of Health Canada. This jurisdictional complication is a major factor in many issues of adequate healthcare delivery for First Nation people, and has major implications for bringing childbirth back to their communities. This will be discussed in further detail below.

At present, the current model that is generally available to on-reserve First Nation people ranges from 'health promotion and public health delivered by nurses and community health representatives (Health Centres), in some communities on a part-time basis only (Health Stations and Health Offices), to community health nursing delivered by nurses with an expanded scope of practice (Nursing Stations)' (Lavoie et al. 2009: 3). On-reserve programming for First Nation pregnant women often includes the First Nations and Inuit Health programmes of Canadian Prenatal Nutrition Program (CPNP), Fetal Alcohol Spectrum Disorder (FASD) and in some communities a Maternal Child Health programme (MCH). Prenatal visits are usually done by nurses at a health centre or nursing station, and women are then sent at approximately thirty-seven weeks' gestation to an urban tertiary centre for 'confinement' until they give birth and travel back to their community. Medical transportation also falls under federal jurisdiction, and funding for transportation for maternal evacuation is only granted for the expectant mother, and she is only allowed provision for an escort if she is under the age of sixteen or has some type of disability. This means that the majority of women travel to the city to give birth alone, without any social support. This relocation, or migration, of women to urban centres to give birth drastically affects the way in which women, families and communities experience birth. Women often describe the experience of maternal evacuation as a 'lonely one, often plagued by insecurity, insufficient or inadequate food, the unfamiliarity of strange surroundings, missing family and other children, and an overall stressful experience' (NAHO 2005: 32). In the province of Manitoba, where I have conducted research, it is estimated that 'as many as 1,100 prenatal women relocate temporarily from First Nation communities in rural and remote regions of Manitoba to Winnipeg or urban tertiary centers to give birth' each year (Phillips-Beck 2010: 11).

Even though the policy of maternal evacuation originates with the federal government, they too acknowledge that this practice has 'multiple 'negative effects' and 'returning safe birthing closer to the community is the right direction for improved health outcomes of mothers, infants, families and communities' (Desjarlais 2008). Despite this acknowledgement, however, the practice of maternal evacuation persists. This leads us to the understanding that this issue is more complex than simply arranging childbirthing facilities in Aboriginal communities, and to fully understand it one must look deeper into the historical and cultural context of both the relationship between First Nations and the state, and the articulation of the importance of the relationship with place of indigenous peoples, and within that, the importance of bringing birth back to those home places. Here, I wish to outline this history, focusing on the movement of people from their communities in order to receive healthcare and fashion their identities through processes of articulated assimilation. From this understanding, the focus moves to the voices of Aboriginal midwives, who challenge state control of both defining birth, and how birth is experienced by mothers, families, communities and nations.

Historical Development of Healthcare for First Nations

During my research, an Aboriginal midwife once touched on the significance of the relationship between history, the state and First Nations regarding healthcare delivery for pregnant women:

> I see that taking the job of midwives and moving birth into the hospital is something that is akin to colonization … [M]ost non-native people, and maybe even some native people, would see this as just something about modern life. But I am not convinced, and I don't think I will ever be convinced that we needed to have modern life that much … Just like taking our land, they took our bodies. And they used women's bodies. And we can look at that through history, that this is the way people conquered … conquered the land, conquered the people … [I]t wasn't always negative, but I think in the case of birth it did become negative, because we [midwives] were made useless.

The midwife's remarks are echoed by others: 'when it comes to health, the past often has something to say about the present' (Hackett 2005: S17). By critically examining this history, state discourses of modernization and medicalization emerge clearly as key points from which the policy of maternal evacuation developed.

Bent et al. (2007: 9) trace the key events regarding entitlements to health-care services for Aboriginal peoples, the first of these being the Royal Proclamation of 1763, in which King George III stated that 'any lands within the territorial confines of the new governments that had not been ceded by the Indian people were reserved for the Indian people'. This was important as it set the stage for treaties to be signed between First Nation peoples and the Crown (Steckley and Cummins 2001: 119). Eleven numbered treaties were signed between 1871 and 1906. Treaty Six has become the most important of these in relation to health services, as it included a provision that 'a medicine chest will be kept in the house of each Indian Agent for the benefit of the Indian people' (Ray et al. 2000: 143). The meaning of this clause was debated, but eventually came to be interpreted as meaning 'free medical care' to Indian people (Bent et al. 2007: 10). The treaties also created Indian reserves, the lands designated to Indian peoples.

The British North America Act of 1867 established the country of Canada. In this Act, the provision of providing healthcare rested with provincial governments, with the exception of Indians. This is explained by the fact that in Section 91(24) of the Act, the legislative authority over 'Indians and the lands reserved for Indians' was the responsibility of the federal government. Also, since the Crown signed the treaties with Aboriginal peoples and not the provinces, including the clause for a medicine chest, the contention was that the responsibility of providing healthcare rested with the federal government (ibid.: 12). In defining the status of registered Indians, the British North America Act resulted in the 'loss of control over their organization and governance and health and social structures' (Carroll and Benoit 2004: 269). This also marks the point of departure from which the provinces constructed policies and programmes that were differentiated from one another. The balance between the provincial approach to healthcare and the federal government's policies and programmes continues to create challenges for Aboriginal peoples across Canada. For example, only four provinces and two territories in Canada have funded midwifery legislation; therefore, access to midwifery care varies dependent on geographic location within Canada.

The First Nations Inuit Health Branch (FNIHB) explain the history of the provision of healthcare in these terms: 'By the 1900s, First Nations and Inuit communities were decimated by smallpox, tuberculosis, and other communicable diseases, but little coordinated effort existed on a national level to address the health crisis. In 1904, the Department of Indian Affairs appointed a general medical superintendent to start medical programs and develop health facilities' (Health Canada 2008). It is important to note that the Canadian government chooses this as its point of departure in its healthcare policy. It places itself in the paternalistic role of coming to the aid of communities in crisis, and I do not wish to suggest that this was not the case, as the rates of infectious disease at the term of the century are well documented. However, as Carroll and Benoit point out, it was the compounding of these epidemics with 'paternalistic government policy ... which contributed to the weakening of Aboriginal peoples' health and well-being' (Carroll and Benoit 2004: 269). It is interesting that this is the first image we receive of the government's role regarding the health of Aboriginal peoples. In choosing this point of departure, the historical summary provided by FNIHB contributes to 'an understanding of Aboriginal society that reinforces unequal power relationships; in other words, an image of sick, disorganised communities can be used to justify paternalism and dependence' (O'Neil et al. 1998: 230).

The Indian Act (1876 and 1958) cannot be ignored as it is a fundamental text that has shaped the relationship between the Canadian state and First Nation peoples. Under the Indian Act, 'Status Indians' became registered, and they were given the right to live on reserves, vote for Chief and Council, share in Band money and inherit reserve property. It also prohibited 'traditional healing practices and ceremonies', a restriction that was in place until the Act was amended in the 1960s (O'Neil and Kaufert 1995: 60). Dickason (1992) notes that communities were assigned government appointed Indian Agents, individuals who were 'often without medical training' and who assumed 'authority over local healers'.

In particular, it is important to understand governmental control in moving people from their communities for medical treatment and other purposes. It is suggested that removing people from their communities for treatment and schooling led to a great mistrust of both the intentions of the federal government in providing healthcare services, and the appropriateness of Western treatment of illness for First Nation people.

Between 1870 and 1996, Aboriginal children were forcibly removed from their homes and taken to residential schools, where the aim was to assimilate them in into mainstream Canadian society (Assembly of First Nations 2011). This not only denied children the right to be raised by their own families, but they were also cut off from their 'traditional knowledge systems, original languages, and traditional cultural practices' (Carroll and Benoit 2004: 256). The schools were characterized by the 'deliberate suppression of language and culture, substandard living conditions and second-rate education, and widespread physical, sexual, emotional, and spiritual abuse' (Smith et al. 2005: 40). When looking at pregnancy and parenting in Aboriginal communities, Smith et al. found that one needs to address the intergenerational impact of residential schools in order to effectively address the current health policies and practices associated with maternal health. Participants in their study articulated the need to 'turn it around', and that in order to adequately address the healthcare needs of Aboriginal parents, this 'could be understood only in the context of their experiences of and efforts to change the [intergenerational impact of residential schools] and related colonizing influences and structures' (ibid.: 40). Indeed, it can be seen that part of the process of 'turning it around' could be a return of the knowledge of childbirth practices to communities, and most importantly allowing the return of women to their homes for childbirth.

Aboriginal Midwifery and the Visioning Workshop

> Being a midwife brought me around the circle, where I wanted to work with women. You have time to work with women, if they want to begin a healing path for themselves. To come full circle, and be able to stand there at other women's births and in that way, be at my own birth. It felt that way for me, because I never got to hear my own birth story. To me, that is something that is a big pull for me, and for many of our women is that we don't know our story. We don't know it and we should know it. We have the right to know our own story right from the beginning. For me, those women can now talk to their children and say this is what happened at your birth, it was a full moon and the wind was blowing and there were stars up in the sky and these are all the things that happened. That informs that baby right from the start. (NAHO 2008: 29)

Aboriginal midwives have become the voice through which the return of childbirth practices back to communities is articulated on both the national and local stage. In their narratives, they recognize not only the past knowledge of their ancestors and their knowledge of birth and healing, but they also allow for the opportunity of new reproductive knowledge to enter the communities. This in turn allows a reframing of indigenous identity through the ongoing relationship to the land from which people come, rather than holding an identity solely governed by the state. The current goals of Aboriginal midwives are not only to bring midwifery practice back to communities, but also to bring back birthing knowledge to the community. As one midwife explains the goals behind her community's education program: 'It is the democracy of knowledge. You bring back that knowledge that once belonged to our communities and give it back to them. And it stays there. Those people don't go home. They are home' (ibid.: 32).

The Aboriginal midwives have organized themselves into a council, the National Aboriginal Council of Midwives (NACM), a branch of the Canadian Association of Midwives (CAM). NACM speaks to both the need for midwifery as part of an overall health strategy for indigenous communities, as well as midwifery as a way to address the historical inequality and relationship between indigenous communities and Western medical care. The mission of NACM is:

> to promote excellence in reproductive healthcare for Inuit, First Nations, and Métis women. We advocate for the restoration of midwifery education, the provision of midwifery services, and choice of birthplace for all Aboriginal communities consistent with the UN Declaration on the Rights of Indigenous Peoples. As active members of the Canadian Association of Midwives, we represent the professional development and practice needs of Aboriginal midwives to the responsible health authorities in Canada and the global community. (CAM 2011: 9)

In this section I explore how this vision statement came into being, and how a workshop to develop a vision and goals for the NACM speaks directly to the issues of knowledge and identity within the context of relocating childbirth.

In October 2009, the NACM gathered in Winnipeg for their yearly meeting. During this, they held a session to try and articulate the goals and vision of their council. To do this, they conducted an art-based exercise in which each midwife drew two pictures. For the first picture, they were instructed to visualize and draw 'the most difficult things that come up in your work with birthing women'.

After a few minutes of contemplation and sketching, each midwife presented and explained their drawing to the group. The first midwife held up her picture and said:

> What I see in the communities I am working in right now is the apprehension of most of the babies, the apprehension of the whole next generation. I am talking about Aboriginal babies, babies from our community. So what I drew is a woman … I call it the trail of tears. I see the trail of tears in my work every day. This woman is in a hospital bed, because most of the time it is a hospital birth. And she is saying, 'Help me somebody, they are going to take my baby away from me. Birth does not feel safe for me and I am overwhelmed by my fear of pain'. And there are the arms of someone they don't know … The baby is in the arms of someone they don't know, and they don't know where that baby is going to go. And the fear of not knowing, fears with the birthing process as we all know, the stress, and it is broken. The whole circle is broken. She is feeling ragged and overwhelmed with not knowing what is going to happen. The women I work with, they tell me that they are broken … Even before they have had their babies, their bodies are numb due to the emotional, spiritual,

sexual and physical violence they have experienced in their lifetime. So they can't see the beauty, they don't know that there is beauty in birth; they don't know the sacredness of birth, because they can't see it because they are so shut down.

The second midwife, a student, held up her picture of a braid. She explained that she started to think about how her grandmother used to braid her hair when she was a little girl, making the braid so tight that it hurt her. In the room, her grandmother, an elderly midwife, was sitting and smiling at her granddaughter as she spoke about this time. She drew the braid to explain what she sees in her work as a midwife:

> There is a disconnection, like long ago families used to be so tight and the men would support the women. Now it seems like everything is loose and coming undone, and it is falling apart ... I found for myself that there was this disconnection. And there is that disconnection, even with the government and the communities ... They are not working together to keep things tight. Everything is coming loose. Long ago when my grandma did deliveries, everyone knew what their title was. Everyone knew that they knew that she was the midwife. There was no doubting her or whatever, they knew she knew what she was doing, and they would call on her ... Now what I see when I go to the hospital ... it is almost like the nurses were like, 'Oh, you know the midwife was here' ... There is a disconnect between the midwives and the doctors and nurses ... You get a sense that they are only being polite, they are not really connecting ... Midwives have to prove themselves, their standards, that they are in line with the doctors. This is what I have been getting the sense of, and I have only been doing this for four years. The first thing that comes to mind is the sweet grass braid. And then how do we get that back? How do we get that connection back and have it tight?

Another midwife explained part of her drawing as:

> Here is the woman. This could be a hospital that she is going to give birth in, so she is not able to stay in her own community. But it is not just about evacuation, she is tired. She is going through this wall. There is a wall that exists between life in the community and the outside life. And there is a wall that divides, and there is no understanding between a lot of people that don't live in the community. They don't know what goes on, what life is like there. And she has to go through that wall, she has to go to the city to give birth, and those are her footsteps. And she is tired, because as you say, she is carrying the weight of the responsibility for her family and

for birth. This is her husband, or her partner, here, who is sitting here, and basically he is depressed. But when I wrote down what my concerns are, I put down family violence, homelessness, poverty, lack of choices for women (especially around birthing), but when I thought about all of those things, the thing that is the most important is the oppression of the women. And it is not just the oppression by the government, but oppression in her own relationships ... I see a woman who is trying to take care of him, she is trying to take care of the kids, she is trying to manage financially, and she has no choices ... she is working so hard and she has no choices. And basically to me, that means she is oppressed ... I think for me, that is what a lot of it comes down to. It is the oppression of women. It is everywhere. I just see it everywhere.

In these descriptions of the issues that Aboriginal midwives face working in their communities, a few common threads emerge. The images of disconnection, of walls, of oppression come together in these drawings. The midwives link the lack of midwifery knowledge in communities to the historical and current structural inequalities that exist in them. The image of disconnection, of 'things coming loose', occurs on many levels. There is a disconnection between women and their families, their health, their history and their identities. As one midwife points out, this disconnection also exists within the bodies of the women they work with. The issue of relocation then becomes more complex than just birth place; rather, in the words of one midwife, birth must be relocated within women's bodies as a safe place as well as a physical shift of birth environment.

In the second part of the workshop, the midwives were asked to visualize a 'landscape of a happy healthy community, where the healthiest babies possible are being born, and the best births are happening'. In this session, descriptions of support, family, community and respect all emerged as key topics. The student midwife held up a colourful drawing with hands and rainbows. She explained:

My granny said, when she was at a birth, she would feel like a lift when you touch the baby. What you are feeling is God, God's presence when you feel this, His love. These are her hands. And the rainbow reminded me of my grandmother. The rainbow represents her, the grannies, the helpers. The house is surrounded by family. You feel the love when you first touch that child. It is His work, and you are feeling His presence. Her spirituality too, whether it is the Creator or God, that is what she is trying to tell me about. The houses are the community. Those are her hands there, the energy she would feel is His work. The warm light in the house ... The house is so warm because of the family ... You are surrounded by people, you are not stranger.

The importance of support and family was also articulated by another midwife. Instead of drawing, she decided to write words down instead. She read from her paper and said:

I wrote I see a young girl in the arms of her mother, her family, and her community. She is considered precious, and when she decides to have a baby it is with a man who respects and cares for her. Together they are guided through the pregnancy and given the necessary preparation for parenthood. At birth time, the young woman is supported and honoured and gives birth her own way. She is aware and active. By doing so, she discovers her strength as a person and as a woman. She mothers her baby closely, and breastfeeds and is given continued support and teachings. She feels whole before and after birth. She is blessed.

This image of being whole and being surrounded by supportive family is in direct contrast to the previous exercise in which the midwives drew the realities they face in their daily work. The return of birth to Aboriginal communities, to the land, was articulated by one midwife who described what her ideal birth experience would be. She explained that she had thought about on many occasions before this exercise:

So I always think of the perfect birth as having all the senses aligned ... The drum is there for our listening, the wind is whirling outside – it's the breath, it's the breathing ... The pine and cedar and sage, the medicines are there for the prayers, maybe there is a sacred fire going so you can smell the fire. And touch again, singing and drumming you in. Love, everyone's heart, all the spirits are there with you ... The ancestors, the star people, the Grandmother Moon is there with you. Your midwife is there beside you, and your family is sitting beside you, and it is a really safe place. And the four directions ... have some significance in your mind ... – what position you give birth in, whether you are facing the east or the north. It is really beautiful, and all of your senses are all awakened so you bring your baby into that safe place.

The emphasis on safety and support extends to the connection between birth and the environment. After the session, I asked this midwife about her thoughts on the connection between birth and the land. She replied:

I think we always went back to identifying with the land ... You know, that whole romanticized version of Mother Earth taking care of us, and all that ... Well, I don't think it is all that romanticized ... It really is a deep part of it. It is for real. Whether it is the Inuit women, or the women down in Oneida in my community ... it is that tie. It is right through Grandmother Moon, right through every fibre of your being, right through your feet, to the very planting in the ground ... That's it. Right through your baby. Every fibre and every cell yearns for that land, and the smells and the wind, and all of that. So, to me, that is your identity, and your relationships, and your language.

During these two sessions, the vision of the collective of Aboriginal midwives becomes clear. They clearly articulate the historical place of midwifery in their communities and relate this to the dislocation that has been perpetuated through state policy. They also collectively visualize a healthy community through notions of safety, support, knowledge and responsibility. This ability to articulate these relationships has led Aboriginal midwives to become a symbol of a movement towards healthier communities, and self determination for Aboriginal peoples.

In conclusion, the relocation of Aboriginal women to give birth exists as part of the complex historical and cultural relationship between indigenous peoples and the state. By looking at the dislocation of people from their communities at the hands of the federal government, issues of acknowledging the authoritative knowledge of midwives and traditional knowledge can be seen as key markers of how these historical inequalities continue to be replayed in the evacuation of women for birth. The assumption that one must seek healthcare outside Aboriginal communities implies that such communities are not places where one can be healthy or become healthy. This chapter has looked at the development of the vision of the NACM as a way to weave these threads together. It has examined how the return of indigenous childbirth practices speaks to healing the past and current systems that cause disconnections which Aboriginal midwives see in their communities, as well as articulating the possibilities for health and healing through birth in home places. The path of the narratives of Aboriginal midwives reveals the loss of control of First Nations peoples over their healthcare and healing practices, the loss of identity through the disconnection with birth and giving birth in their territories, and the potential for healing and restoration that is possible within the repatriation of birth to First Nation communities.

Notes

1.   Indian Act (1985), §.2.

References

Adelson, N. 2008. 'The Embodiment of Inequity: Health Disparities in Aboriginal Canada', *Canadian Journal of Public Health* 96 (Supplement 2): S45–S60.

Assembly of First Nations. 2011. Fact Sheet: Quality of life of First Nations, June 2011.

Basu, P. 2004. 'My Own Island Home: The Orkney Homecoming', *Journal of Material Culture* 9(1): 27–42.

Benoit, C., D. Carroll and R. Eni. 2006. 'To Watch, To Care: Stories of Aboriginal Midwifery in Canada', *Canadian Journal of Midwifery Research and Practice* 5(1): 11–17.

Bent, K., J. Havelock and M. Haworth-Brockman. 2007. *Entitlements and Health Services for First Nations and Métis Women in Manitoba and Saskatchewan.* Winnipeg: Prairie Women's Health Centre of Excellence.

CAM. 2011. 'National Aboriginal Council of Midwives', *Pinard: Canadian Association of Midwives Newsletter* 9.

Carroll, D., and C. Benoit. 2004. 'Aboriginal Midwifery in Canada: Merging Traditional Practices and Modern Science', in I. Bourgeault, C. Benoit and R. Davis-Floyd (eds), *Reconceiving Midwifery.* Montreal: McGill-Queen's University Press, pp.263–87.

Carsten, J. (ed.). 2000. *Cultures of Relatedness: New Approaches to the Study of Kinship.* Cambridge: Cambridge University Press.

CICH. 2000. 'The Health of Canada's Children: A CICH Profile', 3rd edn. Ottawa: Canadian Institute of Child Health.

Couchie, C., and H. Nabigon. 1997. 'A Path Towards Reclaiming Nishnawbe Birth Culture: Can the Midwifery Exemption Clause for Aboriginal Midwives Make a Difference?' in F. Shroff (ed.), *The New Midwifery: Reflections on Renaissance and Regulation.* Toronto: Women's Press.

Davis-Floyd, R., and C. Sargent (eds). 1997. *Childbirth and Authoritative Knowledge: Cross-cultural Perspectives.* Berkeley: University of California Press.

Desjarlais, J. 2008. 'Returning Safe Birthing Closer to Communities', unpublished paper. Office of Nursing Services, First Nation and Inuit Health Branch, Health Canada.

Dickason, O. 1992. *Canada's First Nations: A History of Founding Peoples from Earliest Times.* New York: Oxford University Press.

Douglas, M. 1991. 'The Idea of a Home: A Kind of Space', *Social Research* 58(1): 287–307.

——— 2006. 'Childbirth among the Canadian Inuit: A Review of the Clinical and Cultural Literature', *International Journal of Circumpolar Health* 65(2): 11-32.

Farmer, P. 2005. *Pathologies of Power: Health, Human Rights, and the New War on the Poor*, 2nd edn. Berkeley: University of California Press.

——— 2006. 'Childbirth among the Canadian Inuit: A Review of the Clinical and Cultural Literature', *International Journal of Circumpolar Health* 65(2): 11-32.

Gone, J.P. 2008. 'So I Can Be Like a Whiteman: The Cultural Psychology of Space and Place in American Indian Mental Health', *Culture and Psychology* 14(3): 369–99.

Gupta, A., and J. Ferguson. 1992. 'Beyond "Culture": Space, Identity, and the Politics of Difference', *Cultural Anthropology* 17(1): 6–23.

Hackett, P. 2005. 'From Past to Present: Understanding First Nations Health Patterns in a Historical Context', *Canadian Journal of Public Health* 96 (Supplement 1): S17–S21.

Health Canada. 2008. 'History of Providing Health Services to First Nations People and Inuit'. Retrieved 15 December 2008 from: www.hc-sc.gc.ca/ahc-asc/branch-dirgen/fnihb-dgspni/services-eng.php.

Ingold, T. 2000. *The Perception of the Environment: Essays in Livelihood, Dwelling and Skill*. London: Routledge.

Jordan, B. 1997. 'Authoritative Knowledge and Its Construction', in R. Davis-Floyd and C. Sargent (eds), *Childbirth and Authoritative Knowledge: Cross-cultural Perspectives*. Berkeley: University of California Press, pp.55–79.

Kaufert, P., and J.D. O'Neil. 1990. 'Co-optation and Control: The Reconstruction of Inuit Birth', *Medical Anthropology Quarterly* 4(4): 427–42.

Lavoie, J., E. Forget, G. Rowe and M. Dahl. 2009. 'Leaving for the City', final report, Medical Relocation Project Phase 2. Winnipeg: Centre for Aboriginal Health Research, University of Manitoba.

MacDonald, M. 2006. 'Gender Expectations: Natural Bodies and Natural Births in the New Midwifery in Ontario', *Medical Anthropology Quarterly* 20(2): 235–56.

——— 2007. *At Work in the Field of Birth: Midwifery Narratives of Nature, Tradition, and Home*. Nashville: Vanderbilt University Press.

McHugh, K.E. 2000. 'Inside, Outside, Upside Down, Backward, Forward, Round and Round: A Case for Ethnographic Studies in Migration', *Progress in Human Geography* 24: 71–89.

NAHO. 2005. 'Exploring Models for Quality Maternity Care in First Nations and Inuit Communities: A Preliminary Needs Assessment: Final Report on Findings'. Ottawa: National Aboriginal Health Organization.

——— 2008. 'Celebrating Birth: Aboriginal Midwifery in Canada'. Ottawa: National Aboriginal Health Organization.

O'Neil, J.D., and P. Kaufert. 1990. 'The Politics of Obstetric Care: The Inuit Experience', in W.P. Handwerker (ed.), *Births and Power: Social Change and the Politics of Reproduction*. Boulder, CO: Westview Press, pp.53–68.

——— 1995. 'Irniktakpunga! Sex Determination and the Inuit Struggle for Birthing Rights in Northern Canada' in F.D. Ginsburg and R. Rapp (eds), *Conceiving the New World Order: The New Politics of Reproduction*. Berkeley: University of California Press, pp.59–73.

O'Neil, J.D., J.M. Kaufert, P.L. Kaufert and W.W. Koolage. 1993. 'Political Considerations in Health-Related Participatory Research in Northern Canada', in

N. Dyck and J.B. Waldram (eds), *Anthropology, Public Science, and Native Peoples in Canada*. Montreal: McGill-Queen's University Press, pp.215–32.

O'Neil, J.D., J.R. Reading and A. Leader. 1998. 'Changing the Relations of Surveillance: The Development of a Discourse of Resistance in Aboriginal Epidemiology', *Human Organization* 57(2): 230–37.

Phillips-Beck, W. 2010. 'The Development of a Framework of Improved Childbirth Care for First Nation Women in Manitoba: A First Nation Family Centred Approach', MA diss. Winnipeg: Faculty of Family Social Science, University of Manitoba.

Ray, A.J., J. Miller and F. Tough. 2000. *Bounty and Benevolence: A History of Saskatchewan Treaties*. Montreal: Queen's University Press.

RCAP. 1996. 'Gathering Strength, Vol. 3', final report, Royal Commission on Aboriginal People, Government of Canada. Retrieved 30 September 2009 from: www.ainc-inac.gc.ca/ch/rcap/sg/sim2_e.html.

Robertson, L. 2007. 'Taming Space: Drug Use, HIV, and Homemaking in Downtown Eastside Vancouver', *Gender, Place and Culture* 14(5): 527–49.

Schwarz, M.T. 1997. 'Unravelling the Anchoring Cord: Navajo Relocation 1974–1996', *American Anthropologist* 99(1): 43–55.

Smith, D., C. Varcoe and N. Edwards. 2005. 'Turning around the Intergenerational Impact of Residential Schools on Aboriginal Peoples: Implications for Health Policy and Practice', *Canadian Journal of Nursing Research* 37(4): 38–60.

Statistics Canada. 2006. 'Aboriginal Peoples in Canada in 2006: Inuit, Métis and First Nations 2006 Census: Aboriginal Peoples 2006 Census'. Ottawa: Statistics Canada.

——— 2010. 'Aboriginal Statistics at a Glance'. Ottawa: Government of Canada.

Steckley, J.L., and B.D. Cummins. 2001. *Full Circle: Canada's First Nations*. Toronto: Prentice-Hall,

Unnithan-Kumar, M. (ed.). 2004. *Reproductive Agency, Medicine and the State: Cultural Transformations in Childbearing*. Oxford: Berghahn.

Van Hollen, C. 2003. *Birth on the Threshold: Childbirth and Modernity in South India*. Berkeley: University of California Press.

Notes on Contributors

Sajida Z. Ally is completing her doctorate in Social Anthropology at the University of Sussex. Having conducted fieldwork in Sri Lanka and Kuwait, her current research focuses on subaltern Tamil-speaking and Muslim women who experience health as minority groups in both their countries of origin and destination. She has extensive experience in coordinating and advising migrants' rights advocacy networks and training programmes, primarily in East, South-East and South Asia, as well as in Geneva.

Elizabeth P. Challinor is Associate Researcher at the Centre for Research in Social Anthropology, University of Minho, Portugal. Her current research is on Cape Verdean student mothers in Portugal, examining their institutionalized encounters with health professionals and social workers, looking at issues of power, identity and cultural awareness. She is also involved in a research project entitled 'Care as Sustainability in Crisis Situations'. She is author of *Bargaining in the Development Marketplace: Insights from Cape Verde* (2008).

Mirabelle E. Fernandes-Paul serves as director of the Women's Center in the faculty of Women, Gender and Sexuality at Oregon State University. She holds a graduate degree in Biochemistry and Molecular Biology and received her doctorate from the University of St Thomas, Minnesota. Her research focuses on the challenges involved in cross-cultural medicine, with a focus on obstetrics, and she has studied the glycobiology of Apoptosis (programmed cell death), as seen in malignant tumours.

Laura Griffith is Senior Qualitative Researcher at the Health Experiences Research Group. Her D.Phil. focused on the emotional experiences of Bangladeshi mothers in the East End of London. Her research interests include qualitative research into personal experiences of health and illness, especially in the field of mental health and the provision of health services to address social inequalities. Currently her research is on acute mental health conditions and she is based within the Department of Primary Care Health Sciences at Oxford.

Nguyen Thi Ngan Hoa is a senior researcher at the Centre for Gender and Family Studies, Southern Institute for Sustainable Development, Ho Chi Minh, Vietnam.

Sunil K. Khanna is Professor of Medical Anthropology at Oregon State University. His research examines the complex interrelations of biology, culture, gender, ethnicity and health in South Asia and the US. His most recent research project in India addresses the availability and use of new reproductive technologies for the purpose of pre-natal sex determination and practices of sex selection in urbanizing North India. His current research focuses on son preference and the practice of pre-natal sex selection among Indian immigrants living in North America. He is the author of *Fetal/Fatal Knowledge: New Reproductive Technologies and Family-Building Strategies in India* (2010).

Catherine Locke is Reader in the School of International Development, University of East Anglia, UK.

Rachel Olson holds a PhD in Social Anthropology from the University of Sussex. Her research focuses on Aboriginal midwifery, maternal health and childbirth in Canada's First Nations communities. She is a citizen of the Tr'ondek Hwech'in First Nation of Yukon, Canada. She is Director of the Firelight Group Research Cooperative and has been conducting research in First Nations communities since 1998, working on various projects, from oral history, traditional land use and traditional knowledge to First Nations health issues.

Kaveri Qureshi is Research Fellow at the Institute of Social and Cultural Anthropology, University of Oxford. Her research is primarily on Pakistani and Indian Punjabi migration and diasporas in Britain, exploring the life course, transnational families and politics.

Nguyen Thi Thanh Tam is a senior researcher at the Institute for Family and Gender Studies, Vietnamese Academy of Social Sciences, Hanoi, Vietnam.

Maya Unnithan-Kumar is Professor of Social and Medical Anthropology at the University of Sussex. Her research interests include the anthropology of the body, childbirth and infertility, reproductive technologies, mobility, health inequalities and human rights. She has carried out long-term field research in north-west India, and has written about notions of reproductive entitlement, inequalities associated with procreative technologies, and meanings of agency in reproductive health, including for migrant women. Her recent research has focused on state and civil society understandings of human rights discourse as applied to sexual, maternal and reproductive health in India.

Index